Innovation Studies

Innovation Studies

Evolution and Future Challenges

Edited by
Jan Fagerberg, Ben R. Martin,
and Esben S. Andersen

OXFORD
UNIVERSITY PRESS

Great Clarendon Street, Oxford, OX2 6DP,
United Kingdom

Oxford University Press is a department of the University of Oxford.
It furthers the University's objective of excellence in research, scholarship,
and education by publishing worldwide. Oxford is a registered trade mark of
Oxford University Press in the UK and in certain other countries

Published in the United States of America by Oxford University Press
198 Madison Avenue, New York, NY 10016, United States of America

British Library Cataloguing in Publication Data
Data available

Library of Congress Control Number: 2013942549

ISBN 978–0–19–968634–6 (Hbk.)

ISBN 978–0–19–968635–3 (Pbk.)

Printed and bound in Great Britain by
CPI Group (UK) Ltd, Croydon, CR0 4YY

Contents

List of Figures

List of Tables

List of Contributors

Esben S. Andersen, Professor of Evolutionary Economics, Aalborg University

Giovanni Dosi, Professor of Economics, Scuola Superiore Sant'Anna

Jan Fagerberg, Professor, Aalborg University and University of Oslo; Visiting Scholar, University of Lund

Edward Lorenz, Professor of Economics, University of Nice-Sophia Antipolis

Bengt-Åke Lundvall, Professor Emeritus, Aalborg University, Secretary General of Globelics

Ben R. Martin, Professor of Science and Technology Policy Studies, University of Sussex

Mariana Mazzucato, RM Phillips Professor in Science and Technology Policy, University of Sussex

Richard R. Nelson, Professor Emeritus and Director of the Program on Science, Technology, and Global Development at the Earth Institute, Columbia University

Carlota Perez, Professor of Technology and Development, Technological University of Tallinn; Visiting Scholar, London School of Economics

Luc Soete, Rector Magnificus, Maastricht University

W. Edward Steinmueller, Professor of Information and Communication Technology Policy, University of Sussex

1

Innovation Studies: Towards a New Agenda

Jan Fagerberg, Ben R. Martin, and Esben S. Andersen

1.1. Introduction

Innovation is increasingly recognized as a vitally important social and economic phenomenon worthy of serious research study. Firms are concerned about their innovation ability, particularly relative to their competitors, because they believe their future may depend on it. Politicians care about innovation, too, because of its presumed importance for growth, welfare, and employment. However, to recognize that innovation is desirable because of its assumed beneficial effects is not sufficient in itself. What is required is systematic and reliable knowledge about how best to influence innovation and exploit its effects to the full. Gaining such knowledge is the aim of innovation studies.

The field of innovation studies is at least half a century old, so now is an opportune time to ask what has been achieved and what we still need to know more about. This is what this book sets out to explore. Written by a number of central contributors to the field, it critically examines the current state of the art and identifies issues that merit greater attention. The focus is mainly on how society can derive the greatest benefit from innovation and what needs to done to achieve this. However, to learn more about how society can benefit from innovation, one also needs to understand innovation processes in firms and how these interact with broader social, institutional, and political factors. Such issues are therefore also central to the discussion here. Hence, although this is not a book specifically about how to manage innovation processes in firms, readers primarily interested in innovation management may nevertheless find the discussion in this book stimulating and challenging.

The book is in large part the outcome of a workshop held in the University of Aalborg in February 2012 on 'The Future of Innovation Studies', in which many leading contributors to the field's development over the years took part. At the workshop, the participants were challenged by Bengt-Åke Lundvall, who gave a broad-ranging assessment of the 'state of the art' of the field, and who identified a number of topics in need of greater attention. These were then addressed by the other speakers, who added further points of their own reflecting their particular areas of expertise. In addition, in order to help focus future discussions, three final chapters, containing short interventions on what needs to be done, have been added. One of those who provide such advice is Richard Nelson, the most highly cited scholar in the area, and someone who has been active in this field of research for more than half a century.

1.2. Understanding Innovation: A Brief Historical Sketch[1]

The need for knowledge on innovation and its effects may seem obvious today but it was not always thus. While, 100 years ago, the innovation theorist Joseph Schumpeter (1912, 1934)[2] did his best to propagate the view that innovation is the ultimate source of economic growth and hence worthy of study, he had few followers at the time or indeed for the next few decades. Only after the Second World War did a relatively modest research effort on this topic begin to emerge, to a considerable extent due to initiatives from actors outside of academia who realized the need for a better understanding of innovation and its effects.

In particular, in the USA during the 1950s, the RAND Corporation—research consultants to the US military establishment—made it possible for young economists such as Kenneth Arrow, Richard Nelson, and Sidney Winter to work on the economics of R&D and innovation (Hounshell, 2000).[3] Meanwhile in Britain, the economist Christopher Freeman was recruited by the Federation of British Industries to collect information on R&D activities in British firms. A few years later, the Paris-based Organisation for Economic Co-operation and Development (OECD) employed Freeman as a consultant, with the task of creating a unified framework for collecting statistics on R&D activities on an international scale. This led to the so-called *Frascati Manual*, which is still the basis for the collection of R&D statistics worldwide (OECD, 1962).[4]

---

[1] More details of the history of innovation studies can be found in Fagerberg et al. (2012) and Martin (2012).

[2] The 1934 edition—the first in English—was based on the radically revised second German edition of the book from 1926.

[3] This resulted in a number of now classic works on the economics of R&D, for example Nelson (1959) and Arrow (1962).

[4] See Fagerberg et al. (2011) for more on Freeman's work.

Where university academics began to become interested in technology and innovation, this was often driven by external demand and/or funded by mission-oriented agencies. For example, in the USA, financial support from the economically and politically important agricultural sector helped enable sociologists and economists to study the diffusion of innovations in that sector (e.g. Ryan and Gross, 1943; Griliches, 1957; Rogers, 1962). Sociologists (and more specifically industrial sociologists or industrial psychologists) were also prominent in the nascent field in the UK. For example, Woodward's (1958) influential book on *Management and Technology* was based on the results of a project sponsored by the Department of Scientific and Industrial Research as part of an effort to stimulate the uptake of social sciences in industry.[5] Likewise, it was a project carried out for a voluntary association and funded by industrial firms, unions, and local government that resulted in the widely read book by Burns and Stalker (1961) entitled *The Management of Innovation*.[6]

Much of this early work took place towards the fringes of the academic world.[7] While drawing upon existing disciplines, particularly economics and sociology, attempts to combine insights obtained from different disciplinary frameworks were initially rare. Moreover, when researchers from the different disciplinary 'tribes' (Becher, 1989) did encounter one another, this often gave rise to fierce dispute (Martin, 2012, p. 1235).[8] This began to change, however, with the establishment of the first academic units devoted specifically to the study of science, R&D, and innovation and related policy issues. Due to the nature of the research, these units often found it appropriate to recruit staff with different disciplinary backgrounds. An important catalyst in this development was the establishment of the Science Policy Research Unit (SPRU) at the newly founded University of Sussex in Britain in 1966,[9] with Christopher Freeman as its first director.[10] SPRU took pride in employing not only social scientists but

---

[5] See <http://www.lib.uwo.ca/programs/generalbusiness/WOODWARD.html> (accessed on 4 December 2012).

[6] This was part of an effort to stimulate the entry of Scottish engineering companies into the emerging field of electrically controlled equipment (Burns and Stalker, 2005, p. 215).

[7] For example, Ryan and Gross worked at Iowa State University, as did Rogers until 1962 when he moved to Michigan State University. Woodward undertook her early research at South East Essex College of Technology before joining Imperial College in 1958. Burns was a lecturer in social studies at Edinburgh University, while Stalker was a psychologist, who shortly afterwards left academia to become a management consultant. Griliches was perhaps the exception, carrying out his early work at Chicago University.

[8] See, for example, the debate between Griliches and Rogers recorded in *Rural Sociology* (Griliches, 1960, 1962; Rogers and Havens, 1962).

[9] In fact, the first such dedicated unit had been set up a few months before this at Lund University, where Stevan Dedijer created the Research Policy Institute (see <http://www.lunduniversity.lu.se/o.o.i.s?id=24890&news_item=5132>—accessed on 4 December 2012).

[10] Freeman also took the initiative to found the journal *Research Policy* (in 1971), which over time became the central journal for innovation studies (Fagerberg and Verspagen, 2009). Other specialist journals founded in the early years include *Research-Technology Management*, *R&D Management*, and *Technovation*.

also engineers and natural scientists in its research. Moreover, despite its name, SPRU's research focused not just on science more narrowly defined, but also on innovation in industry and on diffusion processes. From the very start, the centre placed emphasis on both research and post-graduate teaching within its field. It gradually developed into a global hub for innovation studies with a large number of visitors, and it became a source of inspiration for similar initiatives elsewhere. For example, among the centres established in the 1970s were the Fraunhofer Institute for Systems and Innovation Research (ISI) at Karlsruhe, PREST (Policy Research in Engineering, Science and Technology) at Manchester University, and the Center for Policy Alternatives (CPA) at MIT.

During the decades that followed, a lively and heterogeneous scientific field evolved. Initially, this could be characterized as 'multi-disciplinary' in nature, in that it simply drew upon knowledge, methods, perspectives, concepts, theories, or whatever from several disciplines. Gradually, however, it became more 'inter-disciplinary' as researchers began to link, blend, and integrate these various disciplinary inputs (Klein, 2010; Martin, 2011).

From a relatively modest activity in a few places, mainly in the USA and the UK, innovation studies grew into a global research community. More and more centres or departments focusing on innovation were founded worldwide. Several new journals and professional associations devoted to the field also emerged.[11] The 1980s and 1990s saw the emergence of new theories and frameworks for research, such as Nelson and Winter's theory of how firms' learning and innovation activities evolve and are embedded in a process of Schumpeterian (technological) competition (Nelson and Winter, 1982), inspiring a host of new work extending far beyond innovation studies proper, much of which was empirically oriented.[12]

Around the late 1980s, work in the field took a new twist with the development of a more 'systemic' understanding of innovation and diffusion (Freeman, 1987; Lundvall, 1992; Nelson, 1993), which emphasized the complementarities between firms' innovation activities and the characteristics of the environments (national, regional, sectoral) in which they are embedded. This approach quickly attracted interest from policy makers, who saw it as helpful for thinking about the design of science, technology, and innovation policies.

---

[11] Some of the most well known include the International Joseph A. Schumpeter Society (founded in 1986), TIM—the Technology, Innovation and Management Division of the American Academy of Management (1987), IAMOT—the International Association for the Management of Technology (1988), the DRUID conferences (1995), the Triple Helix conferences (1996), and the Globelics Network (2002).

[12] Nelson and Winter's theory found a particularly receptive audience among scholars in business and management (Meyer, 2001), who drew on it as a source of inspiration in subsequent work on firms' capabilities in identifying, absorbing, and creating knowledge and exploiting it commercially (Cohen and Levinthal, 1990; Teece et al., 1997).

Interest in innovation also increased in business and management schools and, as the volume of teaching and research in these grew, the proportion of business and management scholars among the users of and contributors to the innovation literature increased substantially as well. As a result, around the turn of the century, approximately one third of the total number of citations to the core literature on innovation came from business and management journals, about twice the level of the early years of the field's development.[13]

1.3. An Evolving Agenda

As the earlier discussion indicates, the agenda of innovation research has undergone important changes during the field's lifetime. For example, Joseph Schumpeter's early theories (so-called Schumpeter 'Mark I') focused mostly on innovation by individual entrepreneurs and their economic effects. As Lundvall notes (in Chapter 2), this continues to be a primary focus in the rapidly growing field of entrepreneurship studies, and Schumpeter is therefore regarded as an important source of inspiration there, too.[14] Schumpeter (1943) subsequently recognized, however, that more attention needed to be given to understanding innovation processes in large firms (Schumpeter 'Mark II'). In his view, the production of a large set of historically-oriented case studies based on a common design was one way to set about this task (Schumpeter, 1947). Hence, after the Second World War the development of a credible theory of innovation in large firms became central to the research agenda in this area. The most influential theoretical contribution on this topic was to be Nelson's and Winter's (1982) evolutionary theory of economic change, previously mentioned, focusing on the roles of knowledge, routines, and selection processes in firms' innovation activities and growth.

As for empirical work, much of this followed Schumpeter's advice about basing one's theorizing on historically-oriented case studies, and the work of business historians such as Alfred Chandler (e.g. 1962 and 1977) became influential in this respect.[15] Most of the early case studies tended to focus on successful examples of innovation, such as the analysis by Langrish et al. (1972) of 84 winners of the Queen's Awards to Industry for Innovation. A major advance in understanding came in the early 1970s with Project SAPPHO, in which matched pairs of successful and unsuccessful innovations

---

[13] See Fagerberg et al. (2012) for further details.
[14] See Landström et al. (2012) for an analysis of entrepreneurship studies and the influence of Schumpeter.
[15] For an overview of innovation in firms, see Lazonick (2004).

were compared in order to better understand the factors influencing success and failure in innovation (Rothwell et al., 1974).

Another means to cast light on innovation activities in firms of different sizes, and one that increased in importance from the 1980s onwards, is to conduct surveys. As the field developed, evidence from surveys of innovation in firms, such as the Yale survey (Levin et al., 1987) and later the Community Innovation Survey (CIS)[16] in Europe and elsewhere, became more widely available and used by researchers. New evidence emerging from these surveys contributed to a more informed discussion about innovation in firms of different sizes, sectors, nations, and so forth. One of the insights that emerged, which significantly influenced the development of the research agenda, was the often important role played by users in innovation processes (Lundvall, 1985; von Hippel, 1986; Porter, 1990). Another was that, contrary to many economists' beliefs, firms in certain sectors did not regard intellectual property rights (and patenting in particular) as especially important for their ability to profit from innovation. Rather, what they placed emphasis on was the development of capabilities (Teece et al., 1997) that allowed them to stay ahead of competitors. Hence, capabilities became an important issue on the research agenda.[17] However, the research also showed important differences remained across industries and sectors in these and other respects, and the exploration of such differences also attracted much attention and led to the development of new frameworks for research (e.g. Pavitt, 1984; Malerba, 2004).

In general, during the last few decades, the strongly firm-centric focus from the field's early years has given way to a broader perspective that places more emphasis on the environment in which firms operate, in particular the innovation system(s) in which they are embedded. There are several reasons for this. One, as previously mentioned, is evidence from surveys stressing the importance of interactions with users and other parts of the environment for firm-level innovation and its economic effects. Another is the observation that firms' strategies with respect to innovation tend to change over time. Gone are the days when the development of large, in-house R&D departments was seen as the only, or the most effective, way to innovate. In its place have come approaches emphasizing that the knowledge, skills, and resources necessary for innovation tend to be widely distributed, and that the ability to identify, access, absorb, and use these is crucial for innovation (Cohen and Levinthal, 1990; Chesbrough, 2003). A third reason is the realization that the relevant knowledge, skills, and resources may not only reside in other firms, but also in public-sector organizations such as universities, research institutes, and other agencies, and that the interaction between firms and such

---

[16] See Smith (2004).   [17] See Teece (2010) for an overview.

public-sector bodies may be important for innovation. As previously mentioned, these insights have led to the development of 'systems' approaches that put interactions, between different firms as well as between agents in the private and public sectors, at the very centre of the analysis.[18] Andrew van der Ven, in an analysis of what he called 'social systems of innovation', summarized the new perspective well: 'Popular folklore notwithstanding, the innovation journey is a collective achievement that requires key roles from numerous entrepreneurs in both the public and private sectors' (Van de Ven et al., 1999, p. 149).

1.4. Achievements and Challenges

Thus, the research agenda in innovation studies has broadened considerably during the last few decades. But has it broadened enough? There is always a danger—in this as in other areas of knowledge—that today's research will tend to reflect past trajectories rather than future challenges. Are we studying the most relevant and pressing problems and addressing them in the right way? Is the knowledge we produce sufficiently useful for those who need it? These are among the questions raised in this volume, which aims to kick-start a debate about the future of the field.

Bengt-Åke Lundvall, in Chapter 2 of this volume, introduces the discussion by providing an assessment of where the field has got to and identifying a number of challenging issues that are further elaborated upon in subsequent chapters. Lundvall notes that what qualifies as a good theory of innovation is not carved in stone but has to evolve as a result of changes in society and our attempts to understand these changes, and he draws upon his own experiences from research projects over the years to illustrate this. Based on recent attempts to survey the field's development, he goes on to ask whether the scholarly literature on innovation has yet developed a common theoretical core. His conclusion is that that this is not yet the case. However, he does identify three main streams of literature: an evolutionary strand that, following Schumpeter's ambitious programme, attempts to create a new basis for understanding economic change; a 'techno-economic' approach focusing on the conditions for profiting from innovation in different industries and sectors; and finally what he terms a 'socio-economic' theory of innovation that aims at understanding innovation by studying the actors involved and how they interact in the process of innovation. While acknowledging the relevance of all three streams, he finds the third line of thinking, with its

---

[18] See Edquist (2004) for an overview of the literature on innovation systems.

emphasis on interactive learning, particularly promising as a platform for further progress in the area. He also stresses that the field is—and should remain—porous, with open lines of communication to neighbouring scientific fields such as entrepreneurship studies, science and technology studies (STS), working life studies, knowledge management, and creativity studies.

The Learning Society: What Does it Take to Succeed?

On this basis, Lundvall goes on to identify certain topics that deserve to be central to the field's agenda in the years ahead. One of the main topics he identifies, and one further elaborated upon in Chapter 3 by Lorenz, is the relationship between innovation and learning, on the one hand, and the organization of work and social protection schemes, on the other. Lundvall and Lorenz both see innovation as related to learning, so in their view there is much to be gained from an improved understanding of the social conditions under which learning occurs. They argue that in modern knowledge-based societies, working life and social protection need to be organized in a way that maximizes the potential for innovation and learning, and they identify the factors that matter most in this respect. By doing so, they also enter a political terrain of great relevance for contemporary Europe and indeed for the rest of the world as well. For example, Lundvall points to a fundamental contradiction at the heart of the learning economy. On the one hand, it depends heavily on social capital and trust of the sort that thrives in egalitarian societies; on the other, it may accelerate the rise of inequality as low-skilled jobs come under threat.

Innovation: Not Only for the Rich?

All too often, innovation is seen as an activity that occurs primarily in advanced settings, for example in high-tech firms, leading universities, and R&D centres, and in advanced countries. Poor people, and the countries in which they live, are often seen as not very interesting from this perspective. While the benefits of innovation eventually may trickle down to them as well, they are assumed not to be directly involved in the innovation process. But is this way of delineating the relevance of the phenomenon really warranted? Lundvall (Chapter 2) thinks not, a view that is shared by Perez in Chapter 4, entitled 'Innovation Systems and Policy for Development in a Changing World'. She argues that the conditions for innovation by—and for—the poor have changed markedly in recent decades for reasons related to the paradigm shift in technology and the resulting changes in the behaviour of large corporations. Perez points to the need for innovation studies and evolutionary economics to develop an understanding of these changes, in particular by fully incorporating history into the inter-disciplinary mix. She also stresses how evolutionary thinking needs to strike an appropriate balance between universal and changing truths, especially when studying innovation with a view to making policy recommendations.

Challenging Economics

Well before innovation studies began to emerge as a field, Schumpeter had criticized the notion, central to much economic thinking, that the allocation of scarce resources between competing initiatives is what economics is all about. As Dosi (Chapter 5) points out, economics should be as much about innovation-driven changes, how these are brought about, and what their consequences are. He outlines the major building blocks of an interpretation of the economy as a complex evolving system and the role that innovation plays in this. Key to this is understanding how economic agents learn and create, exploit and share knowledge. Indeed, as Lundvall (Chapter 2) points out, understanding knowledge and its role in the economy is where traditional economics fails spectacularly. To rectify this failure, Dosi argues, economists need to borrow heavily from cognitive and social psychology as well as from innovation studies and evolutionary economics. Another central issue that needs to be resolved, according to Dosi, is the role of selection processes. No new initiative can succeed if it is not accepted by the potential users, that is, it must survive a selection process. Yet, as Dosi notes, research shows that selection processes are far more complex than most economists tend to assume. In order to understand these processes, a broad inter-disciplinary and historical perspective is required. Other topics that Dosi points to as being in need of further research are financial dynamics and their relationship with the real economy, and the determinants and dynamics of income distribution.

Is Innovation Always Good?

This is the thought-provoking question raised by Lundvall and taken up in greater detail by Soete in Chapter 6 of this volume. Over the years, there has been a widespread tendency in the innovation literature to make the assumption that innovation is always good. Yet, as Soete observes, innovation does not necessarily benefit society at large. Innovation may often be of the 'destructive creation' type, as he describes it—that is, innovations benefiting the few at the expense of the many—rather than the supposedly more desirable 'creative destruction' type (which may destroy a few incumbents but to the ultimate benefit of society as a whole). Prominent cases of such 'destructive' innovations may be found in the financial sector (as Martin also notes in Chapter 8) as well in manufacturing. Examples in the financial sector include cases allowing actors to realize great gains in the short term while invoking even greater costs for society as a whole at a later stage. In the manufacturing sector, examples include innovations involving planned obsolescence, and innovations leading to unsustainable consumption growth and environmental degradation. All this raises an important problem for policy and scholarly work, namely how to design mechanisms—or selection environments—that prevent such socially destructive innovations from spreading, while at the same time stimulating socially constructive innovations that benefit the many at the bottom of 'the pyramid' and not just the few at the top. To be able deal with these issues, Soete argues, what is required is not 'less state' but a more competent and independent public sector attracting people with advanced qualifications and a willingness to defend public interests and make the most out of the continuous flow of challenges that innovation gives rise to.

1.5. Towards a New Agenda?

The earlier discussion has pointed to a number of challenges that require more attention. How can we ensure that the research community studying innovation is able to take up these challenges in a constructive way? This question, again raised by Lundvall, is discussed in more depth by Steinmueller in Chapter 7, 'Innovation Studies at Maturity'. He suggests that the field of innovation studies may be approaching a Kuhnian juncture as it acquires some of the characteristics and institutions of 'normal science', in other words, a field characterized by a high degree of consensus on theoretical concepts and methodological approaches and on what the important research problems to be addressed are. Steinmueller argues that, to some extent, this should be regarded as a necessary and desirable step in the field's development, and points to the importance of a renewed emphasis on developing appropriate pedagogical and community-building tools, such as introductory texts, training programmes, conferences, and a digital presence, all of which he sees as insufficiently developed at present. However, according to Steinmueller, this process of creating normal science, while necessary, should not be allowed to weaken our ability to address many of the crucial challenges that humanity currently faces, and in which science, technology, and innovation are likely to play key roles. Rather than promoting closure and raising entry barriers to the field, Steinmueller argues, we instead need to embrace diversity, ensuring that the field continues to attract, and be enriched by, people seeking to make a difference in the world, regardless of their prior training or disciplinary background. One potential way forward, Steinmueller suggests, might be to place a greater premium (in the form of a major prize, for instance) on truly path-breaking and creative work in this area.

Fifteen Challenges for Innovation Studies

Starting from a list of major advances over the field's history, and drawing upon the issues raised in earlier chapters, Martin (in Chapter 8) proposes a list of 15 challenges for innovation studies over the coming decades. He argues that the focus of our empirical studies has not always kept pace with the fast changing economy and the world in which we live, in particular the shift from manufacturing to services and the growing need for sustainability as well as economic growth. Moreover, the way in which we conceptualize, define, operationalize, and analyse 'innovation' is rooted in the past, leaving us less able to grapple with other less visible forms of innovation. The relative neglect of financial innovations has left us with little to contribute to the analysis of the current financial crisis and of the growing polarity between rich and poor, or to discussions on how economics needs to shift to a new paradigm if we are to avoid similar problems in the future. Some of Martin's challenges relate to what sort of field we aspire to be, in particular if we are to avoid falling prey to academic 'bubbles' or to disciplinary sclerosis. Picking up the issue raised by Steinmueller, he asks whether we want to become a more academic discipline, or a field that continues to respond to challenges encountered by decision-makers in government, industry, and elsewhere, even if that means operating as an inter-disciplinary 'mongrel' of somewhat lower academic status rather than a disciplinary 'pedigree'. Last, he raises the important question of how innovation scholars can maintain their research integrity, morality, and collegiality in an era of escalating academic competition.

Reflections on the Challenges Ahead

The final three chapters contain contributions that—based on the earlier chapters in the book—reflect on the challenges lying ahead. Chapter 9 is by Richard Nelson, one of the pioneers in this area and author of some of the most influential publications in the field. With respect to the future agenda in this area, Nelson emphasizes three points. Although Schumpeter, he notes, had a broad concept of innovation, most work in this area has focused on a particular subset of this, namely product and process innovation. It is high time, Nelson argues, to give higher priority to other types of innovation (innovation not involving 'Technology with a capital T', as he describes it) such as those in business organization and management practice. This will also stimulate the forging of stronger alliances with scholars in business and management, something that Nelson sees as beneficial for the field's progress. The second point is the study of what factors affect the kinds of innovations that are generated, and how we can influence these. Although this has been an important topic on the research agenda for some time, Nelson argues that our understanding of these phenomena can be sharpened by paying greater attention to historical detail (and consequently engaging in more interaction with historians). The third priority is to gain a better understanding of what determines whether the fruits of innovation are widely shared or accrue mainly to particular groups and interests. This, he notes, is an issue that attracts interest from economists, and therefore increased cooperation with them would be beneficial for this particular goal to be achieved.

Mariana Mazzucato has recently been appointed to the SPRU chair at Sussex University that was originally held by Christopher Freeman, another pioneer in this area. She starts, in Chapter 10, where Nelson leaves off, namely with the relationship between the creation of innovation and the distribution of its rewards, which she flags as perhaps the most important issue for researchers in this area to address in the years to come. The argument that the increasing inequality one can observe in the developed part of the world is mostly a reflection of differences in skills across different strata of the population is, in her view, not sufficient to explain the large differences that have evolved. Another important contributing factor that she identifies, drawing upon evidence from the ICT and pharmaceutical sectors, has to do with the ability of private corporations to capture most of the 'rents' that stem from public investments in the creation of new knowledge, and to transfer these to their management and owners. If only a small percentage of these gains instead accrued to those that made the original investments (i.e. to the state), Mazzucato argues, there would much more scope for new initiatives in other areas of great societal importance, such as 'green' technology. Only by the innovation community showing greater attention to such issues, she contends, 'can we hope to achieve growth that is not only "smart" but also "inclusive"'.

The final contribution, Chapter 11 by Bengt-Åke Lundvall, also author of Chapter 2 in this volume, covers a broader range of issues and in a rather different manner to those of Nelson and Mazzucato. Lundvall's reflections relate to Steinmueller's discussion (Chapter 7) of what kind of framework and resources are required for the field's continuing progress. However, in addition to the factors identified by Steinmueller, Lundvall suggests establishing large research projects with international participation and extensive senior–junior interaction as a possible way forward. In particular, he emphasizes such projects as an ideal tool for research training. Drawing to a large extent on suggestions in earlier chapters of this volume, Lundvall sketches a number of possible themes for such projects, ranging from challenges and opportunities posed by globalization for national systems of innovation, to the sources of—and the barriers constraining—creativity.

Where to Go from Here?

The contributions in this volume contain a large number of suggestions as to what might be done in the years to come. Clearly the field is not running out of ideas, which augurs well for its future vitality. Although it is difficult to prioritize from within this rich portfolio something that ultimately will depend on the choices made by future generations of researchers, we would nevertheless conclude by emphasizing four points.

First, it has been common (and still is many quarters of society, not to mention academia) to view innovation as something that only goes on in advanced, high-tech environments in rich parts of the world, and that is limited to product and process innovation. However, within innovation studies, the insight that innovation is a pervasive phenomenon that can be found in 'low-tech' as well as 'high-tech' sectors, and in poor as well as rich environments, has been gaining strength. Moreover, it is increasingly recognized that it can take many different forms, not just as new products or processes, and that, say, organizational innovation (including new business models and management practices) may be just as important. This broadening of the range of phenomena analysed by innovation researchers needs to continue if the field is to further increase its relevance in society. There is, for example, no specific reason why studies of innovations in the public sector should not be a central part of the field. However, this continuous expansion of what scholars in this area address also poses an important challenge for theory— one that should not be taken lightly. Can innovations in both the private and the public sector, in industry and agriculture, in rich and poor environments, and so on, all be studied through the same 'lens' and, if not, what adaptations are necessary?

Second, the very fact that innovation is a pervasive phenomenon increases its role as a crucial driver of social and economic change and its potency as a problem-solving mechanism in dealing with challenges that occur, such as those posed by climate change. In fact, this is one of the main reasons why innovation attracts so much interest from policy makers and society at large. It is also an important reason why the field, from the very beginning, has managed to attract more than its fair share of 'people seeking to make a difference in the world', as Steinmueller puts it. Innovation researchers should be aware of this important role that the field may play, and constantly ask themselves how theories, frameworks, and research agendas may be adapted to fulfil this role. For example, as pointed out by Mazzucato earlier, a fresh perspective on the role played by the state in innovation, and how this relates to distribution, should be high on the agenda. In doing so, researchers will undoubtedly learn to appreciate Keynes' point about the problem being not so much about developing new ideas as getting rid of old ones.

Third, as noted earlier, innovation studies started as a relatively separate 'specialism' operating within existing disciplines, particularly economics and sociology. It took many years to build stronger connections between these different disciplinary environments and even longer to arrive at the inter-disciplinary focus that characterizes a large part of the field today. This should be regarded as a strength, since the focus of our study, innovation, cannot be properly understood on the basis of a single discipline. However, disciplinary narrow-mindedness has its own internal dynamics, so the continuing existence of a lively inter-disciplinary field is something that cannot be taken for granted, but instead constantly needs to be fought for and further developed, as several authors in this volume point out. The pervasive character of innovation and the broadening of our interests that it leads to, imply that the range of other fields that potentially might be relevant is also increasing. Reaching out to various disciplinary and inter-disciplinary fields that deal with issues of common interest should be a central objective of our future work.

Last, none of the above can be achieved without a well-functioning innovation studies community, and this holds also for several other objectives identified by the authors of this volume. Much praise has been given to how this community functioned in the past (see Lundvall in this volume) when, under the leadership of Chris Freeman, Richard Nelson, and others, the field managed to attract many promising young researchers into an exciting scholarly community engaged in discussing how the important economic, social, and environmental problems of the time could be fruitfully addressed. Since then, the community has grown much larger and more diverse. Although a plethora of organizational resources such as journals, conferences, and training schemes have developed over years, they tend—as pointed out by Steinmueller—to be rather specialized or even 'sectarian', as he puts it. Hence, as noted in a recent empirical study of the field (Fagerberg et al., 2012), there is a possibility that the various components or sub-fields that constitute the broader field may drift apart, with possible negative consequences for scholarly interaction and—if evolutionary logic is to be believed—for future scientific progress in this area. To avoid this outcome, innovation researchers need to create new frameworks for scholarly interaction that manage to attract the interest of innovation researchers more generally, not just one particular 'breed', be they economists, management scholars, or policy researchers.

References

Arrow, K. J. (1962), 'Economic Welfare and the Allocation of Resources for Invention', in *The Rate and Direction of Inventive Activity: Economic and Social Factors*. Cambridge, MA: National Bureau of Economic Research, 609–26.

Becher, T. (1989). *Academic Tribes and Territories: Intellectual Enquiry and the Cultures of Disciplines*. Buckingham: Open University Press.

Burns, T. and Stalker, G. M. (1961). *The Management of Innovation*. London: Tavistock.

Burns, T. and Stalker, G. M. (2005), 'Mechanistic and Organic Systems', in J. B. Miner (ed.) *Organizational Behavior 2: Essential Theories of Process and Structure*. New York: Sharpe, Armonk, 214–25.

Chandler, A. D. (1962). *Strategy and Structure: Chapters in the History of the American Enterprise*. Cambridge, MA: MIT Press.

Chandler, A. D. (1977). *The Visible Hand: the Managerial Revolution in American Business*. Cambridge, MA: Harvard University Press.

Chesbrough, H. W. (2003). *Open Innovation: the New Imperative for Creating and Profiting from Technology*. Cambridge, MA: Harvard Business School Press.

Cohen, W. and Levinthal, D. (1990). 'Absorptive Capacity: A New Perspective on Learning and Innovation', *Administrative Science Quarterly*, *35*: 128–52.

Edquist, C. (2004) *Systems of Innovation—A Critical Review of the State of the Art*. Oxford: Oxford University Press.

Fagerberg, J. and Verspagen, B. (2009). 'Innovation Studies—The Emerging Structure of a New Scientific Field', *Research Policy*, *38*: 218–33.

Fagerberg, J., Fosaas, M., Bell, M., and Martin, B. R. (2011). 'Christopher Freeman: Social Science Entrepreneur', *Research Policy*, *40*: 897–916.

Fagerberg, J., Fosaas, M., and Sapprasert, K. (2012). 'Innovation: Exploring the Knowledge Base', *Research Policy*, *41*: 1132–53.

Fagerberg, J., Mowery, D. C., and Nelson, R. R. (eds) (2004). *Oxford Handbook of Innovation*. Oxford: Oxford University Press.

Freeman, C. (1987). *Technology Policy and Economic Performance: Lessons from Japan*. London: Pinter.

Griliches, Z. (1957). 'Hybrid Corn: an Exploration in the Economics of Technological Change', *Econometrica*, *25*: 501–22.

Griliches, Z. (1960). 'Congruence Versus Profitability: A False Dichotomy', *Rural Sociology*, *25*: 354–56.

Griliches, Z. (1962). 'Profitability Versus Interaction: Another False Dichotomy', *Rural Sociology*, *27*: 325–30.

Hounshell, D. A. (2000), 'The Medium is the Message, or How Context Matters: The RAND Corporation Builds an Economics of Innovation, 1946–1962', in A. C. Hughes and T. P. Hughes (eds), *Systems, Experts, and Computers*. Cambridge, MA: MIT Press, 255–310.

Klein, J. T. (2010), 'A Taxonomy of Interdisciplinarity', in R. Frodeman, J. T. Klein, and C. Mitcham (eds), *The Oxford Handbook of Interdisciplinarity*. Oxford: Oxford University Press, 15–30.

Landström, H., Harirchi, G., and Åström, F. (2012). 'Entrepreneurship: Exploring the Knowledge Base', *Research Policy, 41*: 1154–81.

Langrish, J., Gibbons, M., Evans, W. G., and Jevons, F. R. (1972). *Wealth from Knowledge: Studies of Innovation in Industry*. Basingstoke: Palgrave Macmillan.

Lazonick, W. (2004), 'The Innovative Firm', in J. Fagerberg, D. C. Mowery, and R. R. Nelson (eds), *The Oxford Handbook of Innovation*. Oxford: Oxford University Press, 29–55.

Levin, R. C., Klevorick, A. K., Nelson, R. R., Winter, S. G., Gilbert, R., and Griliches, Z. (1987). 'Appropriating the Returns from Industrial Research and Development', *Brookings Papers on Economic Activity, 1987*: 783–831.

Lundvall, B.-Å. (1985). *Product Innovation and User-Producer Interaction*, Industrial Development Research Series. Aalborg: Aalborg University Press.

Lundvall, B.-Å. (1992). *National Systems of Innovation: Towards a Theory of Innovation and Interactive Learning*. London: Pinter.

Malerba, F. (2004), 'Sectoral Systems: How and Why Innovation Differs Across Sectors', in J. Fagerberg, D. C. Mowery, and R. R. Nelson (eds), *The Oxford Handbook of Innovation. Oxford: Oxford University Press*, 380–406.

Martin, B. R. (2011). 'What Can Bibliometrics Tell Us About Changes in the Mode of Knowledge Production?', *Prometheus, 29*: 455–79.

Martin, B. R. (2012). 'The Evolution of Science Policy and Innovation Studies', *Research Policy, 41*: 1219–39.

Meyer, M. (2001). 'Nelson and Winter's Evolutionary Theory—A Citation Analysis, Mimeo, SPRU, University of Sussex, Brighton.

Nelson, R. R. (1959). 'The Simple Economics of Basic Scientific Research', *Journal of Political Economy, 67*: 297–306.

Nelson, R. R. (ed.) (1993). *National Innovation Systems: A Comparative Study*. Oxford: Oxford University Press.

Nelson, R. R. and Winter, S. G. (1982). *An Evolutionary Theory of Economic Change*. Cambridge, MA: Harvard University Press.

OECD (1962), 'The Measurement of Scientific and Technical Activities: Proposed Standard Practice for Surveys of Research and Experimental Development ('The Frascati Manual') ', DAS/PD/62.47. Paris: OECD.

Pavitt, K. (1984). 'Sectoral Patterns of Technical Change: Towards a Taxonomy and a Theory', *Research Policy, 13*: 343–73.

Porter, M. E. (1990). *The Competitive Advantage of Nations*. New York: Free Press.

Rogers, E. M. (1962). *Diffusion of Innovations*. New York: Free Press.

Rogers, E. M. and Havens, A. E. (1962). 'Rejoinder to Griliches "Another False Dichotomy"', *Rural Sociology, 27*: 330–2.

Rothwell, R., Freeman, C., Horsley, A., Jervis, V. I. P., Robertson, A. B., and Townsend, J. (1974). 'SAPPHO Updated—Project SAPPHO Phase II', *Research Policy, 3*: 258–91.

Ryan, B. and Gross, N. C. (1943). 'The Diffusion of Hybrid Seed Corn in Two Iowa Communities', *Rural Sociology, 8*: 15–24.

Schumpeter, J. A. (1912). *Theorie der wirtschaftlichen Entwicklung*. Leipzig: Duncker & Humblot.

Schumpeter, J. A. (1934). *The Theory of Economic Development*, translated by R. Opie. Cambridge, MA: Harvard University Press.

Schumpeter, J. A. (1943). *Capitalism, Socialism and Democracy*. New York: Harper.

Schumpeter, J. A. (1947). 'The Creative Response in Economic History', *Journal of Economic History*, 7: 149–59. Reprinted in Schumpeter, J. A. (1989), *Essays on Entrepreneurs, Innovations, Business Cycles and the Evolution of Capitalism*, edited by R. V. Clemence, New Brunswick, NJ: Transaction Publishers, 221–71.

Smith, K. (2004), 'Measuring Innovation', in J. Fagerberg, D. C. Mowery, and R. R. Nelson (eds), *The Oxford Handbook of Innovation*. Oxford: Oxford University Press. 148–78.

Teece, D. J. (2010), 'Technological Innovation and the Theory of the Firm: The Role of Enterprise-Level Knowledge, Complementarities and (Dynamic) Capabilities', in B. H. Hall, and N. Rosenberg (eds), *Handbook of the Economics of Innovation*, Vol. 1. Amsterdam: Elsevier, 679–730.

Teece, D. J., Pisano, G., and Shuen, A. (1997). 'Dynamic Capabilities and Strategic Management', *Strategic Management Journal*, 18: 509–33.

Van de Ven, A. H., Polley, D. E., Garud, R., and Venkataraman, S. (1999). *The Innovation Journey*. Oxford: Oxford University Press.

von Hippel, E. (1986). 'Lead Users—A Source of Novel Product Concepts', *Management Science, 32*: 791–805.

Woodward, J. (1958). *Management and Technology*. London: HMSO.

Part I
Evolution, Developments, and Key Issues

2

Innovation Studies: A Personal Interpretation of 'The State of the Art'

Bengt-Åke Lundvall

2.1. Introduction

This chapter examines the status of innovation studies and reflects on where the field might go in the future. As described in Chapter 1, innovation studies emerged in the 1960s and 50 years later had developed into a relatively large field consisting of several thousand researchers with numerous inter-disciplinary research projects, much econometric work, relations with a range of scientific disciplines, and receiving much attention from the outside. A central question is whether this field has yet acquired a core theoretical perspective. It is argued that there are actually three theoretical perspectives that complement each other: the evolutionary economics perspective as presented by Schumpeter and by Nelson and Winter; the techno-economic perspective in which innovation is seen as reflecting the characteristics of technology in terms of technological opportunity and industry characteristics; and the socio-economic perspective that emphasizes interactive learning and innovation systems.

The integration of these different perspectives leads this chapter to confront several major challenges for innovation studies. First, there is the challenge to develop relations with entrepreneurship studies and with science and technology studies (STS) as well as with other adjacent fields such as knowledge management and creativity studies. Indeed, there seems to be a particular need to relate to working life studies in a way that introduces the analysis of work organization into the study of innovation systems, and that links innovation performance to the specificities of labour markets and education institutions. Second, there is the challenge of expanding the engagement of innovation scholars in the analysis of countries at different levels of development. If economic development is seen as capacity building, the links between national competence building and innovation are crucial. Third, there is the challenge of analysing the phenomenon of unsatisfactory innovation. Strengthening the participation of users may be one crucial way to make innovation outcomes more satisfactory, but there seems to be a particular need to give considerably more attention to 'financial innovation' and perhaps to develop the concept of the 'financial industrial complex' to provide a better understanding of why financial innovations are sometimes disruptive. Fourth, given the predominance of standard economics as a source of policy advice, there is a major challenge to make more systematic efforts to produce and disseminate insights that demonstrate the considerable limitations of this type of advice. Fifth, there is the challenge to combine the consolidation of the field of innovation studies with the introduction of mechanisms that make sure that the field remains open and receptive to ideas from users and from other fields of knowledge.

The present chapter does not pretend to give a complete, balanced, and objective survey of the field. The assessment, as well as the ideas for future research, inevitably reflects to a certain extent my own idiosyncratic perspective. One starting point is that personal knowledge emanating from research experience matters and problem-based learning developed in collective research projects is an important driver for knowledge creation in innovation studies. This chapter therefore starts with an overview of the most important findings from research projects that I have been involved in (Section 2.2). In Section 2.3, I discuss, on the basis of my own research experience and more recent research on the topic, what constitutes the theoretical core of the field of innovation studies. In Section 2.4, I sketch a borderline between innovation studies and two adjacent fields—entrepreneurship studies and STS. In Section 2.5, the field is opened up and related to work organization, development studies, and economics. This leads, in Section 2.6, to a discussion of the major challenges confronting innovation studies in terms of institutionalization and research training.[1]

2.2. Learning from Project Research

In academic life, scholars are expected to play the role of impersonal analytical machines.[2] The ideal scholar is one who, given equal access to data, reaches exactly the same conclusions as his/her colleagues. Academic training

---

[1] Some conclusions of the discussion in this chapter are presented in Chapter 11, where I propose a set of international research projects addressing the aforementioned challenges as well as providing suitable training sites for young researchers.

[2] This, at least, is the conventional ideology with respect to the nature of the scientist. However, several decades of work by STS scholars reveals that reality is often far removed from this idealized view.

aims at developing a persona and a language that hides rather than reveals the personal history of the scholar.[3]

There are certainly good reasons for setting limits to subjectivity—even if it is obvious that scholars 'like' some theories better than others, they should be obliged to argue their case. It is useful to act and think 'as if' there is something out there worth looking for that we might refer to as 'reasonably reliable knowledge'.

However, as Michael Polanyi (1958/78) noted, different scientists know different things as their learning experiences have been different—elements of their knowledge are personal rather than general. And some of the personal knowledge emanates not from books but from learning from interactions with other scholars or especially from episodes of problem-oriented and project-based empirical work. This is why I choose to use a sketch of how my current understanding of innovation has been shaped by experiences from specific research projects as the entry point to a more general discussion of the status of innovation studies.

The Formation of the Ike Group

In 1977, Aalborg economists hosted the Annual Conference of Danish Economists. Together with three colleagues, I wrote a paper for the conference on wages and competitiveness (Christensen et al., 1978). The major conclusion was that the countries with the strongest growth in wages were the most competitive. This controversial result later became recognized internationally and known under the heading 'the Kaldor paradox' (Kaldor, 1978).

According to the analysis, the key to this paradox was to understand productivity as endogenous and, under certain conditions, affected positively by a combination of international competition and domestic wage pressure. In the Aalborg paper it was assumed that firms are not X-efficient[4] and that on average they respond to stronger wage pressure either by intensifying their efforts to develop more attractive products or by intensifying their efforts

[3] When you ask Nobel Prize winners in science to identify the most crucial experiences that informed their theoretical work, they often refer to collaboration or apprenticeship relations with outstanding senior scholars in their own field (Nielsen and Kvale, 1999). I personally owe a great deal to three outstanding scholars. The first is the Swedish economic historian, Lars Herlitz, who at the end of the 1960s introduced me to the history of economic thought and especially to the works of Karl Marx. I also owe a lot to Christopher Freeman, who in the beginning of the 1980s helped me to understand the innovation process and showed me how to combine Schumpeter with Keynes and Marx. Chris, with his modesty and lack of tolerance for academic pompousness, became a role model (not an easy one to live up to!). Over the last decades I have had the privilege to draw upon the wisdom of Dick Nelson. Among other things, I have learnt from him the importance of diversity as a source of innovation and the need for diversity in the use of the scientific tools to be applied to the innovation process.

[4] In other words, there is a difference between the efficient behaviour of firms assumed by economic theory and their behaviour in practice (Leibenstein, 1966).

23

to introduce more efficient production methods. The analysis also pointed to the important distinction between product and process innovation in connection with international competitiveness and balance of payment restricted economic growth (Thirlwall, 1979). Product innovation was presented as a key to sustainable strong international competitiveness.

This experience posed interesting research questions about the link between innovation, productivity, and international competitiveness, and the IKE research programme 1977 was formed on that basis. It was defined as a research programme on international competitiveness and industrial development.[5] When Christopher Freeman joined the group as a visiting professor at the beginning of the 1980s, he opened up new analytical perspectives as well as access to the international network of innovation scholars.

Freeman's lectures provided an insight into Schumpeter's work and how it linked to Marx and Keynes. He engaged members of the group in new topics such as innovation as an interactive process and the systemic character of innovation. Freeman also edited a booklet on innovation, competitiveness, and international specialization with contributions from members of the group (Freeman, 1981).[6]

The Mike Project, 1980–83

At the beginning of the 1980s, there was a strong focus upon the emerging technology then referred to as 'microelectronics' in science and technology policy in all countries in Europe. The MIKE project was established 1980 with a three-year grant from the Danish Technology Council. The focus was upon economic performance, assessing the impact of the development and use of information technology on employment, growth, and international competitiveness (Brændgaard et al., 1982, 1984).

The research was organized around units that were referred to as 'industrial complexes'. The four units selected were the:

- agro-industrial complex,
- textile industrial complex,
- office automation complex,
- environmental industrial complex.

To begin with, the project operated with a definition of 'complex' that was close to what is referred to today as a sectoral system of innovation or an industrial cluster. As the research proceeded, it was realized that the term should

---

[5] Today the same acronym 'IKE' refers to Innovation, Knowledge, and Economic Dynamics.

[6] Most of my research has been shaped by discussions within the IKE group. I owe a lot of ideas and inspiration to the founding members—Asger Brændgaard, Bent Dalum, Björn Johnson, and Esben Sloth Andersen.

be interpreted more broadly—closer to the classical reference to the 'military industrial complex' in the USA. One reason for this change in perspective was that we found shared visions among users and producers of technology, and that these visions in several cases led to 'unsatisfactory innovation'. In some of the complexes this reflected an exchange of personnel between functions as regulators and policy-makers, on the one hand, and technology producers and users, on the other. One common pattern observed was that a trajectory originally rooted in rational ideas about how to develop and use technology was taken too far because of the converging common understanding among agents that this must be the right way to go.[7]

In all four complexes, the focus was upon how firms that developed, produced, or supplied the technology interacted with the users of the technology. We observed very different patterns of user–producer relationships and found that the patterns differed between more or less standardized and mature technologies, and between technologies characterized respectively by incremental or radical change. Especially in sectors exhibiting non-disruptive constant incremental change, long-term relationships between users and producers were found to be important. We also found that the role of geographical distance between user and producer reflected the kind of innovation process that predominated.[8]

This project had a major impact upon the direction of the research pursued within the IKE group. Lundvall (1985) was directly inspired by this research experience. This booklet adopted a critical stance towards standard economics, but was also intended to offer a constructive contribution to the study of innovation. It argued that 'pure markets' were not supporting product innovation and that neither neo-classical models nor transaction cost theory could explain the kind of long-term relationships between users and producers that were observed in the real economy.[9]

---

[7] When, in the autumn of 1984, I presented these observations at the TEP-seminar at Stanford University, I was introduced to similar ideas about 'lock in' developed by Brian Arthur and Paul David.

[8] One stereotype in the understanding of scientific procedure is that the inspiration from formal codified abstract knowledge is somehow superior and anterior to what can be learnt from history, from empirical observation, and from revealing good stories. The idea is that you start from existing theory, then you derive hypotheses, and at the end you return to the theory and refine it. Within innovation studies we can observe a reverse learning process, where case studies play an important role in shaping theoretical perspectives. We might refer to this phenomenon as the 'importance of paradigmatic cases'. In innovation studies I propose the following links between scholars and 'paradigmatic case studies'. Schumpeter: railways; Christopher Freeman: chemical industry + Project Sappho; Nathan Rosenberg: textiles and textile machinery; Richard Nelson: the Moon and the Ghetto, Giovanni Dosi: information technology. My own paradigmatic case studies took place in the MIKE project mentioned earlier (Lundvall, 1985). The experience convinced me that it was useful to analyse and understand innovation as an interactive process and to move towards the concept of innovation systems.

[9] The idea that markets are 'organized' and that there are *relationships* between seller and customer has been developed on a different basis by Kirman (1994). See Dosi's contribution to this book (Chapter 5).

It proposed that the best way to understand the observed pattern, where producers are linked to users through network relationships, was to recognize the importance of interactive learning engaging diverse agents. Vertically integrated firms, with both 'customers' and 'suppliers' in-house, would be handicapped since the interactive learning taking place would become too narrow and 'locked-in'. At the other extreme, specialized firms that operated in pure markets would not obtain access to any form of qualitative feedback from suppliers and customers. Firms with long-term network relationships to a multitude of external and diverse customers and suppliers would learn more because of the higher degree of diversity of their partners. While the interaction would involve transaction costs, the 'benefits from interactive learning' may more than compensate for these costs. This is especially the case in sectors and markets where the technology offers a basis for ongoing innovation.

The analysis illustrates the view of Schumpeter (1934) and Nelson and Winter (1982) that standard economics is a theory that works best for a fictional stationary economy where innovation is rare. In an economy without product innovation, the standard economics assumption of 'pure markets' would be more plausible.

The Pike Project, 1989–92

At the end of the 1980s, an extreme version of the Solow paradox ('we see computers everywhere but in the productivity statistics') could be witnessed in Denmark. Between 1986 and 1989 investments and employment were growing quite strongly, but the rate of growth of productivity was *negative in important sectors including manufacturing*. This phenomenon could not be explained by the mainstream economists, and the PIKE project was set up to analyse the background of this productivity mystery.

The project combined quantitative analysis at different levels of aggregation with case studies at the firm level, and it arrived at quite a clear conclusion. It was found that the most important explanation was that the accelerated introduction of information technology in Danish firms had not been matched by change in the organizational structure of the firms and upgrading of the competences of the employees. Firms that did combine the introduction of information technology with organizational change and upgrading of skills experienced a stronger growth in labour productivity than the average firm, while those that did not experienced a negative rate of productivity growth (Gjerding et al., 1990).

The project demonstrated the importance of the mismatch between a radically new technology and the pre-existing organizational structure and skill structure. The fact that this kind of mismatch at the micro-level had a significant impact upon economic growth at the aggregate level gave strong support to the ideas of Freeman and Perez that the growth potential of new techno-economic paradigms is not easily realized because of the slow adaptation of skills and of organizational and institutional settings (Freeman and Perez, 1988).

The Nis Project, 1987–92

Lundvall coordinated a project on national systems of innovation that started before, but ran in parallel with, the Nelson project (described later in Section 2.3). However, the set-up of the project was different. First, the intention was to move towards a theoretical understanding of innovation as an interactive process. Second, the authors who were invited to join were asked to address specific sub-systems or dimensions of the national innovation system, including the openness of the system as well as the policy implications. The fact that most of the authors came from Denmark or other small countries in Northern Europe gave the analysis a specific flavour. For instance, the relative success of the Nordic countries had been attained in spite of a specialization in low technology (exports came mainly from sectors with low R&D intensity). Therefore, there was strong focus upon how competence-building could emerge out of routine activities related to production and marketing.

The starting point of the book is a statement regarding the importance of knowledge and learning—knowledge is the most important resource and learning is the most important process. A prominent role for the structuring of the book was given to the analysis of how users interact with producers and how they form lasting relationships. As I will demonstrate in Section 2.3, Christopher Freeman (who made an important contribution to the book) and others at SPRU had already developed an implicit and sometimes explicit systemic understanding of innovation systems.

Other early contributions on national systems of innovation that led up to the 1992 publication were a book on how the information technology revolution affected small countries (Freeman and Lundvall, 1988) and the three chapters on national innovation systems in Dosi et al. (1988) by respectively Freeman, Nelson, and Lundvall.

The OECD Job's Study, 1992–95

The most important lesson from the Job's Study was a new understanding of the link between globalization, technical change, skills, and inequality (OECD,

1994).[10] The study demonstrated that there was growing inequality in all member states between skilled and unskilled labour in the period studied (the latter part of the 1980s). This took the form of growing differences both in employment rates and in earned income between highly-skilled and low-skilled workers. When explaining this trend, the OECD reports presented two separate alternative causes. One was the impact of skill-demanding technology (especially ICT) and the other was the impact of growing trade from low-income countries.

A third interpretation, however, was the learning economy hypothesis developed in Lundvall and Johnson (1994).[11] Here, the assumption was that the combination of new technology, globalization, and deregulation led to a speeding up of change that gave an advantage to skilled workers, since they were better equipped in terms of the capacity to learn.

This perspective was relevant for the emerging field of OECD activity around the knowledge-based economy. With support from the incoming Clinton administration, OECD was asked to promote the understanding of this new phase in capitalist development. The first conference on this topic took place in Copenhagen 1994 (Foray and Lundvall, 1994). This experience and the follow-up project on knowledge management in the learning society organized by OECD's Center for Education Research and Innovation (CERI) some years later (OECD, 2000) was useful in providing insights into the complexities of knowledge and learning.[12]

The Disko Project, 1996–99

The Disko project was financed by the Ministry of Industry, Denmark, and was an attempt to analyse the Danish innovation system.[13] The project was organized around four broadly defined themes:

- The firm (organizational structure, innovation activities, exposure to competition).

[10] I was employed as Deputy Director at the OECD Directorate for Science, Technology, and Industry between 1992 and 1995. During this period I represented the directorate within the small group of economists who coordinated the Job's Study.

[11] While I worked at OECD, the organization adopted the idea of 'the new economy' after a meeting with Alan Greenspan in 1994. The assumption that the use of information technology would give rise to steep increases in productivity was used to justify lax monetary policy in the USA and elsewhere. The idea was that the productivity increase would eliminate the risk of inflation. This idea was revised after the bursting of the ICT bubble.

[12] When I returned to Aalborg University in the autumn of 1995, I gave an inaugural lecture that reflected on my experiences from OECD. The title was 'The Social Dimension of the Learning Economy', and the role of tacit knowledge was given a prominent place in the lecture (Lundvall, 1996).

[13] One interesting characteristic of the Disko project was that it served as a training site for six PhD students. Such large projects can be excellent frameworks for research training—a point I will return to later. Another interesting feature was that three of the PhD students were financed by the Ministry of Industry and spent some of the project working within the Ministry. This reflected the fact that the Ministry at that time was acting as an 'advanced user' in relation to innovation studies.

- Inter-firm interaction (patterns of domestic and international interaction of innovating firms).
- The firm and the institutional context (education, research, labour market, finance).
- The innovation system as a whole (innovation survey, input–output patterns, economic growth).

Again, a diverse set of research tools, including case studies as well as econometric analysis, was used. One important tool was a postal survey of 2000 firms in the private sector. This survey was conducted on three occasions (1996, 2001, and 2006). The fact that it was organized in collaboration with Danmarks Statistik allowed us to link specific responses to a vast amount of relevant data. One of the most important data sources was IDA, a complete labour market register covering all firms and all individuals in Denmark. This unique access to data made it possible to test interesting hypotheses linking organizational forms and organzsational change, innovation, and employment patterns to each other.[14]

The major outcomes from this project are summarized in Lundvall (2002). Many of the results deepened our understanding of the original hypotheses on the importance of interactive learning as the basis for innovation. This was the case for the analysis of product innovation and inter-firm collaboration. We found that *all* firms that engaged in product innovation at least occasionally involved as external partners in the innovation process, and that long-term (domestic) relations played an important role. However, we also found that, while interaction with foreign firms was less frequent than interaction with domestic firms, it had a greater impact upon innovation outcomes.

The project also made it possible to return to issues about the role of competition in relation to polarization in labour markets. Firms that responded to increased competition by developing new forms of organization and new products were found to have expanded their employment while those that did not lost jobs. At the aggregate level, the innovative firms even increased the number of unskilled workers employed. This result indicates that, when globalization pressure is met with innovative responses, the tendency towards polarization in the labour market may be more than compensated for.

---

[14] IDA is the acronym for the integrated database for labour market research. For details, see <http://www.dst.dk/en/Statistik/dokumentation/Declarations/integrated-database-for-labour-market-research--ida-.aspx>.

Later on, we used the Disko survey results to study how different kinds of knowledge and different modes of learning relate to innovation. The analysis demonstrated how firms that combine research efforts with promoting experience-based learning are significantly more innovative than those that only engage in research (Jensen et al., 2007). The distinction drawn between STI- and DUI-modes has been useful in explaining why business strategies and economic policy aiming at promoting innovation should not focus exclusively on science as a source or driver of innovation.[15]

The Locnis Project, 2002–05

The LocNis project was designed in collaboration with the EU Commission, and the idea was to combine insights from a number of EU-supported projects and produce a cross-disciplinary and cross-sectoral synthesis. In the LocNis project we invited representatives from projects covering respectively the labour market, management, education, and innovation studies to a series of seminars. At the end the different contributions were brought together in Lorenz and Lundvall (2006).

In the LocNis project one of the most interesting contributions came from Lorenz and Valeyre (2006). They used survey data from the third Working Condition Survey 2000, organized by the European Foundation for the Improvement of Living and Working Conditions, to construct a taxonomy of modes of work organization and found very dramatic differences between different parts of Europe. This provided an insight into a previously rather neglected aspect of national innovation systems, and was later used to demonstrate that national systems with a high proportion of jobs offering learning opportunities were countries with a large share of innovative firms (Arundel et al., 2007).

Lessons Learnt[16]

The most important lesson of my research experience is that it is essential to understand innovation as an interactive process. The analysis of constellations of user–producer interactions in connection with product innovation

---

[15] STI (Science, Technology, and Innovation) refers to a learning mode with the focus upon codified knowledge, while DUI refers to tacit and experience-based knowledge emanating from learning by Doing, Using, and Interacting. Later I will argue—with reference to the seminal paper by Cohen and Levinthal (1990)—that these concepts might be used to develop a better understanding of what constitutes the absorptive capacity of a firm.

[16] My own personal knowledge differs from that of colleagues working in the field of innovation studies. It reflects what I have learnt from doing research in a small Nordic welfare economy and from the design and execution of specific research projects. For instance, with the exception of the contribution by Lorenz, the other contributors to this book do not pay much attention to

has over time made this perspective more visible and explicit. This perspective helps us understand why economic theory idealizing the 'pure market' is woefully inadequate. Understanding innovation as an interactive process creates a more useful platform for the institutional design of management strategies and public policy.

As already mentioned, Christopher Freeman pioneered both the idea that interactive learning was important for innovation and the systemic perspective on innovation (see also Section 2.3). Making the analysis between the two levels explicit and detailed as in Lundvall (1985) and Lundvall (1988) contributed to the analytical foundation of the innovation system. More recent research projects deepened and broadened the understanding of national innovation systems. In the Disko project (Lundvall, 2002), the role of learning organizations in the system was studied while the Loc Nis project (Lorenz and Lundvall, 2006) focused on the role of national education and labour markets.

In Lundvall (2002) it was shown that *interaction within firms* is crucial for innovation and that such interaction is at the core of what have been referred to as 'learning organizations'. Later Lorenz and Lundvall (2006) showed that *learning at the workplace* matters for innovation and that workplace learning will depend, in turn, upon how countries organize labour markets and education.

The concept of the 'the learning economy' was inspired by a similar concept developed by the Swedish pedagogical professor Husén (1974), who referred to 'the learning society' as a normative concept (Lundvall and Johnson, 1994). The idea behind the concept is simple. It refers to an assumption that there is a speeding up of change that requires a speeding up of learning.

Recent research with Edward Lorenz has focused upon how the learning economy is organized differently in different parts of Europe. In the more egalitarian Nordic countries, we find a broad participation of workers. In the UK and in the South of Europe, the participation gap between thinkers and doers is wider. More or less ambitious welfare states and differences in social distance explain why modes of innovation are different in different innovation systems (Lundvall and Lorenz, 2011). Patterns of inequality influence innovation modes, and waves of innovation then affect inequality (Freeman, 2001).

the organization of work as an important dimension of innovation studies. On the other hand, this chapter illustrates that my engagement with science and technology studies (STS) is perhaps rather less than that found among colleagues from SPRU.

2.3. The Theoretical Core of Innovation Studies

This section discusses, with reference to a similar attempt within entrepreneurship studies, whether it is possible to define a 'theoretical core' of innovation studies. It is argued that it is indeed possible to do so, and that the core is based around a perspective in which innovation is seen as an interactive process. This interpretation is qualified through a discussion of the theoretical contributions of the works most frequently cited in handbooks on innovation studies. I will use the results from Fagerberg, Fosaas, and Sapprasert, (2012) and refer to the five most cited works for each of three periods (up to 1969, 1970–90, and after 1990).

Innovation as an Interactive Process: A Theoretical Core to
Innovation Studies?

Innovation studies covers a broad field of research where scholars with varying disciplinary backgrounds address issues at different levels of aggregation by means of a great range of analytical tools. Two recent attempts, using different methodologies, to analyse the community of innovation scholars and the knowledge base they share (Fagerberg and Verspagen, 2009; Fagerberg, Fosaas, and Sapprasert, 2012) both emphasize that the field is divided into a number of sub-fields or clusters. According to Fagerberg, Fosaas, and Sapprasert (2012) there is one cluster that brings together scholars who link innovation to management and firm performance, and another that comprises economists and other social scientists interested in the relationship between innovation and R&D, economic growth, and public policy. These two studies also show that, while the field of innovation studies has its roots in economics, it also attracts numerous scholars who study innovation from a management, organizational, political science, historical, philosophical, or sociological perspective.[17]

Is it meaningful to look for a theoretical core in such a diverse and complex field of knowledge? I will argue that such a core can indeed be discerned and that this core has become more visible over recent decades. My inspiration for raising the issue of 'a theoretical core' comes from contributions by Shane and Venkataraman (2000), two of the most frequently cited authors in entrepreneurship studies. They contend that it is of strategic importance to define what constitutes the theoretical core of the similarly heterogeneous

---

[17] While Fagerberg and Verspagen (2009) made use of surveys and asked scholars to define their own position, Fagerberg, Fosaas, and Sapprasert (2012) instead drew upon handbooks of innovation studies to map the field. The fact that the two methods yield broadly similar results enhances the credibility of the respective studies.

field of entrepreneurship studies. They argue that the key building blocks in the theoretical core of entrepreneurship studies are respectively the *individual* and the *opportunities* that he/she encounters. The process of entrepreneurship that needs to be studied is one where individuals perceive, assess, and act in relation to opportunities. Hence, it is important to understand both the individual entrepreneur and the context within which he/she acts. The context may, for instance, be more or less fertile when it comes to offering opportunities, and the individual may be more or less able to exploit them as they arise.[18]

I would suggest that the closest we get to such a core in innovation studies is the conceptualization of *innovation as an interactive process* involving many actors and extending over time. The focus of the analysis is upon individuals with heterogeneous skills or upon organizations with heterogeneous capabilities that interact with one another. They typically engage in information exchange, problem solving, and mutual learning as part of the process of innovation. In the course of this, they establish 'relationships' that may be interpreted as forming organizations, networks, clusters, or even 'innovation systems'.[19]

This definition of the theoretical core assumes that it is useful to regard the innovation process as one that starts with combining elements of existing knowledge and ends with new knowledge as an important output. Innovation may be seen as a 'new combination' of more or less disparate elements of knowledge. The more disparate the elements are, the more radical the innovation. Radical innovation may reflect a combination of insights from 'distant' disciplines in natural science (e.g. physics and biology) or from combining 'distant' technologies (e.g. ICT and genetic engineering). Incremental innovations may combine more or less distant forms of experience-based

---

[18] The structure of the model has something in common with a production function approach to technical change, where 'firms' can make choices between different techniques that are more or less intensive in the use of labour and capital respectively. One major difference compared with mainstream economics is, of course, that entrepreneurship scholars (in common with innovation scholars) recognize that agents operate under conditions of fundamental uncertainty.

[19] The proposed theoretical core may be compared to Dosi's reference to the SYS-synthesis—a combination of research outcomes from Sussex, Yale, and Stanford (Dosi et al., 2006, p. 1451). According to Dosi, the SYS-synthesis represents a common understanding of certain characteristics of the innovation process: uncertainty and serendipity in search processes; the long time-lag from 'discovery' to 'application'; sometimes technology runs ahead of science; the outcome has elements of a public good; the important role of tacit knowledge and experience-based learning; and context (in particular, the technology or sector) matters. This list of 'stylized facts' is useful because it sums up a number of important insights emanating from historical and empirical studies of innovation processes. It is also helpful in explaining why neo-classical economics is so inadequate when it comes to understanding and explaining what goes on in an economy where innovation is ubiquitous. However, it does not really constitute a theoretical core as defined by Shane and Venkataraman.

knowledge (e.g. marketing experience and production experience) as well as the outcomes of learning by interaction across organizational borders.

Interaction may be studied as the exchange of information, as a process of interactive learning, or as cooperation within or across organizational borders. In order to understand the character of interaction and knowledge sharing, it is essential to make distinctions between different forms of knowledge. At any point in time, an innovation system may be characterized by a set of relationships between agents. The process of innovation will reflect these relationships, and the process leads to an ongoing construction, reproduction, and destruction of relationships.

Looking for the Theoretical Core Using the Most Cited Works as Source

In this section I will give a brief presentation of fifteen works that emanate from three different periods. I will discuss if and how they contribute to a theoretical core for innovation studies, and test our hypothesis that a perspective in which innovation is seen as an interactive process constitutes such a core. In doing so, I will refer to other contributions that may be seen as complementary or as a follow-up to the selected works. This mode of proceeding should also provide a sense of the evolution of the field.[20]

THE PERIOD UP TO 1969

In Fagerberg, Fosaas, and Sapprasert (2012), the most highly cited works on innovation have been listed for three different time-periods—see Tables 2.1–2.3. The period up until 1969 includes the seminal work on innovation diffusion by the sociologist, E. M. Rogers (1962), the contribution on innovation management by Burns and Stalker (1961), the analysis by Kenneth Arrow of the appropriability of scientific efforts (1962b), and the two most important contributions by Joseph A. Schumpeter (1934, 1942). One's first impression is that these works are rather different in character and represent quite disparate perspectives on innovation. Here, I will discuss how each of them has served as a stepping stone for the development of innovation studies as the field exists today.

Arrow's contribution signalled that economic theory and economic policy should pay more attention to science and technology. Until then, the

---

[20] We should expect an evolution in the theoretical core. This evolution may encapsulate refinements of the theory, reflecting new insights based upon historical and empirical research. However, as argued in Chapter 4 by Carlota Perez, theory also needs to adapt to fundamental changes in historical context. For instance, the stronger emphasis upon interaction in innovation theory may reflect a movement towards a network society. It is consequently not meaningful to insist upon a 'general theory' valid for all historical époques.

Table 2.1. The core literature for the period up to 1969

1	Rogers (1962)	*Diffusion of Innovations*
2	Schumpeter (1934)	*The Theory of Economic Development*
3	Arrow (1962)	Economic Welfare and the Allocation of Resources for Invention
4	Schumpeter (1942)	*Capitalism, Socialism, and Democracy*
5	Burns and Stalker (1961)	*The Management of Innovation*

Source: Adapted version of table 7 in Fagerberg, Fosaas, and Sapprasert (2012).

Table 2.2. The core literature, 1970–89

1	Nelson and Winter (1982)	*An Evolutionary Theory of Economic Change*
2	Freeman (1974)	*The Economics of Industrial Innovation*
3	Pavitt (1984)	Sectoral Patterns of Technical Change
4	Freeman (1987)	*Technology Policy and Economic Performance*
5	Von Hippel (1988)	*The Sources of Innovation*

Source: Adapted version of table 7 in Fagerberg, Fosaas, and Sapprasert (2012).

Table 2.3. The core literature, 1990–2009

1	Nelson (1993)	*National Innovation Systems: A Comparative Study*
2	Porter (1990)	*The Competitive Advantage of Nations*
3	Lundvall (1992)	*National Systems of Innovation*
4	Cohen and Levinthal (1990)	Absorptive Capacity: A New Perspective on Learning and Innovation
5	Saxenian (1994)	*Regional Advantage*

Source: Adapted version of table 7 in Fagerberg, Fosaas, and Sapprasert (2012).

economic arguments for investing in science had mainly been delivered by scientists or engineers such as John D. Bernal (1939) in the UK and Vannevar Bush in the USA. Now Arrow (1962b) provided arguments based upon welfare economics as to why governments should assume a responsibility for directly or indirectly funding basic research. It played a similar role in creating a demand for innovation studies as Solow's analysis of economic growth, which revealed a major unexplained 'residual' that he referred to as technical progress (Solow, 1956, 1957).

Arrow's paper may also be seen as an early economic formulation of 'the linear model of innovation' as it was originally presented by Vannevar Bush (1945) and indirectly of what I will refer to as 'the techno-economic theory of innovation'. Appropriability—that is the possibility for innovators to reap the benefits that come from the introduction of an innovation—and regimes of intellectual property protection have become classical themes in innovation studies. An important step forward was the Yale Survey that asked managers to assess a series of issues related to appropriability and technological opportunity (Levin et al., 1987). The most striking result coming out of the Yale study was that the means and effectiveness of instruments for protecting knowledge differed quite strongly across sectors and technologies, as well as between process and product innovation. The realization that such differences may be reflected in different forms of technological competition remains central to many current contributions to innovation studies.

The contribution by Burns and Stalker (1961) established a link between the rate of change in the environment of the firm and its most appropriate form of organization. They argued that 'organic organizations' with a more fluid division of labour and with horizontal interaction were more innovative and better able to respond to change than organizations characterized by a formalized and more rigid specialization characterized by vertical communication.[21] In that their analysis made a distinction between different forms of interaction and communication within organizations, it relates to the theoretical core as defined earlier. As a follow-up to their work, others developed further distinctions between organizational types that play an important role in modern innovation studies. Mintzberg's (1979) taxonomy has proved to be especially fruitful:

- simple structure characteristic of an entrepreneurial organization,
- machine bureaucracy,
- professional bureaucracy,
- diversified form,
- adhocracy or innovative organization,
- missionary organization.

The analysis of the organizational dimension of innovation has developed further in recent years. With inspiration from Mintzberg, Alice Lam has analysed how the character of knowledge and organizational forms are interdependent, and also how this can be illustrated by studying organizational structure in different national labour markets and innovation systems (Lam, 2000; Lam and Lundvall, 2006).

The work on innovation diffusion by Everett Rogers was rooted in a specific tradition of agricultural innovation diffusion that took off in the 1940s with a study of the spread of hybrid corn in the USA (Ryan and Gross, 1943). Valente and Rogers (1995) give an overview of how this field of research emerged and

---

[21] One important point made later by Cohen and Levinthal (1990) was that the organizational forms that contribute to flexibility and to the absorption of new ideas are not so different from the organizational forms that promote innovation and the creation of new ideas. This point is supported by empirical work showing how firms characterized by organic forms such as 'adhocracy' are both more innovative and more organizationally flexible than others (Lundvall, 2002).

then gradually disappeared. One interesting feature of Rogers' own contribution is the importance that he attaches to the formation of networks and his criticism of the narrow focus on characteristics of the individual farmer. His emphasis upon how information exchange takes place in networks and in geographical space may thus be seen as a forerunner to the perspective whereby innovation is seen as an interactive process.

Compared to more recent contributions, it is worth noting that none of the three works listed here is very specific when it comes to the technological dimension of innovation. In the case of Rogers, innovation is used in an extremely broad sense, referring mainly to the diffusion and use of new ways of doing things.

Schumpeter is more specific and defines innovation as encompassing:

> The introduction of new goods…new methods of production…the opening of new markets…the conquest of new sources of supply…and the carrying out of a new organization of any industry. (Schumpeter, 1934, p. 66)

In his *Theory of Economic Development* (1934), he also refers to innovations as 'new combinations', sometimes further specified as reflecting a change in the production function. This book and his subsequent work on *Capitalism, Socialism and Democracy* (1942) are fundamental because they link innovation to economic development and not least because of the fundamental criticism of mainstream economic theory that they deliver.

In as far as there is a theory of entrepreneurship and innovation in *Theory of Economic Development*, it is arguably closer to the theoretical core of modern entrepreneurship studies than to that of modern innovation studies. Schumpeter's entrepreneurs are individuals with specific personal traits that make them stand out from other economic agents who are imitators or even who resist change. Entrepreneurs are those who see opportunities and introduce new combinations. The theory of innovation is thus sociological and based mainly upon a hypothesis regarding diversity among economic agents. This sociological focus is also reflected in his famous article on the survival of capitalism (Schumpeter, 1936/91), in which he outlines the major threat to the system as coming from a change in social patterns and lifestyle in which the traditional bourgeois family is weakened and subversive critical intellectuals become more dominant.

Schumpeter demonstrates why a theory of capitalist development must place innovation at the very centre of analysis. Not only will capitalist dynamics in the form of growth and business cycles reflect waves of innovations and entrepreneurial initiative; according to Schumpeter, capitalism itself could not exist without innovation. Innovation creates differential rents that take the form of profits, and without profits there would be no capitalism. This implies, of course, that an economic theory relevant for capitalism needs to recognize the inevitability of uncertainty, since it is clear that all future possible outcomes of innovation processes cannot be known in advance. It also implies that it is inconsistent to operate with models assuming general equilibrium, since innovation is by its very nature a dis-equilibrating phenomenon.

In the innovation literature, Schumpeter (1942) is mainly referred to as reflecting the author's change of view regarding the 'entrepreneurial function'. It is no longer the heroic individual who is seen as bringing new processes and products to the market (often referred to as 'Schumpeter Mark I'). Innovation is instead now seen as the outcome of systematic efforts pursued by big and often oligopolistic firms that have sufficient resources to engage in research and development. This trend, of course, makes it even more important to understand what takes place inside organizations. The expansion of work on innovation management inspired by Burns and Stalker (1961) may be seen as a follow-up to what has been referred to as 'Schumpeter Mark II'. More generally, the new perspective opens up the possibility to think about 'collective entrepreneurship' and to adopt a pragmatic approach to methodology in which action by individuals is not the only legitimate starting point for the analysis.

Schumpeter's understanding of the innovation process has had a substantial influence on modern innovation studies. First, the distinction between his Mark I and Mark II perspectives gave rise to a rich debate on firm size, market power, and innovation performance. This debate yielded the preliminary result that there is an inverted U-shaped relationship between size and innovation performance; in industries with weak competition more intense competition will stimulate firms to engage more in innovation, while in industries with strong competition, innovation performance might become weaker as competition is intensified. Some interesting contributions, such as Richardson (1996), have criticized the static understanding of competition underpinning these analyses and argued that in technologically dynamic sectors 'monopolies' may remain extremely active innovators in spite of their market power, offering low price as well as high quality products.

More interestingly from the point of view of modern innovation studies, the debate ended with an emerging view that the two modes may coexist and be more or less frequent in different sectors and at different stages of the technology life cycle. Dosi (1988), in his seminal paper on the microeconomics of innovation, pointed to technological opportunity, cumulativeness of technology, and appropriability as three variables that influence what mode becomes dominant in a specific sector. Malerba and Orsenigo (1997) later introduced the concept of 'technological regimes', and this concept remains central to Malerba's work on sectoral innovation systems.

Schumpeter's second major influence on modern innovation studies came through a debate sparked by a reaction to his rather one-sided focus upon the supply side. Schumpeter assumed *that the demand side does not play an active role in innovative change.*[22] It is true that he defines the opening of new markets as one kind of innovation. However, even in this case he thought that it was the supply side that persuades consumers and users to adjust their previous routine behaviour. In general, he believed that it was the Schumpeterian entrepreneurs or firms that designed innovations and made them successful. Indeed, it can be argued that the innovation system perspective came partly out of a criticism of Schumpeter's relative neglect of the demand side.

Schmookler (1966) took almost the opposite view to Schumpeter. He used a host of empirical data on inventions as well as various secondary sources to demonstrate that inventions and innovations tend to flourish in areas where demand is strong and growing. One important outcome of the ensuing debate was *a new perspective on innovation as reflecting the interplay between technology-push and demand-pull* (Mowery and Rosenberg, 1979).

The 'chain-linked model', in which both supply-push and demand-pull are considered in relation to scientific knowledge, may be seen as one contribution to the new perspective (Kline and Rosenberg, 1986). The perspective on innovation as a process of interaction between producers and users may be seen as a micro-dimension of this new perspective (Lundvall, 1985). And, as we shall see, Christopher Freeman played a crucial pioneering role in introducing a systemic view of innovation

THE PERIOD, 1970–89

The most cited work from this period is Nelson and Winter's book, *An Evolutionary Theory of Economic Change*. It makes an attempt to realize the intentions of Schumpeter, that is to develop an economic theory that forms an alternative to neo-classical economics that is able to explain what goes on in an economy where innovation and change are pervasive. The book gives a broad and realistic introduction to a microeconomic theory with reference to empirical insights as to how individuals and firms learn and make decisions. On this basis it builds simulation models based upon an evolutionary perspective that make it possible to understand how the innovation, retention, and selection of routines (and firms) shape aggregates and industrial development.

---

[22] Another point where Schumpeter's approach differs from the NSI approach is his neglect of the importance of knowledge and learning for understanding the innovation process. Schumpeter's entrepreneurs are activists who bring new combinations to the market. How the new combinations specifically come about is left unanswered (Witt, 2003, p. xiv).

While the work reflects the experience acquired by the authors from carrying out research on innovation, its primary intention is not to present a theory of innovation. Nonetheless there is an implicit and sometimes explicit theory of how firms engage in innovation processes underlying the analysis. This perspective is developed in some detail in the authors' earlier article entitled 'In search of a useful theory of technological innovation' (Nelson and Winter, 1977). An important assumption is that firms use heuristics (routines for searching) and that those directly involved in technical innovation tend to follow particular technological trajectories. A central theme is that the conditions for innovative activities are very different across sectors and that this has to do with the character of the technology, the demand for the technology, and the institutional setting. In line with the interactive perspective, it is recognized that the innovation process includes an active role for users. But there is little reference to this interaction and relationships. For instance, the natural trajectories are seen as evolving on the supply side; the fact that they become more anchored and difficult to change through long-term relationships with users is not discussed.[23]

The prominent position of the two books by Freeman and of the seminal article by Pavitt (1984) putting forward a sectoral taxonomy, reflects the fact that in the 1970s the Science Policy Research Unit became the leading European research unit in relation to innovation studies. It is important to note that SPRU was inter-disciplinary from the very beginning, and that it combined expertise in economics and social science with experience in the specific fields of science and technology. Freeman referred to the 'economics of innovation' in the title of his 1974 book, which was richer in terms of references to the characteristics of different technologies than Schumpeter and also went further in characterizing the innovation process.

As pointed out in the analysis of Freeman's contribution to innovation studies by Fagerberg et al. (2011), Freeman's starting point was an attempt to study and understand the links between science and industrial innovation. Early on, however, he defined a broader research agenda that might be seen as the early origin of what I define as the theoretical core. In its very first annual report, the Unit's purpose was described as contributing 'to a deeper understanding of the complex social process of research, invention, development and innovation. It aims to study this process in industry and in government, as well as in universities, and in the context of the environment

---

[23] It is also interesting to note that there is reference neither to Burns and Stalker nor to Mintzberg in Nelson and Winter (1982). The theory of organization presented is inspired by the literature on decision-making under bounded rationality by March and Simon (1958). Decentralization is discussed as a management issue while activating ordinary employees in 'learning organizations' is not considered as a way of reducing the need for detailed control and monitoring by management.

in developing countries, as well as in industrial societies' (SPRU, 1967, p. 5, cited in Fagerberg et al., 2011, p. 900).

The 'mission statement' from SPRU's 1971 annual report is even more explicit in recognizing the systemic character of innovation:

> The Unit's central interest is in policy for the professional research and development network and the way in which this social subsystem interacts with society as a whole. This interest includes both technological innovation arising from R&D, and the narrower concept of 'science' as fundamental research. It extends to the diffusion process of innovations in social systems. (SPRU, 1971, p. 6, cited in Fagerberg et al., 2011, p. 900)

In Freeman (1974), the section on how firms engage in innovation presents results from Project SAPPHO (see Rothwell, 1972, 1977) highlighting the importance of interaction between individuals and departments within firms as well as the importance of interaction with suppliers, customers, and science institutions. Freeman's (1987) book on Japan was the first publication to explicitly refer to a national system of innovation, and it gave strong emphasis both to the role of networking and to the importance of organization of work. So while the historical work by Rosenberg (1976) on the role in innovation of users of machinery was preparing the ground for the chain-linked model, Freeman's experiences from Project SAPPHO prepared the ground for the innovation system perspective.

Both the two remaining contributions in the top five for this middle period—those by Pavitt (1984) and von Hippel (1988)—refer to the division of labour in innovation processes. Pavitt makes a distinction between sectors while von Hippel refers to the micro-level where certain innovations are initiated and sometimes realized by users while others are created by suppliers or producers.

The original Pavitt taxonomy distinguishes between sectors that are:

- supplier-dominated,
- production-intensive,
  - scale-intensive,
  - specialized suppliers,
- science-based.

In the supplier-dominated sectors, innovations tend to be imported in the form of machinery from specialized suppliers or in the form of new materials or complex systems from scale-intensive firms or science-based firms. Scale-intensive firms are dependent on having an in-house production engineering capacity, but also depend on the successful absorption of innovations from specialized suppliers and science-based firms. Both specialized suppliers and science-based firms tend to be active innovators. The specialized suppliers are highly dependent on their interaction with customers, while the science-based firms are dependent also on interaction with science institutions. Pavitt explains the observed patterns in terms of differences in source of technology, user needs, and appropriability.

Von Hippel (1988) represents a major contribution to the understanding of the division of labour between users and producers of innovation. He uses some of the same variables as Pavitt to explain why certain innovation activities take place among users. In some of his work the location of 'appropriability' appears to be the crucial factor. Later on, he introduces the location of specialized knowledge that takes the form of 'sticky information' as the most important underlying explanation.[24]

While these contributions by Pavitt and von Hippel help to understand the importance of the systemic interdependence and the division of labour in innovation processes, they give less attention to how this interdependence is reflected in processes of cooperation and patterns of interaction.

THE THEORETICAL CORE, 1990–2009

All the works listed earlier were published in the first half of the 1990s and they seem to form a more homogenous set in term of theoretical perspectives than those from the other two periods.

This is certainly the case for the three most cited works. Nelson (1993) presents a series of case studies of national innovation systems, Porter (1990) studies what constitutes national competitive advantage, while Lundvall (1992) is an attempt both to study sub-systems within the national innovation system and to give the national system of innovation a theoretical underpinning at the micro-level. However, as we shall see, there is also important overlap between these works, which deal with the national level, Cohen and Levinthal (1990), who focus at the level of the firm, and Saxenian (1994), who studies institutions and interactions at the regional level.

Nelson is, together with Freeman, the most important founder of modern innovation studies, and his style of research may serve as a model for future generations of innovation scholars. Together with Sidney Winter, he has followed up on Schumpeter's ambitions and developed the most ambitious attempt so far to establish a new economic paradigm that is more effective than the neo-classical one when it comes to explaining how the economy really works (Nelson and Winter, 1982). But he has also pursued and organized an impressive series of major research projects, and conducted empirical studies comparing innovation processes related to different technologies as

---

[24] This terminology is confusing since it is usual to define information as the least 'sticky' form of knowledge—as knowledge that can be communicated by means of digital media.

well as related to the same technology in different national contexts (see, for instance, Nelson, 1984).

Nelson's (1993) book was the outcome of a major project that brought together a number of scholars from different countries who were asked to develop an analysis of their own national innovation system. The authors were given quite considerable freedom to design their own chapter and the main coordination of the content took place at meetings with other participants. This explains why the different chapters placed emphasis upon different dimensions of the national innovation system. But many of the contributions highlight the interaction between industry and knowledge institutions, and in the introduction to the volume Nelson refers to the national specificity of user–producer relationships as motivating the focus on national rather than regional or global innovation systems.

Porter might not normally be regarded as a central figure in innovation studies, but his work on competitive advantage (Porter 1990) had several affinities with the work on national innovation systems by Freeman, Nelson, and Lundvall as presented in Dosi et al. (1988).[25] One line of argument is that competition is important for firm performance and for national competitive advantage. National economies that house several outstanding firms in the same economic sector will tend to remain dynamic and innovative in the sector. To this more traditional industrial economics approach, Porter added the importance of interaction with supplier industries and user industries. Vertical relationships and the formation of clusters were seen as necessary for transforming technological competition into sustained competitiveness.

Lundvall's (1992) publication was the outcome of the project on national innovation system mentioned previously (Section 2.2). The subtitle— 'towards a theory of innovation and interactive learning'—signalled the intention to move towards a theoretical understanding of innovation as an interactive process. The scholars invited to join were asked to address specific sub-systems or dimensions of the national innovation system, including the openness of the system. Examples of sub-systems were the public sector, the financial sector, and the science system. Therefore, there was a strong focus upon how competence-building could emerge out of routine activities related to production and marketing. The idea that learning by doing, using, and interacting (DUI) was as important as R&D was immanent in the analysis.

Cohen and Levinthal (1990) provided a new definition of, and perspective on, the important concept 'absorptive capacity'. In the literature referring to the article, this concept is linked strongly to in-house R&D efforts. It is argued that one major reason for developing in-house R&D is that it is necessary in

---

[25] Actually, there was some direct spillover, in that Porter involved scholars from the IKE group in Aalborg in his project at the end of the 1980s.

order to be able to exploit external knowledge sources quickly and effectively. However, in the first half of the article the authors present a more complex and complete understanding of knowledge creation and learning (Cohen and Levinthal, 1990, pp. 128–37).[26]

Interactive learning, in this case within regional networks, also plays an important role in Saxenian (1994). She shows that networking—along with the institutions supporting networking—constitutes one of the major differences that explain why semiconductor firms grew much more rapidly on the basis of innovation in Silicon Valley than on the East Coast (Route 128). Indeed, scholars within economic geography were among 'early adopters' of the notion that innovation is an interactive process. They were also quick to pursue research on how different forms of knowledge and learning relate to location. This may reflect the fact that scholars in geography such as Torsten Hägerstrand had been among the pioneers in studying innovation diffusion (Hägerstrand, 1952, 1967). As a result, there is now a voluminous literature on regional innovation systems and innovative clusters (Polenska, 2007).

Is there a Theoretical Core in Innovation Studies?

It is not possible to distil a single theoretical core for innovation studies on the basis of the 15 most highly cited works covering the last century. We can nevertheless distinguish three major theoretical components to the development of such a core.

1. Many contributions, including the evolutionary economics model developed by Nelson and Winter, represent attempts to build an alternative theoretical paradigm for economics by complementing Schumpeter with insights emanating from innovation studies.

2. The work on appropriability can be said to have started with Arrow (1962), but it originally had a narrow focus on information. It developed into something like a (techno-) economic theory of innovation through the early works of Nelson and Winter as well as through the contributions of Freeman (1974), Pavitt (1984), the Yale Survey (Levin et al.,

---

[26] In the first part of the article there is a recognition that competence may be built on the basis of problem-solving, including learning by doing and learning by interacting within and across the borders of the firm. There is only one paragraph that may be read as an argument for narrowing the focus of the empirical part to R&D (Cohen and Levinthal, 1990, p. 134). In that paragraph, it is argued that 'learning by doing' is problematic since it may reduce diversity. This neglects the fact that interactions among heterogeneous experts and departments within the firm and especially interactions with diverse customers may lead to new combinations. In this respect, Jensen et al. (2007)—who show that the most innovative firms combine R&D-efforts with systematic attempts to stimulate learning by doing, learning by using, and learning by interacting—offer a more satisfactory empirical illustration of the theoretical discussion of absorptive capacity as developed in Cohen and Levinthal (1991).

1987), and Von Hippel (1988). This theory can be seen as constituting the theoretical base for the analysis of sectoral innovation systems.

3. Innovation as an interactive process was implicit in the contributions by Burns and Stalker (1961) and Rogers (1962). It was important in Freeman's work and in the last period it was a central element in all the top five contributions. This points to a socio-economic theory of innovation. It forms the theoretical foundation of national and regional innovation systems.

While both the techno-economic and the socio-economic theory of innovation may be formulated in general terms (there are a few key concepts that constitute the theory), they have in common the fact that they end up demonstrating the importance of historical and local context for how innovation actually takes place. In the case of techno-economic theory, the difference between sectors and underlying technologies is fundamental. In the case of socio-economic theory, the institutions of corporate, local, regional, and national systems differ and give rise to different patterns of interaction and interdependence.

The division of Schumpeter's work into respectively 'Mark I' with an emphasis on the role of the individual entrepreneur and 'Mark II' where big companies with a significant research capacity are the most important drivers of innovation (Phillips, 1971) illustrates the point made by Carlota Perez in Chapter 4 that theories have to adapt to changes in the real world. While it may be useful to study innovation as an interactive process and innovation systems in different historical époques, we would assume that the critical interfaces for the interaction will change from one period to the next. In evolutionary economics we should expect that the mechanisms that give rise to diversity and selection will differ as the techno-economic context changes.

2.4. Innovation Studies: Drawing the Boundaries to Adjacent Fields

In the last section we made an effort to characterize innovation studies by looking for its theoretical core. In this section we will define it by reflecting on its boundaries in relation to two adjacent fields—entrepreneurship studies and science and technology studies (STS). We will start by asking: who are the innovation scholars and where does the research on innovation take place? Fagerberg and Verspagen (2009) defined the core literature by using citation patterns in *Research Policy* and they combined it with an e-mail survey with responses from around 1000 individuals who defined themselves as innovation scholars. Recently Fagerberg et al. (2011) conducted a study of the field using citation patterns as reflected in authoritative 'handbooks' as the source. The latter project involved other colleagues who used the same method to map respectively STS (Martin and Nightingale) and entrepreneurship studies (Landström and colleagues). The results have been brought together in Fagerberg, Landström, and Martin (2012). In what follows, I present some reflections on the differences between innovation studies and these two neighbouring fields.

The Borderline between Innovation Studies and Entrepreneurship Studies

While entrepreneurship research and innovation research both have strong roots in the work by Joseph Schumpeter, the overlap between the communities that currently are associated with the respective fields is relatively limited.[27] This is surprising given that the theoretical core of entrepreneurship studies is quite close to what we referred to earlier as the techno-economic theoretical core of innovation studies. In both cases the focus is upon how agents exploit opportunities in contexts with varying appropriability conditions. One difference is that the techno-economic perspective gives rather more attention to how opportunities as well as appropriability levels differ between technology fields.

Another and more fundamental difference relates to the distinction between individual and collective entrepreneurship. In mainstream entrepreneurship studies, the traditional focus of analysis has tended to be on individual agents engaging in action in order to exploit opportunities. In such studies methodological individualism tends to go relatively unchallenged, and indeed some proponents explicitly insist that the focus *should* be on individual rather than collective action (e.g. Casson, 1985). This is reflected in the fact that analysis of the personal characteristics of the typical entrepreneur is an important sub-field in entrepreneurship studies that has no equivalent in innovation studies. Innovation is the outcome of entrepreneurial action, so innovation studies also studies innovation agents, but here the agent may be collective as well as individual.

These differences between the entrepreneurship and the innovation research communities may reflect specific historical *alliances* with particular sub-fields that have resulted in a *bias* making them less compatible. The entrepreneurship

---

[27] Taking the top ten references appearing on Google Scholar for respectively 'innovation' and 'entrepreneurship' points to two largely separate communities of scholars. Among those most cited for their work on innovation, you will find Nelson, Von Hippel, Cohen and Levinthal, Freeman and Soete, Tidd, Bessant and Pavitt, Nelson, Lundvall, Hobday, and Rogers. Among those most cited in entrepreneurship, one finds Shane, Kirzner, Baumol, Drucker, Levine, and Aldrich. None of those listed appear on both top ten lists, although this does not rule out there being some overlap and interaction between the two fields (for a more systematic analysis, see Bhupatiraju et al., 2012).

literature early on became linked to research on the role of *small businesses* in the economy. The alliance with small business research was reinforced in the post-war era in the USA when influential contributions (e.g. Birch, 1979, 1987) were successful in linking the process of creating new firms and the small business sector to job creation and employment. This linking was sometimes justified on rather dubious grounds (Davis et al., 1993). On the other hand, innovation research had its roots more in *science policy research*. Christopher Freeman at the Science Policy Research Unit (SPRU) at Sussex University, as well as Richard Nelson in the USA, pointed to R&D efforts as crucial for *technical* innovation. This led innovation researchers to pay considerable attention to large organizations with sufficient resources to establish R&D laboratories. The different alliances of the two types of research may help to explain why entrepreneurship research is closer to the Schumpeter Mark I perspective while innovation research pays more attention to Schumpeter Mark II.

The alliance with science policy and the confrontation with the linear model of innovation have encouraged the innovation research community to make efforts to understand the role of knowledge in relation to innovation and economic development. In more recent work this has resulted in important distinctions between forms of knowledge and modes of learning. Innovation is seen neither as growing out of science nor as the outcome of a single individual's actions. Instead, it is viewed as a process in which agents learn by doing, using, and interacting. The interactive learning processes result in a transformation both of agents and of the relationships between those agents (i.e. 'relational learning').[28]

Innovation Studies and STS: On the Role of External Users and Critical Perspectives

The STS community and the innovation studies community have in common the analysis of the role of science in society and economic development.

---

[28] The boundary is perhaps not quite as clear as is suggested by the distinctions made earlier. In research teams such as IKE and more recently CIRCLE, scholars have contributed to both fields. For instance, entrepreneurship scholars do make distinctions between high-tech entrepreneurial firms (Storey and Tether, 1997) and the rest; they study 'collective entrepreneurship' carried out by entrepreneurial teams (Reich, 1987); and they also bring in the notion of 'learning' with reference to the importance for entrepreneurial success of earlier experience from sector-specific employment relationships (Dahl and Reichstein, 2007). On their side, innovation scholars contribute to the entrepreneurship literature through analysing the role of new firms in specific sectoral innovation systems and in specific stages of the technology cycle. Their work on the role of the financial sector in innovation systems, including the study of venture capital, overlaps with the analysis of entrepreneurship studies. It is worth noting that, while both fields are open to inputs from behavioural science, entrepreneurship studies favour psychology, since it helps to understand the individual traits of entrepreneurs, while in innovation studies the preferred behavioural disciplines would be (or at least should be!) sociology and social psychology, as represented, for instance, by John Dewey and George Herbert Mead.

Nonetheless, the work by Martin and Nightingale (2012) and by Bhupatiraju et al. (2012) shows that there is even less overlap between these two fields in terms of their respective core literatures. My focus here is on differences having to do with external users and on the role of critical perspectives.

The research by Fagerberg and colleagues makes an attempt to characterize users according to academic disciplines and in terms of journals. The bibliographic methodology they employ covers only academic publishing and does not permit any analysis of the breakdown of *external users* between the private and public sector. One would hope that this might perhaps be included in subsequent bibliometric or other research. There are unique characteristics of innovation studies that stem from combining close interaction with external users with critical perspectives in a way that is found neither in entrepreneurship studies nor in STS.

Innovation studies is a relatively young field of research and it developed in close interaction with international organizations such as OECD in Paris and the Rand Corporation in the USA. The two most important founders, Christopher Freeman and Dick Nelson, were both involved in those public policy institutions while they were establishing the foundations of the field, and to a considerable extent their analysis was motivated by public policy concerns. That interaction with external users has continued and has stopped the field from becoming too abstract and losing its connection with what happens in the real world.

But such a 'socio-engineering' approach, in which it is seen as legitimate and even positive to come forward with proposals that could be implemented by private or public sector agents, is not uncontroversial. Significantly, neither Marx nor Schumpeter saw it as the task of scholars to offer advice to 'decision-makers' in the private or public sector. In this respect Freeman and Nelson have more in common with Keynes.[29] The STS community differs from innovation studies in paying much more attention to the negative consequences of new technology and of public science policy. Scholars in this tradition are notably less engaged in looking for solutions to policy or management problems.[30]

This difference might reflect the fact that innovation scholars who have their roots mainly in economics are more committed to economic objectives, such as economic growth and international competiveness, while the STS tradition is more rooted in a critical sociological tradition, where science is seen as serving wider objectives. However, it might also reflect the fact that innovation scholars implicitly or explicitly regard the economic environment

---

[29] Indeed, when I asked Christopher Freeman who he regarded as the greatest economist, he cited Keynes, not Marx or Schumpeter.

[30] Recently, I proposed this distinction in correspondence with Andrew Stirling, and he responded that he saw a more important distinction in that innovation studies tend to assume the innovation process to be unidirectional, while the STS perspective acknowledges that it can take a variety of directions.

as constituting a selection regime that dominates over competing selection regimes emanating from the political and normative side.

Relating Innovation Studies to Other Adjacent Fields

The work by Fagerberg, Landström, and Martin (2012), in which the content of innovation studies is compared to that of entrepreneurship studies and of science and technology studies, is helpful in understanding the specific character of each of these fields. The two adjacent fields are especially relevant for comparison since they have much in common when it comes to the processes that they study. Potentially this kind of comparative work could be helpful in renewing the field of innovation studies. Transferring insights and ideas from adjacent fields is one mechanism of renewal.

One strength of these comparative studies has been the application of a single and relatively simple methodology (looking at citation patterns in relation to 'handbooks'). Nonetheless, it would be interesting to combine this method with other approaches that make it possible to study how the specific field is organized when it comes to how scholars interact with non-academic users. It is reasonable to assume that the unique evolution of the field will depend as much upon interaction with external users as it does upon interaction within the academy. This would also provide important insights on the societal role of specific knowledge fields.

There are other adjacent fields that could contribute to the enrichment and renewal of innovation studies. In particular, the three fields of knowledge management, creativity research, and working life studies come to mind. Knowledge management overlaps with 'management of innovation', but it goes deeper into the understanding of knowledge and learning. Most creativity studies have traditionally focused upon individual creativity but there is also a growing literature on 'collective creativity' and on the role of the creative class (Florida, 2002). Innovation processes may be seen as processes where disparate forms of knowledge are combined in new creative ways, and therefore it is important to understand how innovation studies relate to these fields of research.

2.5. Opening Up the Borders of Innovation Studies

Several of the chapters in this book bring in new perspectives on innovation by opening up innovation studies to the world of workplace learning (Lorenz), economic development (Perez), and economics (Dosi). In what follows I will offer some reflections on how innovation studies can interact and evolve in relation to each of these areas.

Innovation, Work Organization, and Systems of Social Protection

Working life studies have previously operated at quite some distance from innovation studies. This field has been dominated by sociologists and the main focus has been upon the quality of working life and upon working conditions related to health or stress. If taken into consideration at all, new technology and innovation have been seen more as a threat than a promising opportunity for workers. Innovation scholars have, with a few honourable exceptions, neglected working life. The next section presents some arguments for linking the two fields and for regarding the organization of working life as an important dimension of innovation systems.

The classical economists saw labour or work as perhaps the most fundamental category in the economy. When they used working time as a measure of value, it reflected the fact that the means of production as well as knowledge require human activity to enable them to contribute to wealth creation. Experiences people encounter at work are fundamental for their wellbeing.[31] Learning-by-doing at the workplace is an important source of knowledge creation.

Innovation is also the outcome of work. Most of the time scientists spend in laboratories is devoted to routine activities. From time to time their efforts result in new insights that may lay the foundation for technical breakthroughs. The same is true for engineers who work mainly on getting technical processes to operate smoothly. However, some of them are from time to time engaged in specific projects aimed at finding new solutions to bottleneck problems in the production process or at creating new products that respond to the requirements of customers. The work of marketing staff will combine selling standard products with marketing new products and providing feedback and inspiration to product developers in their own firm.

This is all relatively uncontroversial and it contributes to the conventional picture where innovation is represented as an elite activity in which managers, scientists, engineers, and policy-makers are the critical actors. It also corresponds to a narrow definition of the innovation system as one represented by a 'triple helix', where the focus is upon the interaction between business leaders, universities, and government officials (Etzkowitz and Leydesdorff, 1995, 2000). Innovation is seen as a process that mainly involves the creative class as defined by Florida (2002). What is more controversial and less

---

[31] Standard welfare economics assumes that consumption increases welfare and that work represents negative utility for the individual. In a learning economy this is a caricature that fails to capture what is going on in the real economy (Lorenz and Lundvall, 2006). Certain types of work require investment in skills and the learning involved may have an intrinsic value.

obvious is that the innovation process also depends on how work is organized for the majority of workers including those often referred to as 'unskilled workers'.

In innovation studies there have been few attempts to show how innovation relates to the work process. The most important link may be the studies of technological unemployment. The TEMPO project where Freeman, Soete, and others analysed the impact of information technology on the labour market was perhaps the most serious attempt to link innovation both to employment and to the work process (Freeman and Soete, 1987). Since then, the majority of innovation studies have neglected the role of workers and instead have focused upon the role of policy-makers, scientists, engineers, and managers.

The literature on the sociology of work, linking technology to work organization and skill development, arrived at quite pessimistic conclusions. This is true for classical contributions such as Braverman (1975) but also for more recent attempts to generalize about trends in working life, such as Sennett (1998). Assuming that automation and process innovations were central, Braverman concluded that the process of deskilling labour would be the dominant one, while Sennett emphasizes how the transformation of working life undermines craftsmanship and the very identity of industrial workers.

Research comparing different national systems in Europe reveals a more nuanced picture than these studies, which were based mainly on US data. International differences in terms of worker participation are quite dramatic and seem to be correlated to national innovation performance (Arundel et al., 2007). In most countries, more participatory forms of worker engagement tend to go hand-in-hand with higher degrees of work satisfaction (Lorenz, 2006). It is important to understand that alienation is not a general tendency linked to innovation and that the implementation of new technology involves a political choice between different modes of innovation with more or less inclusive worker participation.

Understanding the work process in relation to innovation and learning is also important for understanding the innovation process. While crucial steps in this process may engage managers, scientists, and engineers, the outcome of the process in terms of intelligent and efficient use of resources depends upon the overall organization of the firm. In organizations with less social distance between workers and bosses and in innovation systems with porous walls between thinkers and doers, certain types of innovations may thrive while others may not. In most cases, systems with more inclusive participation will ensure a more speedy process of innovation. Workers will be more ready to provide feedback on how new processes work and more willing to solve problems with new technologies on their own.

The mapping of work organizations developed by Lorenz and Valeyre (2006) opens up a new line of research that makes it possible to understand economic development as a transformation of working life. We find that the degree and form of active participation of workers is very different in respectively the South, West, Centre, and North of Europe. In Arundel et al. (2007) we demonstrate that there is a correlation across nations in Europe between the rate of participation at the workplace and the frequency of radical innovation.

The European data from 2000 show that the Nordic countries have very few jobs left that are organized according to Taylorist principles, while the proportion of such jobs is much higher in the countries in Southern Europe that are now most exposed in the Euro crisis. An optimistic interpretation would be that economic development will gradually make working life more democratic and participatory.

The Social Dimension of the Learning Economy

The concept of 'the learning economy' refers to a specific phase of capitalist development, where a combination of factors such as globalization, deregulation of finance, and the widespread use of information and communication technologies *speeds up the rate of change* in different dimensions (on the demand side, the user needs change rapidly, and on the supply side there is acceleration in the creation, diffusion, and use of new technology) (Lundvall and Johnson, 1994).

We see the growing emphasis in the management literature on 'learning organizations' as reflecting the new context. In a period of rapid change, flat organizations with extensive horizontal communication are more efficient than hierarchical organizations with barriers between functions (Senge, 1990; Drucker, 1993). One can see references to 'the network society' (Castells, 1996) and 'open innovation' (Chesbrough, 2003) as pointing to another important dimension of the learning economy. In an era of growing complexity and rapid change, it is becoming increasingly difficult to locate all the necessary competences inside the organization.

As already mentioned, one of the most interesting results coming out of the OECD Jobs Study (OECD, 1994) was the general tendency towards labour market polarization in member states. This has been explained in terms of both trade patterns and skill-biased technical change. The learning economy perspective offers another interpretation. The fact that employees with education are becoming better off reflects the fact that education has increased their capacity to learn. Important theoretical contributions that support this view are to be found in Nelson and Phelps (1966) and Schultz (1975).

Nelson and Phelps (1966) present a simple growth model in which people with higher education contribute to economic growth through two mechanisms. First, they are able to pursue regular activities more efficiently than the average worker. Second, and this is the new insight provided by the paper, *they are more competent when it comes to exploiting new technical opportunities*. The conclusion from the analysis is that the marginal productivity of the highly educated will reflect the rate of technical change (exogenously specified in the model). Schultz (1975) follows a similar line of thought but takes the reasoning several steps further. In particular, he argues on the basis of empirical observations that education makes individuals better prepared to deal with disequilibria.

There is an inherent contradiction in the learning economy. On the one hand, it depends upon social capital—for instance in the form of 'generalized trust'—that typically thrives in homogenous and egalitarian societies. On the other hand, it tends to give rise to growing inequality because the low skilled will be weakened in labour markets. This contradiction points to the importance of state intervention to redistribute skills and learning opportunities in favour of the low skilled. In several papers I have referred to this as a call for a 'new new deal' (e.g. Lundvall, 1996).

Innovation, Education, and Labour Market Policy

In Lundvall et al. (2008) it is shown that countries with education systems that are open and that balance theoretical and practical elements tend to go hand-in-hand with wide participation in workplace learning. In Holm et al. (2010) it is shown that learning organizations thrive in countries with 'flexicurity' in labour markets.[32] It is a major challenge for innovation scholars to contribute to an understanding of how the different institutional set-ups characterizing education and labour market systems shape innovation processes. They might find inspiration in the work on different national business systems by Whitley (1994), and one ambition might be to develop a taxonomy for national systems that is richer and more relevant for understanding innovation than the one offered in the literature on varieties of capitalism (e.g. Hall and Soskice, 2001).

The Nordic countries (and other small European welfare economies) have been quite successful in terms of wealth production. In the post-war period these egalitarian welfare states have ranked among the world's leaders in

---

[32] Flexicurity refers to a combination of high mobility in the labour market and few restrictions on hiring and firing, on the one hand, and relatively generous support for those that become unemployed, on the other. In Europe, Denmark and Holland have been seen as examples of countries having labour markets characterized by flexicurity.

terms of GNP per capita and the UNDP index as well as in more qualitative competitiveness rankings. In the most recent rankings presented by the European Innovation Scoreboard, Denmark, Sweden, and Finland are, together with Germany, identified as the EU's 'innovation leaders'. They have in common that they combine low degrees of income inequality with high degrees of worker participation in processes of change. Their education systems are open and balance theory and practice, their labour markets are characterized by flexicurity, and they are welfare states where victims of change are offered retraining. The observed correlations are systemic and it does not follow that the Nordic model can be exported to the rest of Europe and even less so to the rest of the world.

Nonetheless, the Lisbon Strategy from 2000 gave signals in this direction when it referred to 'more social cohesion' and 'better jobs' as strategic goals. But by 2005 the strategy had already become narrower and focused only upon growth and employment (Lundvall and Lorenz, 2011). Currently, there is a tendency in Europe to move backwards towards cruder competitiveness strategies where lower wages and taxes are seen as the major means to attract capital and boost exports. The economic crisis has reinforced this tendency through austerity programmes and campaigns to lower wage costs.

The rather disappointing experiences of diffusing good practices such as 'flexicurity' within Europe, and the recent return to narrower competitiveness strategies, raise challenges for innovation research. Given the systemic character of innovation, what are the possibilities for international policy learning? Can measures aimed at income equality and ambitious welfare systems be implemented and stimulate innovation in countries that are bigger and less homogeneous? Have we entered a new era of global competition where such 'nice strategies' are reaching their limits? Or is the return to non-innovative competitive strategies merely reflecting the strength of vested political interests and the recourse to dubious economic theory.

This points to a need for a research agenda that studies and compares the outcomes of alternative competitiveness strategies in the current context of global competition. Such a research agenda might broaden the understanding of which policies have an impact upon innovation performance, including labour market and education policy. Knowledge creation that relates to work experience should be taken into account. For example, what is the impact of income distribution on the social distance between workers and bosses and upon worker participation in processes of technical change?

A Research Agenda Linking Innovation and Economic Development

Recently there have been major research efforts to understand the process of 'catching-up' as it relates to emerging economies such as India, Korea,

China, and Brazil (Malerba and Nelson, 2011). In these countries, economic activities are increasingly based upon technological knowledge, and many concepts developed by innovation scholars in the context of developed economies can be applied. Yet regional and sectoral development is very uneven in these economies, and they tend to include substantial informal sectors characterized by low productivity and low skills (Cassiolato and Vitorino, 2009; Lorentzen, 2009). To understand the mediation of knowledge and skills between the formal and highly productive sector and the informal sector remains a major challenge for the innovation system perspective.

To analyse the role of innovation and competence-building in the least developed economies that remain dominated by agriculture and raw material almost certainly requires new concepts. There are both classical research issues in development economics that can be illuminated from an innovation system perspective, and new ones that have to do with the globalization of production and the new role of information technology. First, there is a need to understand how these economies can transform economic growth based upon stronger demand for raw materials into durable capacities in related industries and services. The tendency to equate innovation with science-based activities and to regard universities as the major source of knowledge in a 'triple helix' constellation is especially problematic in these countries. It is a major challenge for innovation research to understand the role of engineering and design capabilities in economic development. Is it possible to develop the necessary related activities through a coordinated strategy of competence-building that combines formal training at different levels with the promotion of experience-based learning?

Another issue has to do with the increasing presence of foreign capital in agriculture and in raw material exploitation emanating both from the West and from the 'BRIC' countries. This may be seen as a potential source of technological learning. To understand under what circumstances the least developed countries may take advantage of this source is an important issue. This has to do both with the absorptive capacity in terms of competences and with the capacity to negotiate with major foreign investors.

In Chapter 4 by Carlota Perez, new opportunities for small-scale firms operating in less-developed countries are seen as coming from new communication technologies, from lower transport costs, and from new business models. Specific conditions of scarcity may give rise to solutions that can become products and services with a significant demand from outside the poor countries. In a context of global resource scarcity, recycling is an important case.

Finally, the role of the informal sector needs to be understood from the perspective of innovation and competence-building. As illustrated by several recent studies, activities in this sector may be strongly influenced by the use of information technology. Mobile phones may help fishermen to locate market demand and they may be linked up to financial systems and other services.

Innovation Studies and the Criticism of Standard Economics

Economists operating in the field of innovation studies are often frustrated by the lack of recognition from the economics mainstream. Even when the mainstream borrows ideas from the innovation community, they seem absentmindedly to forget to mention the source. This frustration began with Schumpeter himself, who had the ambition to develop a coherent theory of capitalist development but who never received the recognition that he strove for. Such frustration detracts from the efforts of innovation scholars to develop their understanding of the economy. Perhaps it would be better to neglect the economics mainstream and to focus instead upon explaining to the public why mainstream neo-classical ideas are inadequate in an economy that is knowledge-based and where innovation is ubiquitous.

Standard economics has also proven surprisingly resistant to criticism demonstrating that theories are inconsistent, abstractions misleading, and assumptions unrealistic. In a period where the tenets of standard economics have undoubtedly contributed to a major crisis, and where its practitioners have little to offer by way of solutions to that crisis, this should not weaken our efforts to establish a more satisfactory theoretical framework through critical analysis.

One of the weakest points of standard economics is its treatment of knowledge and learning—concepts that are at the very core of innovation studies. This has to do with the historical origin in science and technology analysis and, of course, with the fact that knowledge is important both as an input to and an output from the innovation process. To understand the different forms of knowledge that are used and produced in the process is therefore fundamental both for understanding innovation and for understanding the limitations of standard economics. It is also important to make distinctions between tacit and codified knowledge and between learning based upon experience and learning based upon systematic scientific research. In Lundvall and Johnson (1994) we proposed a pragmatic taxonomy of knowledge distinguishing between know what, know why, know how, and know who. Another important issue is the distinction between more or less individual and collective knowledge and the sharing of knowledge within and across organizational borders, as well as local and generic knowledge. Winter (1987), in an exploratory paper on knowledge management, referred to 'a paucity of language' when it comes to characterizing knowledge, and there is still a need for a more refined vocabulary.

To say that knowledge is diffused or transferred from one context to another underestimates the efforts needed to absorb knowledge in a distinct context. To understand how learning may take place and the most important barriers to it, including those based upon unequal power and legal rules of knowledge protection, is important for understanding the possibilities for linking innovation to economic development. While some knowledge may move almost literally at the speed of light, other kinds might require that people or teams of people actually move from one place to another. To operate on the basis of methodological individualism or on the assumption of a global generic knowledge base is misleading in a world where most relevant knowledge is located in discrete 'knowledge pools' with unequal and limited access (Arrow, 1994). Thus, to develop our basic understanding of knowledge and learning is fundamental both for qualifying innovation studies and for making the criticism of standard economics more effective.

Is the Rate of Innovation in the Learning Economy Too High?

In Chapter 6, Luc Soete refers to two particular instances where innovation appears to have negative repercussions. One has to do with technological competition leading to more destruction than creation, and the other is concerned with financial innovation. To these may be added other instances where the constellations of technology and user–producer relationships lead to 'unsatisfactory innovations' and raise the issue of the optimum speed of change.

There is a certain bias in the way change is viewed in economics. Economists normally tend to see it as equivalent to progress. Sociologists who are more concerned with how individuals can benefit from the stable reproduction of communities tend to be less sanguine and more ready to consider the negative impact of change. Among economists, Anne P. Carter, who made important contributions both to input–output analysis and to innovation studies, is an exception in attempting to measure 'the costs of change'. She grouped all work that was oriented either at imposing change on others or at managing the consequences of change and used this category as an indicator of the costs of change. In Carter (1994, 1996), she questions whether the acceleration of innovation and change results in greater wellbeing.

This issue is topical in relation to the current state of the world. In a world where governments regard their own economy as competing internationally, it is difficult to imagine ways to slow down change at the national level. Therefore it is interesting to consider what kind of global agreements might result in a more satisfactory rate of change. Global warming and financial instability may be seen as problems that require either a slowing of, or new directions for, innovation processes. A new regulation regime with a Tobin tax might be one way to reduce the speed of financial transactions as well as the rate of financial innovation, while global regulation aiming at resource saving and less pollution combined with a CO_2 tax may be necessary to slow down global warming.

The Financial Industrial Complex

It is of particular interest to analyse the financial–industrial complex from this perspective. As pointed out in Chapter 6 by Luc Soete, recent swarms of 'financial innovations' are perhaps the most striking example of how innovations can have hugely destructive consequences. In the financial–industrial complex, user–producer interactions have become increasingly incestuous over the last decade as financial innovations provided new instruments for leveraging. Those financial innovations made it possible for an increasing share of transactions to take place inside the complex while taxing the rest of the economy. To provide entrepreneurial and industrial customers with credit became of secondary importance. Data-sets on national banking available at OECD reveal that between 2000 and 2007 the proportion of both gross income and net profit that came from ordinary credit activities (net interest margin) was shrinking in all countries, while the share of profit emanating from leveraging was rapidly escalating.

Even after the discrediting effect of the crisis, the financial–industrial complex has considerable power and it continues to play a destructive role in the economy. The strength of the financial–industrial complex emanates from several sources. It wields enormous financial resources that can be used to buy political power, while regulators are closely connected to the interests of the sector. The fact that the sector, while nationally rooted and sometimes even quite local (the City and Wall Street), is operating worldwide makes it difficult to regulate. However, most important is the fact that the complex constitutes a kind of scaffolding for the whole economy. If it crumbles, the whole economy may sink into a serious depression. This unique position and the resulting arrogance are reflected in the inordinate sums of money paid to top executives in spite of popular anger.

The capacity to engage in extortion in relation to policy-makers is reinforced by the fact that those who have a deep insight into how this complex works—the scholarly experts on finance—often receive much of their income from the sector. Policy-makers are almost helpless; in critical situations where there is a need for intervention, they are reluctant to act, since action may undermine confidence and hence start a run on the weakest parts of the financial system. To this should be added the fact that the sector has become the primary motor of the whole economy, especially in the case of the UK and the USA.

In this situation it is no longer legitimate to argue that scholars specialized in innovation studies have no responsibility for what happens in the analysis of finance in relation to the crisis. Here, we should listen to the words of Chris Freeman. In a late interview (Sharif, 2006), he told us that it was more important to launch an attack on neo-classical macroeconomics than to find ways of promoting specific technologies or clusters.[33] In one of his last important papers, he focused upon the financial dynamics and foresaw the ICT-financial bubble in the US economy (Freeman, 2001). It is time we paid closer attention to his warnings and advice.

2.6. The Future of Innovation Studies

One of the main points in Chapter 7, by Ed Steinmueller, is his somewhat pessimistic observation that many young scholars today tend to see innovation studies not as a pioneering and exciting field but rather as something becoming more like 'normal science'. In this section I will reflect upon how the field may be organized in such a way that it combines sustainability in terms of its infrastructure with a renewal of content and methods that makes it attractive for future generations of scholars.

The Organization of the Research Field

In their article on innovation studies, Fagerberg and Verspagen (2009) raise a question about the future of the field:

> In this respect the most relevant question that the research undertaken here might lead to is the following: are the current institutions and organizations in the field strong enough to allow the knowledge of the field to evolve in a cumulative fashion? This may not have been a problem previously, but with the field's continuing growth (and diversity), one would expect these requirements to become more stringent. As we have shown, the only channel of communication that reaches the entire field is the journal Research Policy. There is no meeting

---

[33] 'Most of the people working on innovation systems prefer to work at the micro-level and they are still rather frightened of the strength of the neo-classical paradigm at the macroeconomic level, even though that's where they have to work. There needs to be an attack on the central core of macroeconomic theory. It is happening but only to a limited extent—the case at present is not sufficiently strongly argued' (Sharif, 2006).

place or association that spans the entire field. This may be the most challenging limitation for the field's continuing development. (p. 230)

In a more recent paper, Fagerberg, Fosaas, and Sapprasert (2012) set out to map the field of innovation studies, and they found that the literature can be grouped into three clusters:

- economics of R&D,
- organizing innovation,
- innovation systems.

One interesting finding is that the third cluster seems to function as a link between the first and the second. This is significant since that third cluster has its roots in earlier SPRU research and engages mainly European researchers as authors and users, while the first two are dominated by US scholars and US institutions. In their conclusions, Fagerberg, Fosaas, and Sapprasert, (2012) raise the following question:

what accompanied this broadening of the field was an effort by leading academics throughout the 1970s and 1980s to take each others' positions seriously and to create sufficient room for inter-action and debate. Will such informal integration suffice in the much larger (and more diversified) community of scholars that has now developed? If not, as seems more likely, it is possible that the different parts that now constitute the field may drift further apart and, eventually, pursue altogether different trajectories, with possible negative consequences for scientific progress in this area...A relevant question, therefore, for scholars in this area is what new forms of integration...may be needed to ensure that the various parts of the field stay connected and the field as whole continues to thrive. (p. 1147)

One purpose of this book is to attempt to provide a response to these questions. Before discussing institutional and organizational issues, however, it is useful to reflect on why it is relevant to study and understand innovation. As already pointed out, the field of innovation studies has, for good or bad, coevolved with its external use in practice in business and in public policy. This is reflected in the clustering patterns referred to earlier, in which there is one macro-cluster centering on the economics of technical change and another on innovation management.

Why Study Innovation?

The dominant external demand for innovation studies comes from policy-makers who need grounds for doing what they do in order to stimulate economic growth, and from business leaders who want to know how to organize activities in order to make a profit from innovation. This might lead to the conclusion that innovation studies could eventually end up as a sub-branch of economics and management respectively. A development in that direction would undoubtedly reinforce the problems identified in Chapter 7 by Steinmueller. Inter-disciplinarity is crucial for different reasons connected with the nature of the field and the topics studied, and without a continuing degree of openness to a range of disciplines the field may not survive.

Technical innovations are rooted in specific branches of science and technology. To understand why innovation processes are diverse, there is a need for a minimum of insight in specific technologies. Therefore innovation studies needs to engage scholars with a background in *natural science and engineering*.

One reason for studying innovation is that by focusing upon change, including radical change, it provides a specific kind of insight into how societies are structured and how they evolve. To study the process of social transformation connected with a technological revolution may offer deep insights into social realities. This is very much in line with what Carlota Perez argues in Chapter 4, and it points to the need to integrate *historians* as well as *futurologists* in our research networks and in teaching curricula.

Studying innovation and innovation policy in a historical perspective should contribute to an improved understanding of the role of the state in the economy. As Ben Martin (Chapter 8) points out with reference to the important work by Mariana Mazzucato (2013), the conventional assumption that governments' sole role is to fix market failure is far from what governments actually do and from what they should do. This line of research requires collaboration with *political scientists*.

As pointed out by Luc Soete in Chapter 6, we need to develop a critical perspective on innovation. Innovations that result in destructive creation rather than creative destruction are a significant problem that merit closer study. This may be particularly difficult for a field that is interacting closely with external users mainly interested in economic growth and profit. This requires that there are institutions and research programmes within innovation studies that encompass or interact with scholars from *STS studies*.

There is also great potential in understanding the role of participation and democracy in relation to the innovation process. Both at the level of the firm and at the regional level, there is a tendency to think about the main actors in terms of a 'triple helix'—as being managers, scholars, and public servants. To understand alternative modes of innovation embracing an active role for consumers and workers requires expertise on *work organization, labour markets, education, and welfare systems* as well as experts on *consumer organizations and marketing* if we are to explore the potential for more 'democratic innovation'.

At the level of the nation state, innovation is generally seen as a means of contributing to economic growth and international competitiveness.

The widespread adoption of the concept of the national innovation system reflects essentially national interests. Here, there is a need to rebalance the strong emphasis upon research supporting national innovation policy with assessments of the impact upon global stability, growth, and wellbeing. This requires *expertise on the international economy and politics as well as on economic development and underdevelopment.*

Both in this connection and when it comes to understanding innovation in the local and regional context, the role of knowledge in geographical and cultural space is important. This requires collaboration between experts on knowledge and learning, on the one hand, and *economic geographers*, on the other. To understand processes of interactive learning, we also need to engage with experts on trust and social capital with roots in *sociology and social psychology.*

It is quite obvious that not even the biggest innovation research units, such as SPRU, the Manchester Institute of Innovation Research or CIRCLE in Lund, could hope to cover all these dimensions. Networks linking diverse institutions and groups must be an essential part of the organizational set-up. It is also apparent that innovation studies, even if it aimed at it, is unlikely to become very discipline-like and self-contained. Individual researchers, research teams, and research institutions will surely continue to have different profiles and agendas drawing on different disciplinary paradigms and perspectives.

A more modest objective is signalled in the question posed earlier about an 'integrative function'. What is needed are more or less formal mechanisms and conventions that facilitate communication and cooperation between sub-communities in order to stimulate 'new combinations' and creativity. Does the current organizational and institutional structure sufficiently serve this purpose?

Building an Open and Diverse Community

There are regular gatherings at conferences convened by such organizations as the Schumpeter Society, DRUID, and Globelics. Each conference has its own profile; for example, while the Schumpeter Society attracts economists, DRUID conferences have a strong participation of business economists and geographers, and Globelics conferences bring together experts on innovation with experts on economic development, with a particularly strong presence of scholars from the South. The DRUID network covers only a part of the larger community that studies technology and innovation management (with conferences such as the TIM division of AoM), arguably now the largest component of innovation studies. There are also the well attended Triple Helix conferences.

It is clear from the mapping exercises carried out by Fagerberg, Verspagen, and others that SPRU and *Research Policy* have played unique roles in the formation of the field. SPRU has also been one of the most multi-disciplinary units of research operating in the field. This historical record could motivate SPRU to take on the task of becoming a meeting place that brings together scholars from the different sub-communities—for instance, in the form of an annual gathering that differs in style and content from the regular meetings referred to earlier. The annual Aalborg symposium would then be used to give special attention to central cross-disciplinary topics on the research agenda.

There have been early efforts to build institutional frameworks for research training in the field of innovation studies. ETICS—with its origins in EUNETICS, established in the early 1990s—has offered research training especially for European students but does not exist anymore. The annual Globelics Academy brings together PhD students working on innovation and economic development from all over the world both at the global and the level of regions (Africa, Latin America etc.). The DRUID Academy is a conference where PhD students make presentations and receive feedback on their work. In the USA, the Consortium for Competitiveness and Cooperation (CCC) network fills a similar function. However, most of the systematic research training still takes place at the local level.

One important issue is how to exploit synergy among scholars and institutions in offering research training.[34] This is especially important for those PhD students who are not connected to any of the major centres. The ideal format would be one where students both are allowed access to scholars who are leading experts in their field of research and are exposed to some of the diversity that characterizes the field. Globelics is expanding its efforts to organize research training worldwide. For Europe specifically there seems to be a need for new research training initiatives to follow after the DIME-ETIC era is over. The aim of the training would be both to offer access to advanced expertise in research tools and methods used by the students and to introduce students to advanced research on diverse topics within innovation studies.

'Who is Us?'

This was the question that Robert Reich (1990) raised to provoke the US public in connection with international trade. We might raise a similar

---

[34] Jan Fagerberg has recently established a website hosted by the IKE-group in Aalborg that circulates information within the innovation studies community (<http://www.innoresource. org/>). This can play an important role in linking diverse research groups and communities.

question when it comes to 'innovation studies'. It is important to note that when Fagerberg, Verspagen, and colleagues define and map innovation studies as a 'scientific field', they are engaging in a form of social construction. They have been honest and open about the methods used and there is, of course, something there to map. But it is also true that the mapping itself contributes to creating a category of 'innovation scholars', increasing their self-awareness and offering identity and a sense of professional and emotional belonging.

One important question is whether it is possible to develop a stronger innovation community without reducing the heterogeneity and the openness to those perceived as 'outsiders'. And would the benefits of such a consolidation be worth the costs of diminished diversity and openness? One important element that has kept the community together is the existence of mentors such as Dick Nelson and Chris Freeman. In their careers they did not restrict their field of research to innovation studies. My own research experience has been equally diverse and I have generally gleaned the most interesting insights from interacting with new fields of knowledge.

On this basis we should ask ourselves why we might want a new generation of 'innovation scholars' to operate within a discipline-like scientific field? The implication is that institutional solutions should not move towards closure. Therefore, I am in favour of developing further the existing 'soft' forms of organization and combining this with establishing new meeting places, websites, and not least major research projects bringing together scholars and students from major centres of research. Such a strategy where we remain open to new fields of knowledge and to collaboration in different directions might not be ideal when it comes to 'consolidating' the field in academic terms and it might be seen as weakening its position with regard to academic infighting. Yet it might be where we should go.

Acknowledgements

As outlined in Chapter 1, this book is the outcome of a wintry event in Aalborg in February 2012. It marked my withdrawal as research director for the IKE group and the passing of my 70th birthday. I am most grateful to Esben Sloth Andersen and Jan Fagerberg who initiated and organized the event, and to the friends and colleagues who took time off to participate and contribute to the symposium and to this volume. I also want to thank Ben Martin and Richard R. Nelson for critical and useful comments to draft versions of this chapter.

References

Arrow, K. J. (1962a). 'The Economic Implications of Learning by Doing', *Review of Economic Studies*, *29*: 155–73.

Arrow, K. J. (1962b). 'Economic Welfare and the Allocation of Resources for Invention', in R. R. Nelson (ed.) *The Rate and Direction of Inventive Activity: Economic and Social Factors*. Princeton: Princeton University Press, 609–26.

Arrow, K. J. (1994). 'Methodological Individualism and Social Knowledge', *American Economic Review*, *84*, Papers and Proceedings, 1–9.

Arundel, A., Lorenz, E., Lundvall, B.-Å., and Valeyre, A. (2007). 'How Europe's Economies Learn: a Comparison of Work Organization and Innovation Mode for the EU-15', *Industrial and Corporate Change*, *16*: 1175–1210.

Bernal, J. D. (1939). *The Social Function of Science*. Cambridge, MA: MIT Press.

Bhupatiraju, S., Nomaler, Ö., Triulzi, G., and Verspagen, B. (2012). 'Knowledge Flows—Analyzing the Core Literature of Innovation, Entrepreneurship, and Science and Technology Studies', *Research Policy*, *41*: 1205–18.

Birch, D. L. (1979). 'The Job Generation Process', MIT Program on Neighborhood and Regional Change.

Birch, D. L. (1987). *Job Creation in America: How Our Smallest Companies Put the Most People to Work*. New York: The Free Press.

Brændgaard (1984). *Strukturproblemer, Teknologipolitik, Sociale Innovationer*. Aalborg: Aalborg Universitetsforlag.

Brændgaard et al. (1982). *Mikroelektronik og Samfundsøkonomi*. Aalborg: Aalborg Universitetsforlag.

Braverman, H. (1975). *Labour and Monopoly Capital—The Degradation of Work in the 20th Century*. New York: Monthly Review Press.

Burns, T. and Stalker, G. M. (1961). *The Management of Innovation*. London: Tavistock.

Bush, V. (1945). *Science: The Endless Frontier: A Report to the President on a Program for Postwar Scientific Research*. Washington, DC: United States Office of Scientific Research and Development.

Carter, A. P. (1994), 'Production Workers, Meta-investment and the Pace of Change', Paper prepared for the meetings of the International J. A. Schumpeter Society, Munster, August.

Carter, A. P. (1996). 'Measuring the Performance of a Knowledge-Based Economy', in D. Foray, and B.-Å. Lundvall (eds), *Employment and Growth in the Knowledge-Based Economy*. Paris: OECD Documents, 61–67.

Cassiolato, J. and Vitorino, V. (2009). *BRICS and Development Alternatives: Innovation Systems and Policies*. London: Anthem Press.

Casson, M. (1985). *The Entrepreneur—An Economic Theory*. Totowa, NJ: Barnes & Noble.

Castells, M. (1996). *The Rise of the Network Society*. Oxford: Blackwell.

Chesbrough, H. (2003). *Open Innovation: The New Imperative for Creating and Profiting from Technology*. Boston, MA: Harvard Business School Press.

Christensen, P. et al. (1978). *Lønniveqau og konkurrenceevne*. Aalborg: Aalborg Universitetsforlag.

Cohen, W. M. and Levinthal, D. A. (1990). 'Absorptive Capacity: A New Perspective on Learning and Innovation', *Administrative Science Quarterly*, *35*: 128–52.

Dahl, M. S. and Reichstein, T. (2007). 'Are You Experienced? Prior Experience and the Survival of New Organizations', *Industry and Innovation*, *14*: 497–511.

Davis, S. J., Haltiwanger, J., and Schuh, S. (1993). 'Small Business and Job Creation: Dissecting the Myth and Reassessing the Facts', NBER Working Paper, 4492.

Dosi, G. (1988). 'Sources, Procedures, and Microeconomic Effects of Innovation', *Journal of Economic Literature*, *26*: 1120–71.

Dosi, G., Freeman, C., Nelson, R. R., Silverberg, G., and Soete, L. (eds) (1988). *Technical Change and Economic Theory*. London: Pinter Publishers.

Drucker, P. (1993). *The Post-Capitalist Society*. Oxford: Butterworth-Heinemann.

Etzkowitz, H. and Leydesdorff, L. (1995). 'The Triple Helix—University-Industry-Government Relations: A Laboratory for Knowledge-Based Economic Development', *EASST Review*, *14*: 14–19.

Etzkowitz, H. and Leydesdorff, L. (2000). 'The Dynamics of Innovation: From National Systems and "Mode 2" to Triple Helix of University-Industry-Government Relations', *Research Policy*, *29*: 109–23.

Fagerberg, J. and Verspagen, B. (2009). 'Innovation Studies: The Emerging Structure of a New Scientific Field', *Research Policy*, *38*: 218–33.

Fagerberg, J., Fosaas, M., Bell, M., and Martin, B. R. (2011). 'Christopher Freeman: Social Science Entrepreneur', *Research Policy*, *40*: 897–916.

Fagerberg, J., Fosaas, M., and Sapprasert, K. (2012). 'Innovation: Exploring the Knowledge Base', *Research Policy*, *41*: 1132–53.

Fagerberg, J., Landström, H., and Martin, B. (2012). 'Exploring the Emerging Knowledge Base of "the Knowledge Society"', *Research Policy*, *41*: 1121–31.

Florida, R. (2002). *The Rise of the Creative Class*. New York: Basic Books.

Foray, D., and Lundvall, B.-Å. (1996). *Employment and Growth in the Knowledge Based Economy*. Paris: OECD.

Freeman, C. (1974). *The Economics of Industrial Innovation*. Harmondsworth: Penguin.

Freeman, C. (ed.) (1981). *Technological Innovation and National Economic Performance*. Aalborg: Aalborg University Press.

Freeman, C. (1987). *Technology Policy and Economic Performance: Lessons from Japan*. London: Pinter Publishers, 330–34.

Freeman, C. (1988), 'Japan: A New National Innovation Systems?', in G. Dosi, C. Freeman, R. R. Nelson, G. Silverberg, and L. Soete (eds), *Technology and Economic Theory*. London: Pinter Publishers, 330–34.

Freeman, C. (2001). 'A Hard Landing for the "New Economy"? Information Technology and the United States National System of Innovation', *Structural Change and Economic Dynamics*, *12*: 115–39.

Freeman, C. and Lundvall, B.-Å. (eds) (1988). *Small Countries Facing the Technological Revolution*. London: Pinter Publishers.

Freeman, C. and Perez, C. (1988), 'Structural Crises of Adjustment: Business Cycles and Investment Behaviour', in G. Dosi et al. (eds), *Technical Change and Economic Theory*. London: Pinter Publishers, 38–61.

Freeman, C. and Soete, L. (eds) (1987). *Technical Change and Full Employment*. Oxford: Basil Blackwell.

Gjerding, A. N. et al. (1990). *Den forsvundne produktivitet*. København: DJØFs forlag.

Hägerstrand, T. (1952). 'The Propagation of Innovation Waves', *Lund Studies in Human Geography, Series B, 4*: 3–19.

Hägerstrand, T. (1967). *Innovation Diffusion as a Spatial Process*. Chicago: University of Chicago Press.

Hall, P. A. and Soskice, D. (2001). *Varieties of Capitalism: The Institutional Foundations of Comparative Advantage*. Oxford: Oxford University Press.

Holm, J. R., Lorenz, E., Lundvall, B.-A., and Valeyre, A. (2010). 'Organisational Learning and Systems of Labour Market Regulation in Europe', *Industrial and Corporate Change, 19*: 1141–73.

Husén, T. (1974). *The Learning Society*. London: Methuen.

Jensen, M. B., Johnson, B., Lorenz, E., and Lundvall, B.-Å. (2007). 'Forms of Knowledge and Modes of Innovation', *Research Policy, 36*: 680–93.

Kaldor, N. (1978). 'The Effect of Devaluations on Trade in Manufactures', in *Further Essays on Applied Economics*. London: Duckworth, 99–116.

Kirman, A. P. (1994). *Economies with Interacting Agents*, Santa Fe: Santa Fe Institute.

Kline, S. J. and Rosenberg, N. (1986). 'An Overview of Innovation', in R. Landau and N. Rosenberg (eds), *The Positive Sum Game*. Washington, DC: National Academy Press, 275–305.

Lam, A. (2000). 'Tacit Knowledge, Organisational Learning and Societal Institutions: An Integrated Framework', *Organization Studies, 21*: 487–513.

Lam, A. and Lundvall, B.-Å. (2006). 'Learning Organizations and National Systems of Competence Building', in E. Lorenz, and B. Lundvall (eds), *How Europe's Economies Learn: Coordinating Competing Models*. New York: Oxford University Press, 109–39.

Leibenstein, H. (1966). 'Allocative Efficiency versus Efficiency', *American Economic Review, 56*: 392–415.

Levin, R. C., Klevorick, A. K., Nelson, R. R., and Winter, S. G. (1987). 'Appropriating the Returns from Industrial Research and Development', *Brookings Papers on Economic Activity, 1987*: 783–831.

Lorentzen, J. (2009). 'Learning and Innovation: What's Different in the (Sub)Tropics and How Do We Explain It? A Review Essay', *Science, Technology & Society, 14*: 177–205.

Lorenz, E. and Lundvall, B.-Å. (eds) (2006). *How Europe's Economies Learn*. Oxford: Oxford University Press.

Lorenz, E. and Lundvall, B.-Å. (2011). 'The Organisation of Work and Systems of Labour Market Regulation and Social Protection: A Comparison of the EU-15', in M. Ekman, B. Gustavsen, B. Asheim, and Ø Pålshaugen (eds), *Learning Regional Innovation: Scandinavian Models*. Basingstoke: Palgrave Macmillan, 50–69

Lorenz, E. and Valeyre, A. (2006), 'Organizational Forms and Innovation Performance: A Comparison of the EU15', in E. Lorenz, and B.-Å. Lundvall (eds), *How Europe's Economies Learn*. Oxford: Oxford University Press, 140–60.

Lundvall, B.-Å. (1985). *Product Innovation and User-Producer Interaction*. Aalborg: Aalborg University Press.

Lundvall, B.-A. (1988). 'Innovation as an Interactive Process: From User-Producer Interaction to the National System of Innovation', in G. Dosi et al. (eds), *Technical Change and Economic Theory*. London: Pinter, 349–69.

Lundvall, B.-Å. (ed.) (1992). *National Systems of Innovation: Towards a Theory of Innovation and Interactive Learning*. London: Pinter Publishers.

Lundvall, B.-Å. (1996). 'The Social Dimension of the Learning Economy', Aalborg University, Department of Business Studies.

Lundvall, B.-Å. (2002). *Innovation, Growth and Social Cohesion: The Danish Model*. Cheltenham, UK, and Northampton, MA: Edward Elgar.

Lundvall, B.-Å. (2006). 'Interactive Learning, Social Capital and Economic Performance', in D. Foray, and B. Kahin (eds), *Advancing Knowledge and the Knowledge Economy*. Cambridge, MA: MIT Press, 63–74.

Lundvall, B.-Å. (2011). 'Notes on Innovation Systems and Economic Development', *Innovation and Development*, 1: 25–38.

Lundvall, B.-Å. and Johnson, B. (1994). 'The Learning Economy', *Journal of Industry Studies*, 1: 23–42.

Lundvall, B.-Å., Rasmussen, P., and Lorenz, E. (2008). 'Education in the Learning Economy: A European Perspective', *Policy Futures in Education*, 6: 681–700.

Malerba, F. and Nelson, R. (2011). 'Learning and Catching up in Different Sectoral Systems: Evidence from Six Industries', *Industrial and Corporate Change*, 20: 1645–75.

Malerba, F. and Orsenigo, L. (1997). 'Technological Regimes and Sectoral Patterns of Innovative Activities', *Industrial and Corporate Change*, 6: 83–117.

March, J. G. and Simon, H. A. (1958). *Organizations*. New York: Wiley.

Martin, B. R., Nightingale, P., and Yegros-Yegros, A. (2012). 'Science and Technology Studies: Exploring the Knowledge Base', *Research Policy*, 41: 1182–1204.

Mazzucato, M. (2013). *The Entrepreneurial State: Debunking Private vs. Public Sector Myths*. London: Anthem Press.

Mintzberg, H. (1979). *The Structuring of Organizations*. Englewood Cliffs, NJ: Prentice-Hall.

Mowery, D. and Rosenberg, N. (1979). 'The Influence of Market Demand upon Innovation: A Critical Review of Some Recent Empirical Studies', *Research Policy*, 8: 102–53.

Nelson, R. R. (1984). *High-technology Policies—A Five-Nation Comparison*. Washington, DC: American Enterprise Institute.

Nelson, R. R. (ed.) (1993). *National Systems of Innovations: A Comparative Analysis*. Oxford: Oxford University Press.

Nelson, R. R. and Phelps, E. S. (1966). 'Investment in Humans, Technology Diffusion and Economic Growth', *American Economic Review*, 56: 69–75.

Nelson, R. R. and Winter, S. G. (1977). 'In Search of a Useful Theory of Innovation', *Research Policy*, 6: 36–76.

Nelson, R. R. and Winter, S. G. (1982). *An Evolutionary Theory of Economic Change*. Cambridge, MA: The Belknap Press of Harvard University Press.

Nielsen, K. and Kvale, S. (1999). 'Mesterlære som aktuel læringsform', in K. Nielsen and S. Kvale (eds), *Mesterlære, Læring som Social Praksis*. Copenhagen: Hans Reitzels Forlag, 9–53.

OECD (1994). *The OECD Jobs Study—Facts, Analysis, Strategies*. Paris: OECD.

OECD (2000). *Knowledge Management in the Learning Society*. Paris: OECD.

Pavitt, K. (1984). 'Sectoral Patterns of Technical Change: Towards a Taxonomy', *Research Policy, 13*: 343–73.

Phillips, A. (1971). *Technology and Market Structure*. Lexington, MA: Heath Lexington Books.

Polanyi, M. (1958/78). *Personal Knowledge*. London: Routledge/Kegan Paul.

Polenska, K. (ed.) (2007). *The Economic Geography of Innovation*. Cambridge, MA: Cambridge University Press.

Porter, M. (1990). *The Competitive Advantage of Nations*. London: MacMillan.

Reich, R. B. (1987). 'Entrepreneurship Reconsidered: The Team as Hero', *Harvard Business Review, 65*: 77–83.

Reich, R. B. (1990). 'Who is Us?', *Harvard Business Review, 68*: 53–64.

Richardson, G. B. (1996). 'Competition, Innovation and Increasing Returns', Department of Industrial Economics and Strategy, Copenhagen Business School.

Rogers, E. M. (1962). *Diffusion of Innovation*. New York: Free Press.

Rosenberg, N. (1976). *Perspectives on Technology*. Cambridge, MA: Cambridge University Press.

Rothwell, R. (1972). 'Factors for Success in Industrial Innovations: Project SAPPHO—A Comparative Study of Success and Failure in Industrial Innovation', Science Policy Research Unit, University of Sussex, Brighton.

Rothwell, R. (1977). 'The Characteristics of Successful Innovators and Technically Progressive Firms', *R&D Management, 7*: 191–206.

Ryan, B. and Gross, N. C. (1943). 'The Diffusion of Hybrid Seed Corn in Two Iowa Communities', *Rural Sociology, 13*: 15–24.

Saxenian, A. (1994). *Regional Advantage*. Cambridge, MA: Harvard University Press.

Schmookler, J. (1966). *Invention and Economic Growth*. Cambridge, MA: Harvard University Press.

Schultz, T. W. (1975). 'The Value of the Ability to Deal with Disequilibria', *Journal of Economic Literature, 13*: 827–46.

Schumpeter, J. A. (1934). *The Theory of Economic Development: An Inquiry into Profits, Capital, Credit, Interests and the Business Cycle*. London: Oxford University Press.

Schumpeter, J. A. (1936/91). *Can Capitalism Survive?* New York: Harper and Row.

Schumpeter, J. A. (1942). *Capitalism, Socialism and Democracy*. London: Unwin.

Senge, P. (1990). *The Fifth Discipline: The Art & Practice of the Learning Organization*. New York: Random House.

Sennett, R. (1998). *The Corrosion of Character: The Personal Consequences of Work in the New Capitalism*. London: W.W. Norton & Company.

Shane, S. and Venkataraman, S. (2000). 'The Promise of Entrepreneurship as a Field of Research', *Academy of Management Review, 25*: 217–26.

Sharif, N. (2006). 'Emergence and Development of the National Innovation Systems Concept', *Research Policy, 35*: 745–66.

Solow, R. M. (1956). 'A Contribution to the Theory of Economic Growth', *Quarterly Journal of Economics, 70*: 65–94.

Solow, R. M. (1957). 'Technical Change and the Aggregate Production Function', *Review of Economics and Statistics, 39*: 312–20.

SPRU (1967). Annual Report, University of Sussex.

Storey, D. J. and Tether, B. (1997). 'Smaller Firms and Europe's Growth of New Technology-Based Firms High Technology Sectors: A Framework for Analysis and Some Statistical Evidence.' Paper presented at the Firm Dynamics and High Tech Industries-Conference, Zentrum für Europäische Wirtschaftsforschung, Mannheim, 9–10 June.

Thirlwall, A. P. (1979). 'The Balance of Payments Constraints as an Explanation of International Growth Rate Differences', *Banca Nazionale del Lavoro Quarterly Review*, *32*: 45–53.

Valente, T. W. and Rogers, E. M. (1995). 'The Origins and Developments of the Diffusion of Innovations Paradigm as an Example of Scientific Growth', *Science Communication, 16*: 242–73.

von Hippel, E. (1988). *The Sources of Innovation*. Cambridge, MA: MIT Press.

Whitley, R. (1994), 'Societies Firms and Markets: The Social Structuring of Business Systems', in R. Whitley (ed.), *European Business Systems*. London: Sage Publications, 5–45.

Winter, S. (1987), 'Knowledge and Competence as Strategic Assets', in D. Teece (ed.), *The Competitive Challenge: Strategy for Industrial Innovation and Renewal*. Cambridge, MA: Ballinger Publishing Company, 159–84.

Witt, U. (2003). *The Evolving Economy: Essays on the Evolutionary Approach to Economics*. London: Elgar.

3

Innovation, Work Organization, and Systems of Social Protection

Edward Lorenz

3.1. Introduction

Much of the core research on the determinants of innovation has tradition-ally focused on the role of formal processes of R&D and on the importance of the skills and expertise of scientists and engineers with third-level educa-tion. In research on national innovation systems there has been a parallel tendency to focus on the institutions and organizations responsible for the production and diffusion of formal scientific and technical knowledge. At the level of measurement, these emphases are reflected in the classic definition of innovation presented in the 1996 edition of the *Oslo Manual* as technical product and process innovation (TPP), and at the level of innovation policies they can be seen in the priority regularly given to increasing national R&D intensity. More recently, there have been notable efforts to widen the scope of innovation research so as to more fully take into account the role of work pro-cesses, systems of labour market protection, and more generally the impact of welfare state institutions. This chapter focuses on these changes in scope and seeks to identify key challenges for researchers in innovation studies.

The chapter begins by examining how work organization has been ana-lysed in the developing field of innovation studies, including the factors that account for the growing interest in the 2000s in measuring and analysing processes of organizational innovation. It is argued that a key challenge still facing researchers in innovation studies is developing an adequate under-standing of the interdependencies between work organization and processes of technical change and innovation. The chapter then turns to the analysis of national systems, arguing that there is a need for developing more robust typologies of innovation systems that integrate the role of labour markets and welfare state institutions. A related challenge is developing multi-level governance frameworks that serve to clarify the interconnections between these social institutions at the levels of nations and regions. The chapter concludes by discussing the obstacles to putting work organization and organizational innovation more firmly on the EU policy agenda.

3.2. Work Organization and Organizational Design

The analysis of work organization and organizational design was addressed in some of the early contributions to innovation studies and notably in Freeman's (1987) classic study of the Japanese innovation system.[1] Freeman focused on the characteristics of the Japanese firm as an innovative organization, arguing that the factory was used as a laboratory for innovation, and that the success of innovations and their rate of diffusion were strongly related to different forms of work organization. In his 1995 paper on globalization and innovation systems, Freeman emphasized the importance of the interdependencies between technical and organizational innovations in the diffusion of radical innovations, arguing that, 'a theory of technical change which ignores these interdependencies is no more helpful than a theory of economics which ignores the interdependencies of prices and quantities in the world economy' (Freeman, 1995, p. 18). Subsequently, as Lundvall has observed (pp. 50–2 this volume), innovation studies scholars have given relatively little attention to the role of workers and work organization in innovation processes, and the emphasis has rather been on the role of formal R&D and on the skills and expertise of engineers, scientists, and managers. In this light, it is relevant that Fagerberg and Verspagen (2009), in their use of citations in *Research Policy* to identify the core literature in innovation studies, recognize only two publications focusing on the organization of the firm, the classic studies by Cohen and Levinthal (1989, 1990) on absorptive capacity. Interestingly, none of the literature specifically focusing on routines or dynamic capabilities finds its way onto the core list. More generally, the management strategy literature dealing with the relation between organization design and enterprise performance is absent. A first conclusion is that the analysis of work organization and organizational design has been rather marginal to the development of the field of innovation studies.

The 2000s, though, have seen a growing interest in the organizational dimension of innovation processes, notably at the level of measurement. A major impetus for this has been the recognition that existing measures

---

[1] Also see Freeman and Soete (1984).

poorly capture innovation processes in services, which are typically less technological and R&D-intensive compared to manufacturing innovation and are often relational in character, having to do with changes in the organization of relations between service providers and users (Tether, 2003; Tidd, 2003; Miles, 2008). Acknowledging these differences, the 2005 version of the *Oslo Manual* abandoned the established definition of technological product and process (TPP) innovation and developed expanded definitions of innovation covering not only product and process innovation, but also organizational and marketing innovation. Organizational innovation is defined broadly to include the implementation of a new organizational method in the firm's business practices, workplace organization, or external relations (*Oslo Manual*, 2005, p. 50). The use of these new definitions in the design of successive waves of the Community Innovation Survey (CIS) after 2005 means that researchers now have access to data for the EU-27 measuring the frequency and the amount of expenditure, not only on product and process innovations, but also on organizational and marketing innovations.

While these new measures have been useful for estimating the frequency of and correlations between different types of innovations across manufacturing and service sectors (e.g. Schmidt and Rammer, 2007), it is far less clear that they have contributed to progressing Freeman's (1995, p. 18) agenda of developing a better conceptual understanding of the interdependencies between organizational change, on the one hand, and product and process innovation, on the other. In my view, this can be explained in part by the measurement framework adopted for organizational innovation in the 2005 version of the *Oslo Manual*, which lends itself to the idea that workplace organization is a separate 'social' or 'non-technological dimension' that can be analysed independently from the 'technological dimension' of innovation processes. This bracketing and separation of the organizational dimension is reflected in the separate indicators of 'technological' and 'non-technological' innovation that can be downloaded from Eurostat's electronic data base, where the former refers to core product and process innovations and the latter to organizational and marketing innovations.[2] While the widening of the scope of the definition and measurement of innovation promoted by the OECD and the European Commission is clearly to be welcomed, the tendency to classify product and process innovation as technological, and organizational innovation as non-technological, gives the mistaken impression that the former can be understood independently of organizational arrangements and that they are somehow non-social.

There are, of course, limitations to what one can measure with a single survey instrument, and CIS indicators of organizational and marketing innovation

---

[2] For measures of technological and non-technological innovation for the EU-27 based on CIS-2008, see <http://appsso.eurostat.ec.europa.eu/nui/setupModifyTableLayout.do>.

were essentially add-ons to a survey framework that was designed to measure the frequency and amount of expenditure on product and process innovations. Still, it isn't clear what researchers and policy-makers are supposed to make of the very broad measures the CIS provides of how much organizational change or innovation has taken place over a three-year period within private sector enterprises. Organizational innovations are defined to include changes in managerial systems, changes in work organization, and changes in the structure of relations with other organizations. From both the research and policy angle, obvious questions are: changes in what direction? And what are the rates of adoption of specific types of managerial practices and forms of work organization that correspond to particular organizational designs? The conceptual and measurement shift that I am arguing for is much in keeping with Freeman's (1995) argument about the importance of analysing the interdependencies between organizational change and technical innovation. Rather than focusing on organizational innovation as a separate type of innovation, the organizational dimension should be treated as a context within which employee-learning and knowledge creation takes place. A key question, then, is what kinds of organizational designs and forms of work organization promote product and process innovation? And the policy challenge is how to promote the adoption of these good designs and forms. Obtaining information relevant to these questions and policy agendas would require a different specialized survey.

At the national level there are enterprise-level surveys that provide this sort of information on organizations. For the most part they have been developed and administered by researchers outside the innovation studies community and in general they do not provide the information that would allow researchers to explore the relations between organization and innovation.[3] A notable exception is the DISKO survey designed and administered at Aalborg University, where there has been a unique collaboration between researchers in innovation studies, human resource management, and industrial relations. A clear impetus in the design of the survey was the interest of Lundvall and his colleagues at Aalborg in developing measures of 'learning organizations' as central components of the learning economy. Thus the DISKO survey questionnaire includes not only indicators of product and process innovation, but also indicators of the use of a variety of managerial practices and forms of work organization that can be used to capture styles and rates of employee learning. This provides the basis for a statistical analysis of the interrelations between organizational forms and styles of employee learning on the one hand, and the frequency of product and process innovation on the other. A number of publications based

---

[3] For a comprehensive overview of organizational surveys undertaken in Europe and North America, see 'GRID Report', EU Meadow project background document No. 2 (downloaded from <http://www.meadow-project.eu/images/docmeadow/back_gridreport.pdf>).

on DISKO have identified positive correlations between the frequency of product and process innovation and the use of 'high-involvement' work practices such as autonomous teams, flexible demarcations in work tasks, and systems of employee involvement (Nielsen and Lundvall, 1999; Foss and Laursen, 2003; Jensen et al., 2007; Lundvall and Nielsen, 2007).

While these results and others based on specialized national-level enterprise surveys support the view that work organization and organizational practice are important determinants of innovative outcomes, they leave unexplored the wider issue of identifying and analysing the impact of inequalities in the distribution of the learning capabilities of individuals and organizations across regions and nations. In the absence of a harmonized EU-level enterprise survey providing relevant measures, the most ambitious attempts to map national differences in learning capabilities have been based on the results of successive waves of the European Working Conditions Survey (EWCS) carried out at the employee-level (Lorenz and Valeyre, 2005; Holm et al., 2010; Lorenz and Lundvall, 2010). The use of employee-level data to characterize work processes and organization has advantages and disadvantages relative to enterprise-level data. While the employee's perspective is limited in terms of capturing the overall structure and strategy of the enterprise, it provides a much richer characterization of daily work activity and how it relates to individual skills development and learning than can be provided by a questionnaire directed to an upper-level manager or employer.

Table 3.1, which draws on the results of the 3rd EWCS carried out in 2000, presents an index of inequalities in access to learning opportunities in the workplace for the EU-15 for employees working in private sector establishments with ten or more employees. The index is based on the results of a cluster analysis performed on a set of indicators of work organization that serves to identify the frequency of what is referred to as the as the 'discretionary learning' form of work organization, characterized by high levels of learning, problem-solving, and employee control over how work is carried out and over the pace of work.[4] The first column of figures in Table 3.1 gives the frequency of discretionary learning for all employees across the EU-15. Columns 2 and 3 show the percentages of 'managers' and 'workers' with access to discretionary learning, and the fourth column uses these results to construct an inequality index. The index shows that access to learning in the workplace tends to be much more equal in the Nordic nations and in the Netherlands than it is in the Southern European nations, while the position of most of the Continental European nations is intermediary. Interestingly, both the UK

---

[4] For a detailed description of the indicators and clustering technique used, see Lorenz and Valeyre (2005).

Table 3.1. Inequalities in access to learning, EU-15

	Share of all employees in discretionary learning	Share of managers in discretionary learning	Share of workers in discretionary learning	Learning Inequality index*
North				
Netherlands	64.0	81.6	51.1	37.3
Denmark	60.0	85.0	56.2	35.9
Sweden	52.6	76.4	38.2	50.3
Finland	47.8	62.0	38.5	37.9
Centre				
Austria	47.5	74.1	44.6	39.9
Germany	44.3	65.4	36.8	43.8
Luxembourg	42.8	70.3	33.1	52.9
Belgium	38.9	65.7	30.8	53.1
France	38.0	66.5	25.4	61.9
West				
UK	34.8	58.9	20.1	65.9
Ireland	24.0	46.7	16.4	64.9
South				
Italy	30.0	63.7	20.8	67.3
Portugal	26.1	59.0	18.2	69.2
Spain	20.1	52.4	19.1	63.5
Greece	18.7	40.4	17.0	57.9

Source: 2nd European Working Conditions Survey, 2000, as presented in Lundvall, Rasmussen, and Lorenz (2008).
* 'Managers' are defined to include managers, professionals, and technicians, while 'workers' include clerks and sales staff and skilled and unskilled manual occupations. The Inequality Index is constructed by dividing the share of 'workers' engaged in discretionary learning by the share of 'managers' engaged in discretionary learning, and subtracting the resulting percentage from 100. If the share of workers and managers were the same, the index would equal 0, and if the share of workers was 0 the index would equal 100.

and Ireland figure among the group of nations that are most unequal in terms of employee access to learning in the workplace.

From columns 2 and 3, it can be seen that the dispersion in access to learning across nations is lower for managers than it is for workers. This implies that the higher overall frequencies of discretionary learning in the Nordic nations have been achieved in part by deepening organizational learning in the sense of extending it down the organizational hierarchy to include manual operators and lower-level sales and service personnel. This is reflected in the fact that there is a strong and statistically significant negative correlation (–0.84) between the share for all employees and the inequality index.

Elsewhere we have shown that access to learning matters for the quality of working life and that those employees engaged in discretionary learning tend to be more satisfied with their jobs than those working in jobs with less discretion and scope for learning (Lorenz et al., 2004). But how much does it matter for innovation performance? Here we face the limitations of using employee-level data and the analysis can only be carried out at the aggregate level. In

Arundel et al. (2007) , using aggregate data from the 3rd CIS we showed that in nations where work is organized to support high levels of discretion in solving complex problems, firms tend to be more active in terms of innovations developed, at least to some degree, through their creative in-house efforts. In countries where learning and problem-solving on the job are more constrained, and little discretion is left to the employee, firms tend to be engaged in a supplier-dominated innovation strategy. Going beyond this macro-level of analysis to explore at a micro-level the relations between innovation performance, on the one hand, and organizational design and forms of work organization, on the other, would require a new European survey carried out at the enterprise level.[5]

3.3. National Systems of Innovation and Competence Building: What Are the Relevant Institutions?

How can be we account for differences in access to learning at the level of national systems? As the percentages in column 1 of Table 3.1 suggest, while differences in the level of economic development may explain part of the variance—the degree of penetration of discretionary learning is relatively low in the less developed Southern nations—the level of economic development cannot provide a complete explanation. There are wide differences in the frequency of discretionary learning between the Nordic nations, the UK, and the Continental European nations, all at similar levels of economic development. This raises the question of institutional embeddedness and the way in which national-level institutions impact on firm-level outcomes. But what institutions should we focus on?

While I have emphasized that comparative research on work organization and organizational design could benefit from better empirical measures, I would argue there is a need for better theory in innovation systems research as a basis for better typologies of national systems. In some of the earlier work on national innovations systems coming out of the USA, there was tendency to focus on the R&D system understood in terms of the relations among the private and public organizations and institutions responsible for formal R&D (Nelson, 1993). This can be seen as paralleling a focus on formal R&D in micro-level studies of innovation to the neglect of the social or organizational dimension.

More recently, and paralleling efforts to widen the definition and measurement of innovation, there have been efforts to widen the institutional focus in innovation systems research to include a consideration of how the structure of labour markets and national systems of social protection impact on micro-level learning and innovation processes. Lundvall has been an important contributor

---

[5] Arguably the optimal solution would be a linked employer/employee survey that would provide complementary information from both the employer's and employee's perspective. For a proposed linked survey design for developing harmonized measures of organizational change and its economic and social impacts, see the EU MEADOW project (<http://www.meadow-project.eu/>).

to this research agenda and his distinctive approach is closely connected to a theoretical position concerning the changing nature of competitiveness, summarized in the notion of the 'learning economy' (Lundvall and Johnson, 1994). Lundvall argues that advanced economies have moved into a phase where the most important factor in competitive performance is the capacity of individuals and organizations to learn and, further, he advances the view that social capital or trust form an essential underpinning of the learning economy. The importance attached to trust can already be seen in his early work on user–producer relations, where he argues that shared norms and codes of behaviour support interactive learning (Lundvall, 1985, 1988). The idea is more fully articulated in his jointly edited volume on *The Globalizing Learning Economy* (Archibugi and Lundvall, 2001) and in his book on innovation and social cohesion in the Danish model (Lundvall, 2002). He argues that inequalities in the distribution of learning capabilities between individuals and organizations may prove self-reinforcing and may result in polarization, notably at the level of labour markets within national systems. These tendencies towards polarization may, in turn, undermine the very conditions for the learning economy's success by weakening trust and social cohesion within and across organizations. This then leads to an interest in looking at the way differences in national labour markets and systems of social protection impact on the distribution of the costs and benefits of change, and consequently on differences in the dynamics of learning and innovation of national systems (Lorenz and Lundvall, 2006).[6]

Other important contributions to this wider understanding of national systems have come from outside the core of the innovation studies community, and in particular from researchers working on the 'varieties of capitalism' (VoC) (Whitley, 1998; Hall and Soskice, 2001) or on 'social systems of production' (Boyer and Hollingsworth, 1997). I think it is fair to say that innovation has never been the central focus in this latter research. The VoC literature, for example, has arguably been more centrally concerned with the way differences in vocational training systems and the mix of general and specific skills in a nation impact on social policy preferences for different types of social protection (Estevez-Abe et al., 2001; Iversen and Soskice, 2001). The VoC framework has, however, generated novel hypotheses concerning the relation between innovation outcomes and national institutional configurations, with the argument that coordinated market economies (CMEs) such as Germany or Japan will tend to be relatively specialized in incremental innovation, while liberal market economies (LMEs) such as the USA or the UK will tend to be relatively specialized in more radical innovations.

This hypothesis emerged from exploring the implications for innovation of a core notion developed in the VoC literature, namely that national systems will

---

[6] This analysis is also the basis for the idea that a 'New New Deal' is now needed to sustain the learning economy.

display comparative economic advantages corresponding to the nature of the complementarities among their institutions. Following Aoki (1994), institutional complementarities are defined to exist when the presence of one institution increases the efficiency or benefits from the presence of another. Further, although the selection mechanisms are merely hinted at, it is argued that a form of institutional coordination in one sphere of the economy (e.g. corporate governance) will tend to generate complementary forms in other spheres (e.g. labour markets or the organization of work), implying that the configuration of institutional arrangements in a nation will not be random (Hall and Soskice, 2000, p. 18). Thus, extending the insights of Aoki (1986) in his comparative analysis of the Japanese and American firm, VoC theorists have argued that incremental innovation will be favoured in CMEs because of institutional complementarities between corporate governance arrangements that are relatively insensitive to short-term profitability and hence favour long-term employment tenures, well-developed systems of vocational training providing an appropriate mix of firm and industry-specific skills, and industrial relations systems characterized by works councils and consensus decision-making.

LMEs, on the other hand, will have a comparative advantage in radical innovation. Well-developed equity markets with dispersed shareholders in LMEs will facilitate the acquisition of new technologies through mergers and acquisitions. These financial institutions will be highly complementary to relatively fluid labour markets, making it easier for companies to rapidly reconfigure their knowledge bases in order to develop new product lines. Labour market mobility is promoted by a lack of restrictions on hiring and firing in LMEs, combined with weak initial vocational training systems that encourage investments in general over firm-specific skills. Further, the hierarchical structure of companies in LMEs, with power concentrated at the top, will make it easier for senior management to implement new business strategies in comparison to managers in CME enterprises who are constrained by the requirements of consensus decision-making (Hall and Soskice, 2001, pp. 40–41).

Hall and Soskice (2000, p. 42–43) provide empirical support for their hypothesis with patent data from the European Patent Office measuring patterns of technological specialization for the USA and Germany. The hypothesis, however, has not stood up very well to more general empirical tests based on larger populations of nations and using patent citations in the NBER patent database to measure the relative specialization of nations in radical and incremental innovations (Taylor, 2004; Akkermanns et al., 2009). This need not imply, as some authors appear to have argued (Herrmann, 2008; Lange, 2009), that national institutions no longer matter much for corporate strategy in an increasingly global economy. It may simply reflect the fact that the conception of institutional complementarities in the VoC literature, which built explicitly on Aoki's classic comparative analysis of the Japanese and American firm in the 1980s and 1990s, is now outdated. For example, relatively fluid labour markets, by promoting greater variety in knowledge and skills, may well increase the likelihood that firms are well placed to introduce radical innovations. However, as the literature on 'flexicurity' has argued, such labour market arrangements may be complementary to vocational training systems favouring investments in industry-specific skills associated with the generous provision of unemployment protection and consensus decision-making at the firm level. Another case in point is the progressive deregulation of financial markets during the 2000s in a context of considerable national diversity in the strength and characteristics of national labour markets and systems of social protection. These 'hybrid' arrangements fit poorly into models proposing a dichotomous distinction, be it between the A-firm and the J-firm, or between liberal market economies (LME) and coordinated market economies (CME).

The identification of institutional complementarities and the assessment of their performance impacts can provide a basis for developing robust taxonomies of national innovations systems, and I would argue that making further progress in this area is one of the key challenges facing research on national systems within the field of innovation studies. A possible way forward is to start from a cognitive perspective and to examine how institutional complementarities promote the forms of related variety in organizational knowledge that sustain learning and innovation. For example, the cognitive perspective takes into account that highly creative firms draw their capability from the diverse and partially tacit industry-specific know-how and problem-solving skills that are embodied in individual experts. While codified formal professional knowledge will play a role, the expert's problem-solving capabilities may have more to do with his or her diverse experience acquired through interaction, trial-and-error, and experimentation in a variety of company settings (Lam and Lundvall, 2006). Flexicurity systems might promote the accumulation and interorganizational transfer of these capabilities in part because the security they provide through income maintenance can encourage individuals to commit themselves to what would otherwise be perceived as unacceptably risky forms of employment and career paths.[7]

3.4. Regions and Nations: The Need for a Multi-Level Governance Framework

The early work on regional innovation systems (Cooke, 1992; Asheim, 1996; Cooke et al., 1998) drew inspiration from seminal contributions to the research on national innovation systems, in particular work by Lundvall

---

[7] For an econometric analysis identifying positive links between flexicurity systems and high levels of employee learning for the EU-27, see Holm et al. (2010).

(1985) and Freeman (1987). A central idea was that of two sub-systems engaged in processes of interactive learning, one composed of private enterprises, often tightly clustered, and the other comprising the regional supportive infrastructure, composed of a variety of organizations responsible for processes of knowledge generation and transmission, including public research institutions, universities, and vocational training providers.

A central issue addressed in this literature has been the relation between geographic distance and knowledge transmission. One strand of literature has focused on the role of formal knowledge spillovers in the performance of high technology sectors. It has provided evidence that the R&D activities of private-sector enterprises benefit from their location in regions that are well endowed with university research or other public-sector research institutions. Proximity favours the transfer of scientific and technical knowledge both though the recruitment of university-trained scientists and through formal R&D collaboration (Jaffe, 1989; Link and Rees, 1990; Acs et al., 1992).

Another strand of research has emphasized the way proximity contributes to the inter-firm transfer of tacit and industry-specific knowledge among regionally clustered firms (Storper, 1995; Maskell, 1998; Lorenz and Lawson, 1999). Unlike most of the research on national systems, there has been a clear emphasis in the regional systems literature on the role of labour markets in the transfer and exchange of knowledge among firms. The work of scholars like Saxenian (1996) on Silicon Valley is illustrative of this, and more recently an econometric literature has developed that seeks to test propositions concerning the importance of related variety in knowledge for innovation by drawing on linked data sets in order to estimate of the impact of labour market mobility on the firm's skill profile and performance (Boschma, 2009).

To my knowledge, however, little attention has been given in the regional innovation systems literature to the way that differences in welfare state institutions might impact on local patterns of labour market mobility and knowledge accumulation. The reason for this is presumably that these framework conditions are nationally set, and scholars working on regional systems have their eyes firmly focused on the specificities of the local level with a view to explaining differences across regions. From the statistical point a view, an obvious question that has not been addressed is what part of observed differences in the characteristics and performance of firms can be accounted for by differences across nations, and what part can be explained by differences across regions within nations? But the more general challenge is developing a multi-level governance framework that could address the neglected issue of the interrelations between national and regional systems of innovation.

In the European context, the EU constitutes a third level of governance with largely unexplored impacts on the interrelations between regional and national innovation systems. While there is a large empirical literature analysing the growth effects of EU structural funds, the issue goes beyond the question of whether EU policies have promoted regional convergence.[8] One relevant question is whether institution building at the EU level has resulted in the creation of a European system of innovation that can be analysed on its own terms. While recent research on the issue has argued that it is premature to identify a European innovation system that can be analysed on the same terms as national or regional systems,[9] this does not preclude the idea that the emergence of a supranational level of governance and regulation has had significant impacts on the relations between national and local systems. Especially in national contexts, where there are existing intra-national-pressures for the decentralization of policy-making, the emergence of the European level of regulation may create new arenas for negotiation between actors and organizations at the regional and national levels, resulting in greater independence of the regional innovation system. While there is a lively literature on the characteristics of multi-level governance in Europe, the implications for innovation policy and outcomes at the regional and national levels remain to be fully explored.[10]

3.5. Policies for Organizational Change and Innovation

There have always been close connections between innovation studies scholars and the policy community, and it can be argued that the importance attached to research on particular concepts has been affected by the extent to which policy-makers have picked up on and adopted the concepts in their policy discourse. Research on innovation systems has no doubt been bolstered by the importance attached to the innovation systems concept in the policy documents coming out of the OECD, and it can even be debated whether the origins of the concept is mainly the policy community or academic researchers (Sharif, 2006). The emphasis placed on the knowledge-based economy in the European Commission's 2000 Lisbon strategy has no doubt not only provided finance through the Framework Programmes but has also conferred greater legitimacy on research focusing on the dynamics of knowledge accumulation and innovation.

---

[8] For a recent review of the literature, see Mohl and Hagen (2010).

[9] See the collection of essays edited by Borrás (2004) in the special issue of *Science and Public Policy* on a European system of innovation.

[10] For the effects of multi-level governance on science policy in France, see Crespy, Heraud, and Perry (2007). For the case of innovation policies in Sweden, Switzerland, and the Netherlands, see Prange (2008).

There has also been a clear connection between the commitment of resources to the production of new survey data that may be used for research purposes and the policy importance attached to the concepts that the surveys are designed to measure. In the EU context, the considerable investments that have been made in expanding the geographical scope of existing surveys, or in conducting new surveys, during the 2000s is linked to the use of the 'open-method of coordination', which requires harmonized statistical measures at the EU level for the purpose of setting targets and monitoring progress in achieving different policy goals. The CIS's evolution from a survey carried out on a voluntary basis by a handful of nations in the 1990s, to a mandatory two-year exercise for EU member nations at present, can be explained in large measure by the importance attached by the European Commission to monitoring innovation performance in accordance with the goals of the Lisbon strategy.

I argued earlier that our understanding of innovation processes within national systems could benefit from better harmonized enterprise-level survey data on organizational design and managerial practice. In lieu of the historically close connections between policy frameworks and priorities, on the one hand, and the development of survey instruments, on the other, it is useful to speculate on how favourable high-level policy discourse is at present to the commitment of resources to developing a harmonized EU-level organizational survey. The European Commission through Eurostat and the OECD traditionally have worked closely together on the design and development of innovation-related survey instruments, and while the OECD has no formal responsibility for the direction of EU innovation policy, it is nonetheless useful to consider how each institution has articulated innovation-related policy objectives and measures.

While promoting innovation remains a cornerstone of the European Commission's post-Lisbon, Europe 2020 strategy, the Commission's understanding of innovation and its approach to innovation policy appear to be remarkably narrow, focusing primarily on R&D and investments in tertiary-level educational qualifications of researchers. Europe 2020 sets out as one of its five headline targets that 3 per cent of the EU's GDP should be invested in R&D (European Commission, 2010a, p. 5) and the Innovation Union, one of the Commission's flagship initiatives—though containing a large number 'action points'—is to a large extent structured around the 3 per cent objective. For example, the role of education and skills development is analysed in terms of member countries 'training enough researchers to meet their national R&D targets', and the discussion on promoting international labour mobility and cooperation within the EU Research Area is expressed in terms of the 'mobility of researchers across countries and sectors' and the 'cross-border operation of research performing organizations'. Similarly, the importance of improving access to finance, including venture capital, is analysed mainly in terms of closing 'the market gaps in investing in research and innovation' (European Commission, 2010b, pp. 9 and 14).[11] The 2011 *Innovation Competitiveness* report focuses almost exclusively on the 3 per cent R&D target and the contribution of educational investments and proposed reforms to the finance and patenting systems towards achieving the target (European Commission, 2011a). While a 2011 report on progress in attaining the overall objectives of Europe 2020 recognizes that existing differences in industrial structure between EU member states may account for the relatively low levels of R&D intensity in certain member nations, this is interpreted strictly as a weakness with little appreciation that firms operating in low-R&D intensive sectors may be highly innovative, or that many innovative firms, including a large share of service sector firms, do not devote resources to R&D (European Commission, 2011b, p. 5).

The EU 2020 strategy, with its strong emphasis on R&D intensity, stands in sharp contrast to the OECD's 2010 Innovation Strategy, which develops a broad understanding of innovation processes that is much in keeping with recent trends in innovation research. The assessment of innovation policy measures in the Ministerial Report on the OECD's Innovation Strategy begins by observing that while R&D is important, many highly innovative firms do not engage in R&D and that value may be created 'through a wide range of complementary technological and non-technological changes and innovations' (OECD, 2010a, p. 6). The analysis of skills gives recognition to formal initial educational systems but also argues that skills acquisition is a lifelong process that extends beyond formal education and includes informal learning processes on the job. In this latter respect, the report argues that, 'organisational structures and employment policies that shape the workplace are essential for determining how human capital translates into innovation and productivity' (OECD, 2010a, p. 11).

In close association with the main elements of the Innovation Strategy, the OECD sets out an ambitious Measurement Agenda for Innovation. The measurement agenda report (OECD, 2010b, p. 13) begins by observing that innovation is the result of a range of complementary assets that include not just R&D but also software, human capital, and new organizational structures. The agenda report continues by pointing to the limitations of policies built around targeting spending levels on R&D, and argues that there is a pressing need to go beyond targets and to develop an understanding of why and how innovation happens in firms. This can be furthered by making improvements to existing data infrastructures, and particularly by improving

---

[11] For the 30 action points of the Innovation Union, see: <http://ec.europa.eu/research/innovation-union/index_en.cfm?pg=action-points>.

business registers and by increasing the scope for linking different data sets, including linking innovation surveys with ICT surveys and with administrative data bases measuring firm-level expenditures on capital, earnings, and employment (OECD, 2010b, p. 14). The agenda report also recognizes the need for new survey data and includes a number of 'gap' pages that refer to key areas where there is a lack of high-quality internationally comparable indicators. These include the 'measurement of innovative activity in complex business structures, organisations and networks' and the 'measurement of the skills required in innovative workplaces'. The approach to skills development is sophisticated and goes beyond the traditional emphasis on the supply and demand for tertiary-level educational qualifications that figures prominently in the European Commission's Innovation Union policy documents. The 'gap' page on 'Innovative workplaces and skills for innovation' in the measurement report notably argues that, 'interaction and learning within firms enables employees to share information, challenge existing patterns, and experiment and collaborate to improve products and processes'. Further, it observes that, while 'the potential role of learning and interaction within organizations has been highlighted as a way to strengthen firm performance in the post-crisis environment', these 'concepts remain difficult to quantify and better measurement instruments are needed' (OECD, 2010b, p. 56).

The OECD's Measurement Agenda for Innovation sets out an ambitious programme both in terms of improving and making better use of existing data structures, and in terms of the development of new measurement instruments. The OECD report clearly recognizes that the agenda implies a long time-frame and that it depends on the efforts and engagement, not only of the statistical community and of policy-makers, but also of organizations and businesses, since the statistical system can only collect what is feasible to measure inside organizations. While the necessary efforts and commitments for developing new measurement instruments of organizational change and employee learning may be present in certain EU member nations, the largely traditional and conservative focus of the EU's Innovation Union clearly suggests that they do not exist at present at the EU level. A possible reason for the lack of support and engagement in this sense amongst policy-makers is the widespread perception that policies for organizational change and innovation would constitute an unacceptable infringement on managerial prerogatives. Despite its many forward-thinking elements, this would also appear to be the dominant view within the OECD. The Ministerial Report on the Innovation Strategy, after arguing for the importance of interaction and learning within organizations, hastens to add, 'governments do not play a direct role in the workplace', and the report limits the role of government policy to shaping the framework conditions that support learning and innovation in the workplace (OECD, 2010a, p. 11).

While my discussion in this chapter has focused in part on the importance of institutional framework conditions for learning and innovation, recognition that institutions matter does not preclude more focused micro-policy initiatives. The Nordic nations have a long and rich experience of policy programmes designed to foster organizational change and innovation at the workplace level. These programmes typically operate by providing competitive funding for the implementation of change within individual firms or within networks of organizations, with management and staff actively working alongside outside researchers or experts.[12] Examples include the Value Creation (VC) programme in Norway, the TEKES programme in Finland, and the workplace innovation programmes administered though VINNOVA in Sweden. The approach adopted in these programmes overrides the objection that policies for organizational change constitute an unacceptable infringement on managerial prerogatives. A central feature of the policy approach is that workplace innovation projects are carried out at the initiative of the employer, who seeks competitive funding. Another important aspect of the policy approach is that projects for organizational change and innovation are based on implementation strategies adapted to the local conditions of the plant, which avoids the problem of proposing universal best-practice solutions that may be poorly adapted to the local technological or organizational context. These policy initiatives at the level of the workplace or networks of firms are highly complementary to the emphasis in the Nordic nations on developing broad-based vocational training and life-long learning systems in support of competence building. The complementary nature of these workplace policies and national framework initiatives may well provide part of the explanation for the advances made in the Nordic nations in extending and deepening learning in the workplace.

References

Acs, Z., Audretch, D., Feldman, M. (1992). 'Real Effects of Academic Research: Comment', *American Economic Review*, 82: 363–67.

Akkermanns, D., Castaldi, C., and Los, B. (2009). 'Do "Liberal Market Economies" Really Innovate More Radically than "Coordinated Market Economies"? Hall and Soskice Reconsidered', *Research Policy*, 38: 181–91.

Alasoini, T., Ramstad, E., Hanhike, T., and Lahtonen, M. (2005). 'European Programmes on Work and Innovation: A Benchmarking Approach', Work-in-Net Project, Supported by the 6th Framework Programme of the European Commission.

[12] See Alasoini et al. (2005) for an overview.

Aoki, M. (1986). 'Horizontal vs. Vertical Information Structure of the Firm', *The American Economic Review*, *76*: 971–83.

Aoki, M. (1994). 'The Contingent Governance of Teams: Analysis of Institutional Complementarity', *International Economic Review*, 35, 657–76.

Archibugi, D. and Lundvall, B.-Å. (2001). *The Globalizing Learning Economy*. Oxford: Oxford University Press.

Arundel, A., Lorenz, E., Lundvall, B.-Å., and Valeyre, A. (2007). 'How Europe's Economies Learn: A Comparison of Work Organisation and Innovation Mode for the EU-15', *Industrial and Corporate Change*, *16*: 1175–210.

Asheim, B. (1996). 'Industrial Districts as "Learning Regions": A Condition for Prosperity', *European Planning Studies*, 4: 379–400.

Borrás, S. (2004). 'Systems of Innovation Theory and the European Union', *Science and Public Policy*, *31*: 425–33.

Boschma, R., Eriksson, R., and Lindgren, U. (2009). 'How Does Labour Mobility Affect the Performance of Plants? The Importance of Relatedness and Geographical Proximity', *Journal of Economic Geography*, 9: 169–90.

Cohen, M. and Levinthal, D. (1989). 'Innovation and Learning: The Two Faces of R&D', *Economic Journal*, 99: 569–96.

Cohen, M. and Levinthal, D. (1990). 'Absorptive Capacity: A New Perspective on Learning and Innovation', *Administrative Science Quarterly*, *35*: 128–52.

Cooke, P. (1992) 'Regional Innovation Systems: Competitive Regulation in the New Europe', *Geoforum*, 23: 945–74.

Cooke P., Uranga, M., and Etxebarria, G. (1998). 'Regional Systems of Innovation: An Evolutionary Perspective', *Environment and Planning, A*(30):1563–84.

Crespy, C., Heraud, J.-A., and Perry, B. (2007). 'Multi-level Governance, Regions and Science in France: Between Competition and Equality', *Regional Studies*, *41*: 1069–84.

Estevez-Abe, M., Iversen, T., and Soskice, D. (2001). 'Social Protection and the Formation of Skills: A Reinterpretation of the Welfare State', in P. Hall, and D. Soskice (eds), *Varieties of Capitalism*. Oxford: Oxford University Press, 145–73.

European Commission (2010a). 'Communication from the Commission, Europe 2020, A Strategy for Smart, Sustainable and Inclusive Growth', COM(2010) 2020 final, Brussels.

European Commission (2010b). 'Europe 2020 Flagship Initiative Innovation Union', COM(2010) 546 final, Brussels.

European Commission (2011a). 'Innovation Union Competitiveness Report 2011, Executive Summary', Brussels.

European Commission (2011b). 'Annex, Progress Report on the Europe 2020 Strategy: Annual Growth Survey 2012', COM(2011) 815 final, Brussels.

Fagerberg, J. and Verspagen, B. (2009). 'Innovation Studies—The Emerging Structure of a New Scientific Field', *Research Policy*, 38: 218–33.

Foss, N. and Laursen, K. (2003). 'New Human Resource Management Practices, Complementarities and the Impact on Innovation Performance', *Cambridge Journal of Economics*, *27*: 243–63.

Freeman, C. (1987). *Technology, Policy, and Economic Performance: Lessons from Japan*. London: Printer Publishers.

Freeman, C. (1995). 'The "National System of Innovation" in Historical Perspective', *Cambridge Journal of Economics, 19*: 5–24.

Freeman, C. and Soete, L. (1987). *Technical Change and Full Employment.* London: Blackwell Publishers.

Hall, P. and Soskice, D. (2001). *Varieties of Capitalism.* Oxford: Oxford University Press.

Herrmann, A. M. (2008). 'Rethinking the Link Between Labour Market Flexibility and Corporate Competitiveness: A Critique of the Institutionalist Literature', *Socio-Economic Review, 6*: 637–69.

Hollingsworth, J. and Boyer, R. (1997). *Contemporary Capitalism: The Embeddedness of Institutions.* Cambridge: Cambridge University Press.

Holm, J., Lorenz, E., Lundvall, B.-Å., and Valeyre, A. (2010). 'Work Organisation and Systems of Labour Market Regulation in Europe', *Industrial and Corporate Change, 19*: 1141–73.

Iversen, T. and Soskice, D. (2001). 'An Asset Theory of Social Policy Preferences', *American Political Science Review, 9*: 875–94.

Jaffe, A. B. (1989). 'Real Effects of Academic Research', *The American Economic Review, 79*: 957–70.

Jensen, M., Johnson, B., Lorenz, E., and Lundvall, B.-Å. (2007). 'Forms of Knowledge and Modes of Innovation', *Research Policy, 36*: 680–93.

Lange, K. (2009). 'Institutional Embeddedness and the Strategic Leeway of Actors: The Case of the German Therapeutical Biotech Industry', *Socio-Economic Review, 7*: 181–208.

Lam, A. and Lundvall B.-A. (2006). 'The Learning Organisation and National Systems of Competence Building and Innovation,' in E. Lorenz and B.-A. Lundvall (eds), *How Europe's Economies Learn: Coordinating Competing Models.* Oxford: Oxford University Press, 109–139

Link, A. and Rees, J. (1990). 'Firm Size, University Based Research and the Returns to R&D', *Small Business Economics, 2*: 25–31.

Lorenz, E. and Lawson, C. (1999). 'Collective Learning, Tacit Knowledge and Regional Innovative Capacity', *Regional Studies, 33*: 305–17.

Lorenz, E. and Lundvall, B. Å. (2006). *How Do Europe's Economies Learn: Coordinating Competing Models.* Oxford: Oxford University Press.

Lorenz, E. and Lundvall, B.-Å. (2010). 'Accounting for Creativity in the European Union: A Multi-level Analysis of Individual Competence, Labour', *Cambridge Journal of Economics, 35*: 251–69.

Lorenz, E. and Valeyre, A. (2005). 'Organisational Innovation, HRM and Labour Market Structure: A Comparison of the EU-15', *Journal of Industrial Relations, 47*: 424–42.

Lundvall, B.-Å. (1985). *Product Innovation and User-Producer Interaction.* Aalborg: Aalborg University Press.

Lundvall, B. Å. (1988). 'Innovation As an Interactive Process: From User-producer Interaction to the National System of Innovation', in G. Dosi, C. Freeman, R. Nelson, G. Silverberg, and L. Soete (eds), *Technical Change and Economic Theory.* London: Pinter, 349–69.

Lundvall, B. Å. (2002). *Innovation Growth and Social Cohesion: The Danish Model*: Cheltenham: Edward Elgar.

Lundvall, B. Å. and Nielsen, P. (2007). 'Knowledge Management and Innovation Performance', *International Journal of Manpower*, 28: 207–33.

Lundvall, B.-Å., Rasmussen, P., and Lorenz, E. (2008). 'Education in the Learning Economy: A European Perspective', *Policy Futures in Education*, 6: 681–700.

Maskell, P. (1998). *Competitiveness, Localised Learning and Regional Development: Specialization and Prosperity in Small Open Economies*. London: Routledge.

Miles, I. (2008). 'Patterns of Innovation in Service Industries', *IBM Systems Journal*, 47: 115–28.

Mohl, P. and Hagen, T. (2010). 'Do EU Structural Funds Promote Regional Growth? New Evidence from Various Panel Data Approaches', *Regional Science and Urban Economics*, 40: 353–65.

Nelson, R. (1993). *National Innovation Systems: A Comparative Analysis*. Oxford: Oxford University Press.

Nielsen, P. and Lundvall, B.-Å. (1999). 'Competition and Transformation in the Learning Economy—Illustrated by the Danish Case', *Revue d'économie industrielle*, 88: 67–89.

OECD (2010a). 'Ministerial Report on the OECD Innovation Strategy, Key Findings'. Paris: OECD Publishing (downloaded from <http://www.oecd.org/dataoecd/51/28/45326349.pdf>).

OECD (2010b). *Measuring Innovation: A New Perspective*: Paris: OECD Publishing.

Prange, H. (2008). 'Explaining Varieties of Regional Innovation Policies in Europe', *European Urban and Regional Studies*, 15: 39–52.

Saxenian, A. (1996). *Beyond Boundaries: Open Labor Markets and Learning in Silicon Valley*. Oxford: Oxford University Press.

Schmidt, T. and Rammer, C. (2007). 'The Determinants and Effects of Technological and Non-technological Innovations—Evidence from the German CIS IV', Centre for European Economic Research (ZEW).

Sharif, N. (2006). 'Emergence and Development of the National Innovations System concept', *Research Policy*, 35: 745–66.

Storper, M. (1995). 'The Resurgence of Regional Economies, Ten Years Later—The Region as a Nexus of Untraded Interdependencies', *European Urban and Regional Studies*, 2: 191–221.

Taylor, M. (2004). 'Empirical Evidence Against Varieties of Capitalism's Theory of Technological Innovation', *International Organization*, 58: 601–31.

Tether, B. (2003). 'The Sources and Aims of Innovation in Services: Variety Between and Within Sectors', *Economics of Innovation and New Technology*, 12: 481–505.

Tidd, J. (2003). *Service Innovation: Organisational Responses to Technological Opportunities and Market Imperatives*. London: Imperial College Press.

Whitley, R. (1998). 'Internationalization and Varieties of Capitalism: The Limited Effects of Cross-National Coordination of Economic Activities on the Nature of Business Systems', *Review of International Political Economy*, 5: 445–81.

4

Innovation Systems and Policy for Development in a Changing World

Carlota Perez

4.1. Looking at the Question

Whether innovation systems and policies are only for the rich was the question originally posed to me by the editors of this book. Its implication is clear: the general thrust of innovation has until recently been seen as focused on serving the needs of rich countries. Could innovation systems and policy favour advance in poor countries? Is there a particular reason to ask that question now? Probably, yes. Would the answer be the same today as it was in the 1960s and 1970s? Certainly not! Could it be that this issue is not inherent to innovation or innovation systems themselves (or to capitalism), but that it can change with the stages of diffusion of technological revolutions and the nature of their paradigms? This is what I will suggest, arguing that such a dynamic understanding would have consequences for innovation studies, for evolutionary economics, and for innovation policy.

Such an interpretation is based on an 'appreciative theory' of how the capitalist economy evolves through successive technological revolutions and techno-economic paradigm shifts, as Chris Freeman and I have proposed (Freeman and Perez, 1988; Freeman and Louçã, 2001; Perez, 2002, 2010a). It represents a style of theorizing that has been predominant in innovation studies (Nelson and Winter, 1982, p. 46–48) as well as in the 'high development theory' of Prebisch, Hirschman, and others. Appreciative theorizing attempts to understand important historical processes that cannot be handled by formal analytical tools. The criticisms put forward by Romer (1993) and Krugman (1995) were based on the vain hope that such processes could be formalized by new growth theory and new trade theory. Instead, some of the most important insights of the appreciative theorists vanished due to certain neo-classical restrictions, and the best hope of rescuing them probably lies in the hands of evolutionary economists.

What this alternative form of theorizing does is to avoid isolating the economy from the specific forms that technology and institutions assume as they evolve, and to refuse to restrict itself solely to the quantifiable aspects. Its main role is to provide a set of heuristics to identify relevant questions, to help formulate research hypotheses, and to serve as a framework for judging alternative explanations. Its main virtue, given its evolutionary form, is to recognize change as intrinsic to the workings of the economy and to be able to handle processes of transformation without having to exclude aspects of the causal network merely because they cannot be measured. Consequently, phenomena such as the recent major bubble and collapse, for instance, do not need to be seen as 'black swans' but can be understood as long-term regularities of the system (Freeman, 2001; Perez, 2002, 2009).

The Role of History in the Inter-Disciplinary Mix

The stubbornness of the post-collapse recessionary trends reveals not only that free markets are not the answer to the crisis, but also that 'pure' economics is not able to analyse it. Society cannot afford to continue looking for the lost keys only under the street lamp. In these uncertain times we need an inter-disciplinary—or perhaps rather post-disciplinary—approach, similar perhaps to the appreciative analyses of the German Historical School on which Schumpeter based much of his theoretical work.

As Freeman (1988, p. 2) argued in the introduction to the book by Dosi et al. (1988) that launched the new wave of innovation economics, the interaction between economics, science and technology, and institutions is essential for understanding growth and development. He further insisted that those inter-relationships can best be understood when incorporating history (Freeman, 1984, 1995; Freeman and Perez, 1988; Freeman and Louçã, 2001). This is in line with Schumpeter's view on how ultimately to pursue economics. Indeed, by opening the door to inter-disciplinarity, evolutionary economics and the innovation system perspective have offered much richer theories for understanding the uncertainties of the real economy and its diversified functioning. We can be proud of the achievements in this area. Yet there is one aspect where we have not gone far enough. In order to design effective policies, society needs to understand the big picture, or more specifically the big *moving* picture.

We need to fully incorporate history in the inter-disciplinary mix. The search for eternal unchanging truths, as in physics, is not appropriate when studying social phenomena as complex—and as human—as innovation, growth, and development. This criticism can be levelled against neo-classical economists, but their work is at least consistent with their overall goals and criteria. However, ignoring history is simply unacceptable in evolutionary economics. It would have been unthinkable to Freeman, but also to Marx and Schumpeter. Technical change continuously modifies the conditions for innovation and for development, and we must be at the forefront of explaining such changes and identifying the specific transformations taking place in each period. Only then can we hope to be useful as a science that serves to guide effective policy design and to shape viable political goals.

Changing Answers to the Same Question

So, is innovation only for the rich? There are two traditional answers to this question by appreciative theorists:

1. The Dependency School, in its various versions (e.g. Singer, 1949; Prebisch, 1951; Gunder Frank, 1967; Cardoso and Faletto, 1968; Sunkel, 1970; Amin, 1976), basically held that Third World countries could not define their future but were technologically dependent on the interests and decisions of foreign investors from the advanced world.[1]

2. The appropriate technology movement (e.g. Sen, 1960; Cooper, 1972) recommended the selection of technologies better adapted to the endowments of the developing world, in the sense of being less capital-intensive and using more labour.

In both cases, it was assumed that technical change was continuous and cumulative, that technology came from the North, and that it was up to the developmental states of the South to try to choose the most appropriate technologies among those that were available for acquisition. The context shaped the analysis, the theoretical answers, and the policy recommendations.

Today in developing countries, we are seeing dynamic innovation systems, policies for enabling innovation and catch-up, upgrading the role of local companies in global value networks, new pathways for development, and so on. Why have the answers and the policy goals changed? Because technical change is constant but also discontinuous. From the mid 1970s, the world has been experiencing the Information and Communications Technology (ICT) Revolution, and the resulting paradigm shift has radically changed the opportunities available to all participants. It has enabled flexible production patterns and network organizations; it has induced and facilitated

---

[1] Indeed, the most innovative technology policies at the time, such as those promoted by UNCTAD and those of the Andean Pact, concentrated on regulating the transfer of technology by MNCs, avoiding restrictive clauses and excessive royalties, and trying to guarantee that effective transfer would indeed take place.

globalization, disaggregation of value-chains, and outsourcing; it has made possible catching-up (and even forging ahead) in the developing world; and it has opened up new opportunities for innovation and for diversity across the whole production spectrum (both tangible and intangible). None of these conditions existed in the 1960s and 1970s.

Changing Context; Redefining Problems

Moreover, it is not only the answers to the question that have changed; the content of the question has also experienced a transformation: who specifically are the poor when we ask 'Not only for the rich?' Do we define them in the same way as in the 1960s and 1970s? Probably not. We can indeed still count most of the traditional 'Third World countries' among the poor in contrast with the rich advanced countries, but not all. First the Four Tigers and now the BRICS have broken away from the ranks of the laggards and begun to catch up—some of them might even forge ahead. Does this mean that the Dependency School was wrong all along? Did the South Koreans and the Chinese leap forward because of choosing labour-intensive technologies? Or is it that both the Dependency School and the appropriate technology proponents were right when they assessed the situation during the mature phase of the Age of Mass Production, but ceased to be right when the ICT revolution changed the context radically?

Already in the 1980s and 1990s, Hirschman, Sen, Gunder-Frank, and others recognized that the ideas of Development Economics and of the Dependency School were no longer useful. However, they did not see that it was because conditions had changed that the ideas about how to handle technologies had to change. The main lesson of history was unfortunately lost in that case.[2]

But we can go further in this rethinking. Should we maintain the definition of 'the poor' as referring mainly to countries? Isn't it important now to look at the poor and the impoverished in the advanced world as well? Shouldn't we also try to see how innovation could help overcome the inequalities that characterize some of the emerging country success stories? Currently, within advanced, emerging, and developing countries there are widening differences between the skilled and the unskilled, between urban and rural populations, between emerging and declining regions (where unemployment is rampant), and, within cities, between rich areas and slums.[3] Does technological innovation hold part of the explanation for these trends, and can innovation policy do anything about them? Should the question of 'not only for

[2] See Hirschman (1982) and Sen (1983). Gunder Frank (1991), writing much later, was one who clearly recognized that times were changing and then went on to attempt a major reinterpretation of history.
[3] Of the people who live on less than $1/day, 70 per cent live in middle-income countries (Sumner, 2010).

the rich' address these differences? Adequate industrial, employment, and welfare policies for the current times may need to involve explicit directions for the specialization or respecialization of each country and each region on the basis of its advantages and capacities to address effective demand in the global space. They will also need a strong component of innovation policy to enhance those capabilities.

In the advanced world, from the late 1940s to the 1960s, technology helped the poor to achieve better lives. Charlie Chaplin brilliantly satirized the negative side of the assembly line, but outside the workplace life did get much better after 1945. In those times, the excluded were mainly in the Third World, and those countries could be defined basically as 'the poor'. Now the picture has changed. Technology and globalization have been stripping many Western workers of their expected 'good life'. Can innovation help them? The idea that there is a technological frontier that is constantly advancing and improving lives may need rethinking if conditions require a reconsideration of what are the most socially relevant directions for innovation. Similarly, the extremely rapid growth processes in China and India have been highly polarized, excluding a high proportion of the population from the benefits of development. Should this issue be confronted by innovation theory and policy? Do we need a more sophisticated picture when addressing the opportunities for the poor? It would definitely seem so.

4.2. The Paradigm Shift and Its Effects on the Conditions of Innovation for and by the Poor (and the Weak)

Let us begin by looking at the nature of the shift from the viewpoint of the theory of techno-economic paradigms. What has changed since the 1970s, when ICT began replacing mass production as the prevailing techno-economic paradigm (Perez, 1985, 1986, 2010a)? How do innovation conditions differ from those prevailing until the 1970s? In what sense do the poor and the weak—be they individuals, firms, or countries—find better (or worse) opportunities for employment, wealth creation, innovation, and potential improvements in the quality of life? These questions can be seen as constituting a whole new research agenda, and that is the spirit in which the following section is presented.

ICT, Innovation, and Market Access by Small Firms in Any Country

There are many changes directly attributable to ICT. Access to information is now infinitely easier than before; networking has become simple and cheap at whatever distance; software and other intangibles constitute an increasing element of innovation and of the global product mix; computers and mobile phones facilitate not only software innovation but also product design and testing; and digital equipment can remove the need to acquire skills that previously took many years to master (undoubtedly a loss for many workers from printing to machine-tool operators—paradigm shifts involve processes of creative destruction on many fronts). These new tools mean that the possibilities for innovation and entrepreneurship are now open to individuals and small companies wherever they are located.

Intangible innovation is easy to transport to the point of use, and the 'app mania', however long it may last, has opened possibilities for many brilliant young people, in whichever country they happen to reside. The open source movement has lowered the cost of software for individuals, schools, and companies, but most of all it has provided a collective learning platform for potential innovators. The opportunities for innovating in tangible products have also multiplied due to the replacement of the mass-production world of simple economies of scale for identical products by one in which economies of scope, scale, and specialization coexist within the flexible production model enabled by ICT. This has resulted in hyper-segmentation of markets and the creation of a very 'long tail' of specialized niche products, where small firms can be very profitable (Kaplinsky, 2005; Anderson, 2006). This has been enhanced by developments in logistics and retail trade that facilitate the handling of small quantities at reasonable cost. Both Damart and Tesco, through their purchasing networks and the 'fair trade' movement, have been built upon those new conditions.

Another possible consequence of this new flexibility is the potential—as yet hardly used—to cater for differences in culture, religion, or climate that had previously been almost ironed out by the American (universal) Way of Life. The notion of different lifestyles delivering 'equivalent satisfaction' could enhance the quality of life of many without forcing homogeneity. 'Frugal innovation' and organic products are an early manifestation of that potential.

Flexible Production and Global Networks

Besides making possible greater segmentation of markets, ICT has provided the infrastructure and tools for the giant global corporations to operate. It is now much easier not only to manage enormous and highly complex organizations with units in many parts of the world, but also to do so with a relatively flat structure and with a variety of arrangements such as alliances and contracts with other companies, suppliers, and partners. It is this profound change that has given impetus to the Asian leap forward in its various forms.

The practice of outsourcing has opened up a wide range of possibilities for incorporating producers in all parts of the world. The much greater volumes that are now possible with changing models and varying product mixes have had a huge employment effect. This is one factor underpinning the success of China and other Asian countries on the basis of low-cost labour for the standardized segments of fabricated product markets.

As the process of learning to globalize proceeds, corporations have been experimenting in many countries with the use of local knowledge workers and local innovative talent. India became central with its experience gained from handling the computer problems expected with the year 2000;[4] and soon the software industry was largely globalized (Arora and Gambardella, 2004; Friedman, 2005). Currently, there is increasing outsourcing of R&D (raising possible intellectual property problems that are not yet clearly defined) as well as a trend to develop knowledge-intensive suppliers (Urzua, 2012), even in traditional sectors such as mining.[5]

From the perspective of emerging countries, there are also important new developments. Several Korean, Indian, and Chinese companies have themselves become global corporations, and are investing by buying companies and outsourcing to both advanced and lagging countries. Some Latin American companies are also now investing globally.

Natural Resources: Curse or Opportunity?

There is an assumption dating from the 1950s, inherited from the mass-production era, that development is only about manufacturing and that natural resources are a dead end (Singer, 1949; Prebisch, 1951). In the late 1970s, concerns arose about the 'Dutch disease'—that is, de-industrialization brought about by revaluation due to natural resource exports (*The Economist*, 1977). More recently, research has associated them with corruption and other ills, coining the term 'resource curse' (Sachs and Warner, 1995).

By contrast, natural resources were seen as very important for development during the first globalization, from the 1870s to 1914. The technological revolution that was then taking place, in the age of steel and heavy engineering, was about chemistry and electricity, about transcontinental railways and world-trading steamships, about metallurgy and major engineering projects.

[4] The so-called 'Y2K problem', when the need to modify all software to go from two to four characters for the year (from 19XX to 2000) raised fears that all computer-controlled equipment would stop working, provided work opportunities for thousands of programmers in India (Friedman, 2005).

[5] BHP Billiton in Chile has employed a SPRU PhD to develop local high-tech suppliers for its copper-mining activities (see Urzua, 2011).

It was also about counter-seasonal world markets for meat, wheat, and other agricultural products. In those times, natural resources were considered a blessing not a curse. Australia, Canada, Sweden, the USA, and others partly owe their catching up to their resource endowment.[6] Yet, as Reinert (2004) emphasizes, policy-makers in those countries understood that raw materials alone—without concomitant highly-skilled, technology-intensive activities—would not result in development.[7]

Times are changing once more. The growth of the emerging countries implies such an increase in the demand for natural resources that prices are likely to oscillate at much higher average levels (Dobbs et al., 2011; Farooki and Kaplinsky, 2012), and it will be necessary to engage in a lot of innovation to guarantee supply as well as to serve the 'long tail' in specialized materials, organic and gourmet foods, and many other niche products (Perez, 2010b). This is happening already, together with upstream innovations in equipment, chemicals, and other inputs. But most importantly, the competition for resources among the established companies of the West and those of the emerging countries is likely to open up unprecedented opportunities for developing countries to negotiate better terms. If energy prices are very high, there will be efforts to avoid the transportation of unprocessed materials by locating some downstream processes *in situ*. These changes would also require innovations in order to solve problems of scale and mobility. Such incentives for innovation could underlie a dynamic growth process among natural resource producers (Marin et al., 2010).

The Environmental Challenges as a Guide to Innovation

Finally, there is the issue of the environment. Both the planet and the economy need extensive 'green' innovation. The potential is there in technological terms. The ICT revolution can enable innovation across a wide range of sectors, from smart-grids to specialized materials, from redesigning products for durability and upgradeability to reducing the need for transport. But 'green' products and services are not capable of being immediately profitable, as many ICT products were at the beginning. The way to increase their economic viability is to induce a clear common direction. Convergence and networking can lead to synergies in suppliers and markets, increasing the profitability of the entire network. Markets alone cannot reach that outcome; an active government can.

---

[6] Of course, it makes a huge difference if such resources are to be exported raw or to be used as the basis (or as a source of income) for technological development. Morris et al. (2012) examine the new conditions and the increase in upstream innovation opportunities.

[7] Reinert (2004) proposes to establish Schumpeterian development economics based on these and other criteria.

The need to greatly enhance the productivity of resources could lead, with the right policies, to redesigning products for true durability. This could generate new second-hand markets, enabling the bottom of the pyramid to take a step onto the consumption ladder sustainably and at low cost. This could also revive maintenance as a major source of jobs for the displaced manufacturing workers of the advanced world. Clear policies to favour a 'green' direction in innovation through such measures as regulation, taxes, and R&D funding are likely to be necessary in all countries, including the poorest, where the need to do more with less is even more pressing (United Nations Environment Programme, 2011).

Finally, there are innumerable opportunities for improving the lives of the poor in an environmentally friendly way, with innovations adapted to harsh climates, renewable energy, the use of waste or local materials, and many other appropriate technologies. The policies and conditions that could bring these innovations forth—from private or public sources—and propagate their use surely merit the attention of innovation scholars.

4.3. The Big *Moving* Picture

Research is needed to provide a deeper understanding of recent changes in the conditions for innovation by and for the poor. Such transformations have been long and complex. It has taken considerable competitive pressure to overcome inertia and to move from a world of mature technologies and international corporations operating in oligopolistic markets, which characterized the late 1960s and 1970s, to the current world of even larger corporations spread across the globe and surrounded by a multitude of nimble, small, knowledge-intensive companies. The countries of the mature world have been slow to realize that emerging countries could threaten their lead in certain areas of innovation, and that their internal unemployment and income distribution problems will probably need to be addressed with more active policies.

Historical analysis indicates that such profound changes in conditions have been typical of the diffusion of technological revolutions (Perez, 2002). If radically new industries and technologies were merely added to the existing stock, the transformations would not be so deep or wide-ranging. What warrants the term 'revolution' is precisely that each set of major new technologies rejuvenates the mature ones, opening up important new innovation trajectories for pre-existing industries. The combination of a new infrastructure network expanding markets, and a new paradigm changing behaviours, redefines industry structures and reshapes their regional distribution. The diffusion of a new paradigm can radically change opportunities for laggards (for

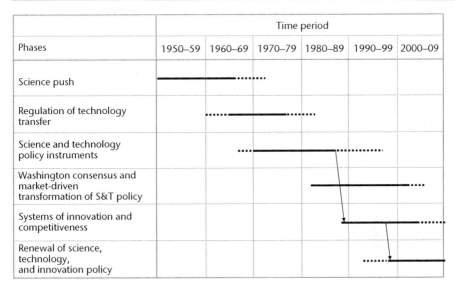

Figure 4.1. Chronology of the phases in science, technology, and innovation policies in Latin America

Source: Sagasti (2011: table 1—translation from the Spanish original).

better or for worse) and this, in turn, requires important changes in development and innovation policies.[8]

In a recent study of the Latin American experience in science and technology policy, Sagasti (2011) identifies five phases. Each encapsulates a different set of fundamental ideas about technology, employs different policy instruments, and creates—or eliminates—different institutions (see Figure 4.1). It is significant that, despite major differences in political conditions between countries (from military dictatorships to democracies), the changes in technology, ideas, and policy instruments described by Sagasti occurred at almost the same time throughout Latin America. There are always some countries that lead and others that lag by a few years, some that design and apply more sophisticated policies, and others that copy and do a minimum, but the fact is that the whole continent went through a similar sequence.

This continent-wide regularity suggests that the transformation may not have been entirely endogenous. The fact that all countries acted in a similar way in relation to technology may indicate that they were experiencing the same set of external forces driving those changes. It may also suggest that the recommendations received—whether from academics, consultants, UN organizations, or whoever—were a response to conditions observed on the

---

[8] For a discussion of opportunities for development as a moving target, see Perez (2001).

ground across the world. This is indeed what would be expected in the framework of successive technological revolutions and paradigm shifts adopted in the current chapter.

According to this interpretation, in the 1970s the advanced world was going through the maturity and decline phase of the main industries of the mass-production paradigm (exacerbated by a dramatic increase in the price of oil) at the same time as it was witnessing the irruption of the ICT revolution and the rise of Japan. The mature industries were setting up final assembly plants in the Third World in order to expand their saturated markets. This was favoured by a set of incentives offered by the import-substitution policies adopted by most underdeveloped countries seeking industrialization. Since mature technologies, by definition, have exhausted their previous trajectories, there was little that could be done in the receiving countries except learning the routines and, as they all did, trying to develop their own science in the hope of arriving at new technologies in a linear process.

Gradually, however, the ICT revolution began to transform the conditions for competitiveness, and mature corporations were forced to introduce not only computers in their offices but also computer-aided equipment in their plants and microelectronics in their products. By the 1980s it was understood, from the Japanese success, that major organizational changes were required in order to reap the expected benefits from new technologies. The Japanese model was then imitated in the offices and plants of advanced countries. This created a problem for the many Tayloristic factories already operating in developing countries, with some of the transferred products becoming obsolete. In addition, the regulation of technology transfer was making conditions more difficult for multinational corporations. Selling the licenses and letting the locals take over was one solution; using low-cost labour for exports from processing zones was another. Tariff barriers stopped being attractive to foreign investors. The opening up of markets encouraged by the 'Washington consensus' policies finally dismantled the model. In the new conditions, in Latin America the inward-oriented economies were unable to resist the pressures or to adopt new competitive practices, and the so-called 'lost decade' set in. By contrast, the 'Four Tigers' in Asia jumped on the new bandwagon with intensive export-oriented learning and rapid implementation of the new paradigm.

In the 1990s and 2000s, there was a revival of official interest in science and technology policies. Seeing the Asian success and relating it to technological learning efforts, the new ideas about science, technology, and innovation policies located within the notion of a national system of innovation began to spread (see Lundvall, Chapter 2, this volume). Technology parks and other 'clustering' attempts became common; innovation funding and entrepreneurial incentives also spread. Global corporations, although not investing much in Latin America, did however modernize their working practices in the remaining local plants and began to outsource to domestic suppliers within their value networks. The experience of Brazil as one of the BRICS established a different view of technological innovation opportunities, which is now being followed across the whole sub-continent.

Hence, we face a 'chicken or egg' situation. Do the circumstances change the thinking about technology and innovation, or does the thinking change the policies? The more likely answer is that there is a continuous feedback loop. Nevertheless, the usual response is to say that 'our knowledge of the processes is increasing' rather than recognizing that the conditions are changing and our previous knowledge no longer captures the new reality. Furthermore, our current knowledge of innovation in the developing world is not a deepening of what we understood in the 1970s. Indeed, it would not have been possible to apply it to design more effective policies in those years. The conditions of the import-substitution model inhibited innovation. When technology was 'acquired' under strict contract clauses that prohibited any changes, and when there were no innovative capabilities in firms and no entrepreneurial models to follow, trying to promote innovation in the way that is effective today would have resulted in frustration.

This brief overview suggests that innovation studies and evolutionary economics share an object of study that is constantly being transformed by the very nature of innovation and by its capacity to go beyond technology to modify organizations, institutions, behaviour, and ideas. It is a truly evolutionary process in need of dynamic theories.

4.4. Does (or Should) Evolutionary Economics also Evolve?

This brings us to the observation made at the start of this chapter regarding the 'obsolescence' of the Dependency School and of the original choice-of-technology discussions, in the light of the paradigm shift in the real economy. Can we analyse the successive changes in the focus of evolutionary economics, of science, technology, and society (STS), and of innovation studies in connection with the changing trends in the economy?

In contrast with other schools of thought, evolutionary economics is naturally open to change, not only due to its theoretical premises but also for the simple reason that it is much more rooted in reality and is constantly studying specific technologies, companies, sectors, and so on. Indeed, it would be interesting to examine the shifts in emphasis in the topics addressed in publications and see how they relate to real shifts in behaviour in the world economy. Could we do something similar for the shifts in emphasis in innovation studies?[9] One might expect to see a process of 'creative destruction' in policy-oriented knowledge as clusters of radical innovations transform the context conditions.

The Balance between Permanent and Changing Truths

This is not to deny that there must be some unchanging basic truths. If the basic tenet is that innovation is the driver of economic growth, then a central task is to identify what one might call the 'laws of change' in market economies, at the micro-, meso-, and macro-level. This defines much of the theoretical work that evolutionary economics has undertaken. Notions as fundamental as technological trajectories and routines,[10] or the processes of learning, or the fact that innovations are interrelated, that the agents in the economy are diverse, and that the process of innovation is a system of interactions[11] are all indispensable for the analysis of any period. Yet even the Pavitt (1984) taxonomy, assuming that the classification can be seen as a stable truth, is likely to change in terms of the industries included in each category.[12] And the same can be said about systems of innovation. The early formulation was very much defined in national terms, but globalization now requires us to analyse more complex networks and interactions across borders.

Distinguishing between fundamental theoretical principles and changing processes should be the normal approach for a truly evolutionary economics. That would be one of the differentiating features enabling it to deal with an economy in evolutionary (and sometimes revolutionary) change, in contrast to the immanent and unchanging constructs of neo-classical economics. Understanding technological opportunities as a moving target and economics as the uneven realization of those opportunities, be it for the rich or the poor, would not only strengthen our academic contribution to the social sciences but also fill a gap in the sort of expertise that policy-makers require. The constant awareness of the interconnection between changing technologies, changing economies, and changing economics would guarantee that we never lose the connection with real life and real processes or replace such realities with mathematics (Drechsler, 2011).

---

[9] The chapters by Fagerberg et al. and Martin in the current volume could serve as an excellent initial basis for the process. See also Morlacchi and Martin (2009).

[10] See Dosi, Chapter 5 of this volume, for an extended discussion.

[11] See Lundvall, Chapter 2 of this volume, for a discussion of interactive learning.

[12] A move in that direction can be found in DeJong and Marsili (2006), but the next technological revolution is likely to make more substantial changes to the sectors in each category.

The Challenges of the Present Moment in History

When we ask about the consequences of technology systems and policy for the poor and the weak, we are not then in some abstract state of limbo where time and place are of no importance. We are at a specific moment in the evolution of the market economies. I have argued elsewhere that the major financial collapse of 2008, which amongst other things morphed into a Euro crisis, is the result of a decoupling of finance from the real economy, which requires the return of an active State, in both advanced and lagging economies (Perez, 2009, 2012). Overcoming the quasi-religious belief in the free market of the old 'First world' and abandoning the Washington consensus in the old 'Third world' will require something to replace it that involves not just going back to policies that served their purpose in the mass-production era. Evolutionary economics, in general, and innovation studies in particular, seem to be ideally placed to provide the necessary new thinking to reshape the economy, reversing the process of income polarization and taking advantage of the new potential for innovation.

Bengt-Åke Lundvall, in Chapter 2 of this volume, urges those working in innovation studies and evolutionary economics to become more involved in policy and politics in order to more effectively confront capitalism, as it is today, as well as to provide alternatives to the interpretations and recipes of neo-classical economics. His plea would be much more easily fulfilled by a scientific community with a keen awareness of historical change and of the dynamic interrelations between changing technologies, changing institutions, and changing economies. This is all the more urgent as we see innovation policy moving from the margins of development strategies to the very core. The BRICS are all incorporating science, technology, innovation, and the promotion of entrepreneurship as a central basis of their economic policy, and developing countries are gradually following their lead.

The Need for Inter-Disciplinarity and Inter-Institutional Collaboration

This new relevance of innovation for development strategies brings to the fore another of Lundvall's propositions to increase innovation studies' relevance: making connections with other social sciences. Indeed, the complexity of the situation warrants not only interaction with other disciplines but also closer collaboration with groups that have approached technology and institutions from different points of view. For instance, innovation studies would benefit greatly from connecting with development studies (e.g. Gereffi and Kaplinsky, 2001; Schmitz, 2004; Gereffi, Humphrey, and Sturgeon 2005) as well as from incorporating the whole issue of transitions. There are easy connections to be made with Dutch scholars in this area (e.g. Geels and

Schot, 2007; Geels, 2010), who have made valuable contributions to theory, methodology, and case-study work. They have also become directly involved in policy-making and experimental processes of change (Grin et al., 2010). Joining forces with the STS community may also enrich the capacity to go beyond technology policy and to cover a broad spectrum from industrial policy to welfare and education policy. And within innovation studies itself there are understudied areas such as finance[13] and institutional innovation (Reinert, 1994, 1999; Schmitz 2004). Their incorporation would enhance the power of the inter-disciplinary mix and facilitate wider collaboration.

Institutional and Policy Innovation as Central Objects of Study

Up to now, there has been a tradition in virtually all PhDs and most journal articles in this field to end with 'policy recommendations'. From my experience as a policy-maker, I can say that these are rarely directly usable.[14] However, at this particular time the need for truly creative policy innovation is considerable. Yet the process of policy innovation has rarely been studied as such by the innovation studies community. Much attention has been given to university industry-links from the 1980s onwards, but virtually none to university–policy links or to learning in policy-making. Do we understand how the social sciences contribute to the effectiveness of innovation policy or to that of the related industrial, science, education, or welfare policies? Over a decade ago, Edquist (2001, p. 17) noted that the system of innovation perspective 'lacks a component (theory) about the role of the State . . . about how innovation policy has actually been designed and implemented and which societal forces have governed these activities'. Since then, this has been partially addressed[15] but many questions still remain. Now is the time to enrich our policy recommendations with a deeper understanding of institutional and policy innovation as an object of study in itself.

Analysing and also Anticipating Context Changes: A Truly Evolutionary Science

Focusing on institutional innovation would be one way of consciously moving to a relevant area; going further by deepening our understanding of the

[13] A recent exception is FINNOV, a project led by Mariana Mazzucato—see Mazzucato (2013), Lazonick (2007), and others in <http://www.finnov-fp7.eu/publications>.
[14] See Radosevic (2012) for a critique of this practice as well as a thorough analysis of the state of the art in innovation policy. See also Bartzokas and Teubal (2002) who propose a more explicit policy orientation.
[15] See, for instance, Nelson (2008) and the earlier work of the Aalborg group such as Gregersen (1992), Johnson (1992), and Gregersen and Johnson (1997) and that of the Tallinn group coming to innovation from Public Administration (Karo et al., 2012).

historical processes of organizational and policy change would guard against obsolescence in recommendations. Furthermore, if we acknowledge the role of major innovations and their diffusion in changing our object of study, then it should be our task to improve our understanding of historical change by looking at the evolution in the focus of research and of ideas within our own field. This implies the construction of a very dynamic science that is constantly aware of its own evolution in relation to the changing nature of technology, of the economy, and of the other phenomena it studies.

Nevertheless, merely following the changing historical context as it unfolds is not enough. We also need to be able to anticipate change, to identify weak trends that are likely to become stronger and to study them as they appear. That is what the pioneers of evolutionary economics and innovation studies did. It is not by chance that the seminal work by Freeman (1974) and by Nelson and Winter (1977, 1982) appeared in the 1970s and early 1980s, followed shortly by the concept of national systems of innovation (Lundvall, 1985, 1988; Freeman, 1987; Nelson, 1993). Truly creative social science identifies trends when they are only just becoming visible. We could, of course, leave the job to historians of science and thus avoid the risk of being accused of speculation. However, the greater risk of offering irrelevant or obsolete recommendations may be too high a price to pay for such academic caution.

4.5. In Conclusion

This chapter has engaged in two levels of discussion. First, at a very general level, it has challenged evolutionary economics and innovation studies to be more consciously and explicitly based in the historical, given the radical changes observable in the context for innovation in the developing world. Second, with specific regard to development-related research, it has given a brief overview of how those conditions have changed in order to outline an agenda and highlight the need for a more inter-disciplinary and collaborative approach to meet the new needs of policy-makers in developing countries

The problems facing innovation policy-makers have changed significantly in recent decades. Not only are there new forms of access to knowledge and technology and new possibilities for the poor and the weak, but both the definition and the location of the poor in the world have changed. These phenomena are themselves natural objects of study for innovation scholars, given their close relationship to technical change and their relevance for innovation policy. Rather than merely extracting policy recommendations from every study, the process of policy innovation itself needs to be seriously studied as well as the university–policy links. Research on the latter would seek to understand how social sciences, and in particular evolutionary economics and innovation studies, support institutional innovation, offering a parallel with what the study of university–industry links has achieved.

Innovation policy used to be a somewhat marginal addition to development policies, more connected to research and education than to growth, employment, and social wellbeing. It has now become a core element in the efforts aimed at catching up and forging ahead in developing and emerging countries. At the same time, the scope of innovation has widened to involve products and processes adapted to the conditions of the poor, such as frugal innovation, direct energy production, and solutions to cater for very harsh climatic conditions, extreme poverty, and other specificities. Given this changed context, it will probably be necessary to differentiate innovation policy for growth and competitiveness from innovation policy for alleviating poverty. In both cases there is a need for research on innovative processes in policy and institutions as well as on technical and organizational innovation for production and wealth creation for and by the poor and the weak.[16] Furthermore, since income polarization has characterized the recent decades in both advanced and emerging countries, it has become crucial to identify innovation policies capable of helping to reverse these trends, taking into account the very different origins, conditions, and levels of such poverty.

Because of this much more complex picture, innovation studies will require the inclusion of both history and political science in the inter-disciplinary mix, and much closer collaboration with complementary schools of thought that focus on historical transitions, development, poverty alleviation, politics, and the role of the State. The challenge will be to maintain coherence while confronting the full complexity of the object of study. The outcome could be truly effective and relevant policy advice.

References

Amin, S. (1976). *Unequal Development: An Essay on the Social Formations of Peripheral Capitalism*. New York: Monthly Review Press.

Anderson, C. (2006). *The Long Tail: Why the Future of Business is Selling More of Less*. New York: Hyperion.

Arora, A. and Gambardella, A. (2004). 'The Globalization of the Software Industry: Perspectives and Opportunities for Developed and Developing Countries', NBER Working Paper, 10538 (downloaded from <http://www.nber.org/papers/w10538>).

---

[16] See Perez (2010b) for an argument in favour of a dual strategy for development, with separate institutions.

Bartzokas, A. and Teubal, M. (2002). 'A Framework for Policy Oriented Innovation Studies in Industrialising Countries', *Economics of Innovation and New Technology*, *12*: 477–96.

Cardoso, F. H. and Faletto, E. (1968). *Dependencia y desarrollo en America Latina*. Mexico: Siglo XXI.

Cooper, C. (1972). 'Science, Technology and Production in the Underdeveloped Countries: An Introduction', *Journal of Development Studies*, *9*: 1–18.

DeJong, J. P. J. and Marsili, O. (2006). 'The Fruit Flies of Innovations: A Taxonomy of Innovative Small Firms', *Research Policy*, *35*: 213–29.

Dobbs, R., Oppenheim, J., Thompson, F., Brinkman, M., and Zornes, M. (2011). *Resource Revolution: Meeting the World's Energy, Materials, Food and Water Needs*. London: McKinsey Global Institute, McKinsey and Co.

Dosi, G. et al. (eds) (1988). *Technical Change and Economic Theory*. London: Pinter.

Drechsler, W. (2011). 'Understanding the Problems of Mathematical Economics: A "Continental" Perspective', *Real-World Economics Review*, 56, March: 45–57 (downloaded May 2013 from <http://www.paecon.net/PAEReview/issue56/Drechsler56.pdf>).

Edquist, C. (2001), 'The Systems of Innovation Approach and Innovation Policy: An Account of the State of the Art', DRUID Conference paper.

Farooki, M. Z. and Kaplinsky, R. (2012). *The Impact of China on Global Commodity Prices: The Global Reshaping of the Resource Sector*. London: Routledge.

Freeman, C. (1974). *The Economics of Industrial Innovation*. Harmondsworth, Middlesex: Penguin Books.

Freeman, C. (1984). 'Prometheus Unbound', *Futures*, *16*: 494–507.

Freeman, C. (1987). *Technology Policy and Economic Performance: Lessons from Japan*. London: Pinter.

Freeman, C. (1988), 'Introduction', in G. Dosi et al. (eds), *Technical Change and Economic Theory*. London: Pinter, 1–9.

Freeman, C. (1995). 'The "National System of Innovation" in Historical Perspective', *Cambridge Journal of Economics*, *19*: 5–24.

Freeman, C. (2001). 'A Hard Landing for the "New Economy"? Information Technology and the United States National System of Innovation', *Structural Change and Economic Dynamics*, *12*: 115–39.

Freeman, C. and Louçã, F. (2001). *As Time Goes By*. Oxford: Oxford University Press.

Freeman, C. and Perez, C. (1988), 'Structural Crises of Adjustment: Business Cycles and Investment Behavior', in G. Dosi et al. (eds), *Technical Change and Economic Theory*, London: Pinter, 38–66.

Friedman, T. (2005). *The World is Flat*. New York: Farrar Straus and Giroux.

Geels, F. W. (2010). 'Ontologies, Socio-Technical Transitions (to Sustainability), and the Multi-Level Perspective', *Research Policy*, *39*: 495–510.

Geels, F. W. and Schot, J. W. (2007). 'Typology of Sociotechnical Transition Pathways', *Research Policy*, *36*: 399–417.

Gereffi, G. and Kaplinsky, R.E. (2001). 'The Value of Value Chains: Spreading the Gains from Globalisation', *IDS Bulletin*, 32 (July), Brighton Institute of Development Studies.

Gereffi, G. J., Humphrey, J., and Sturgeon, T. (2005). 'The Governance of Global Value Chains', *Review of International Political Economy*, *12*: 78–104.

Gregersen, B. (1992), 'The Public Sector As a Pacer in National Systems of Innovation', in B.-Å. Lundvall (ed.), *National Systems of Innovation: Towards a Theory of Innovation and Interactive Learning*. London: Pinter, 129–45.

Gregersen, B. and Johnson, B. (1997). 'Learning Economies, Innovation Systems and European Integration', *Regional Studies*, *31*: 479–90.

Grin, J., Rotmans, J., Schot, J., Geels, F. W., and Loorbach, D. (2010). *Transitions to Sustainable Development: New Directions in the Study of Long Term Transformative Change*. London: Routledge.

Gunder Frank, A. (1991). *Underdevelopment of Development: an Autobiographic Essay*. Stockholm: Bethany Books.

Hirschman, A. (1982), 'The Rise and Decline of Development Economics', in M. Gersovitz et al. (eds), *The Theory and Experience of Economic Development*. London: Allen and Unwin, 372–90.

Johnson, B. (1992), 'Institutional Learning', in B.-Å. Lundvall (ed.), *National Systems of Innovation: Towards a Theory of Innovation and Interactive Learning*. London: Pinter, 23–44.

Kaplinsky, R. (2005). *Globalisation, Poverty And Inequality: Between a Rock and a Hard Place*. Cambridge: Polity.

Karo, E., Drechsler, W., Kattel, R., and Stillings, C. (2012). 'Introduction to the Special Issue: Public Administration, Technology & Innovation', *Halduskultuur— Administrative Culture*, *13*: 4–9.

Krugman, P. (1995). *Development, Geography, and Economic Theory*. Cambridge, MA: MIT Press.

Lazonick, W. (2007). 'The US Stock Market and the Governance of Innovative Enterprise', *Industrial and Corporate Change*, *16*: 983–1035.

Lundvall, B.-Å. (1985). *Product Innovation and User-Producer Interaction*, Industrial Development Research Series. Aalborg: Aalborg University Press.

Lundvall, B.-Å. (1988). 'Innovation as an Interactive Process: From User Producer Interaction to National Systems of Innovation', in G. Dosi, and et al. (eds), *Technical Change and Economic Theory*, London: Pinter, 349–69.

Marin, A., Navas-Aleman, L., and Perez, C. (2010). 'The Possible Dynamic Role of Natural Resource-Based Networks in Latin American Development Strategies', Globelics Working Paper.

Mazzucato, M. (2013). *The Entrepreneurial State: Debunking Private vs. Public Sector Myths*. London: Anthem Press.

Morlacchi, P. and Martin, B. (2009). 'Emerging Challenges for Science, Technology and Innovation Policy Research: A Reflexive Overview', *Research Policy*, *38*: 571–82.

Morris, M., Kaplinsky, R., and Kaplan, D. (2012). 'One Thing Leads to Another— Commodities, Linkages and Industrial Development', *Research Policy*, *37*: 408–16.

Nelson, R. R. (1993). *National Innovation Systems: A Comparative Analysis*. New York: Oxford University.

Nelson, R. R. (2008). 'What Enables Rapid Economic Progress: What are the Needed Institutions?', *Research Policy*, *37*: 1–11.

Nelson, R. R. and Winter, S. G. (1977). 'In Search of a Useful Theory of Innovation', *Research Policy*, 6: 36–76.

Nelson, R. R. and Winter, S. G. (1982). *An Evolutionary Theory of Economic Change*. Cambridge, MA: Harvard University Press.

Pavitt, K. (1984). 'Sectoral Patterns of Technical Change: Towards a Taxonomy and a Theory', *Research Policy*, 13: 343–73.

Perez, C. (1985). 'Microelectronics, Long Waves and World Structural Change: New Perspectives for Developing Countries', *World Development*, 13: 441–63.

Perez, C. (2001). 'Technological Change and Opportunities for Development as a Moving Target', *CEPAL Review*, 75: 109–30.

Perez, C. (2002). *Technological Revolutions and Financial Capital: The Dynamics of Bubbles and Golden Ages*. Cheltenham: Elgar.

Perez, C. (2009). 'The Double Bubble at the Turn of the Century: Technological Roots and Structural Implications', *Cambridge Journal of Economics*, 33: 779–805.

Perez, C. (2010a). 'Technological Revolutions and Techno-Economic Paradigms', *Cambridge Journal of Economics*, 34: 185–202.

Perez, C. (2010b). 'Technological Dynamism and Social Inclusion in Latin America: A Resource-based Production Development Strategy', *CEPAL Review*, 100: 121–41.

Perez, C. (2012). 'Financial Bubbles, Crises and the Role of Government in Unleashing Golden Ages', FINNOV Working Paper 2-12. Forthcoming (2013) in A. Pyka and H. P. Burghof (eds), *Innovation and Finance*. London: Routledge.

Prebisch, R. (1951). *Estudio económico de América Latina* 1949. New York: CEPAL.

Radosevic, S. (2012). 'Innovation Policy Studies between Theory and Practice: A Literature Review Based Analysis', *STI Policy Review*, 3: 1–45.

Reinert, E. S. (1994). 'Catching-Up from Way Behind—A Third World Perspective on First World History', in J. Fagerberg, B. Verspagen, and N. v. Tunzelmann (eds), *The Dynamics of Technology, Trade, and Growth*. Aldershot: Elgar, 168–97.

Reinert, E. S. (1999). 'The Role of the State in Economic Growth', *Journal of Economic Studies*, 26: 268–326.

Reinert, E. S. (ed.) (2004). *Globalization, Economic Development and Inequality: An Alternative Perspective*. Cheltenham: Elgar.

Romer, P. M. (1993). 'Idea Gaps and Object Gaps in Economic Development', *Journal of Monetary Economics*, 32: 543–73.

Sachs, J. and Warner, A. M. (1995). 'Natural Resource Abundance and Economic Growth', NBER Working Paper, 5398.

Sagasti, F. (2011). *Ciencia, tecnología, innovación: Políticas para América Latina*. Lima/México: Fondo de Cultura Económica.

Schmitz, H. (ed.) (2004). *Local Enterprises in the Global Economy: Issues of Governance and Upgrading*. Cheltenham: Elgar.

Sen, A. (1960). *Choice of Techniques: An Aspect of the Theory of Planned Economic Development*. Oxford: Blackwell.

Sen, A. (1983). 'Development: Which Way Now?', *Economic Journal*, 93: 745–62.

Singer, H. W. (1949). 'Economic Progress in Underdeveloped Countries', *Social Research: An International Quarterly of Political and Social Science*, 16: 9–11.

Sumner, A. (2010). 'Global Poverty and the New Bottom Billion: What if Three-Quarters of the World's Poor Live in Middle Income Countries?', mimeo, Institute of Development Studies, Brighton.

The Economist (1977). 'The Dutch Disease', *The Economist,* 26 November: 82–3.

United Nations Environment Programme (2011). *Towards a Green Economy: Pathways to Sustainable Development and Poverty Eradication.* Nairobi: UN Environment Programme.

Urzua, O. (2011). 'The Emergence and Development of Knowledge Intensive Mining Service Suppliers in the Late 20th Century', PhD thesis, SPRU, University of Sussex.

Urzua, O. (2012). 'Emergence and Development of Knowledge-Intensive Mining Services (KIMS)', The Other Canon Foundation and Tallinn University of Technology, Working Papers in Technology Governance and Economic Dynamics, No. 41.

5

Innovation, Evolution, and Economics: Where We Are and Where We Should Go

Giovanni Dosi

5.1. Introduction

In this chapter, I outline the major building blocks of an interpretation of the economy as a complex evolving system and the role innovation plays in it, together with an assessment of the achievements of the evolutionary research programme thus far and some challenges that lie ahead.[1] An evolutionary perspective attempts to understand a wide set of economic phenomena—from microeconomic behaviour to features of industrial structures and dynamics, and the properties of aggregate growth and development—as outcomes of far-from-equilibrium interactions among heterogeneous agents, characterized by endogenous preferences, 'boundedly rational' but capable of learning, adapting, and innovating with respect to their understanding of the world in which they operate, the technologies they master, their organizational forms, and their behavioural repertoires. Although far from being disdainful of formal modelling and statistical analysis, the research programme is largely *inductive*, taking seriously the empirical regularities at all levels of observation that inspire and bound the modelling assumptions.

---

[1] This work draws upon Dosi and Winter (2002); the Introduction to Dosi (2013) (and its INET version in Dosi, 2011); and Dosi and Nelson (2010), which provides more detail.

5.2. Coordination and Change

Before discussing the evolutionary research programme, let me start by identifying some fundamental questions addressed by the economics discipline and the answers to such questions that contemporary theory offers. In my view, the two basic questions at the core of economics since its inception relate to the *drivers and patterns of change* of the capitalistic machine of production and innovation, and to the mechanisms of (imperfect) coordination among a multitude of self-seeking economic agents often characterized by conflicting interests.[2] Of crucial importance are the answers that diverse theories offer to these two questions, but equally important are the relations presupposed by each theory between the two questions.

Adam Smith begins his *Wealth of Nations* with an analysis of the drivers of change—in particular, the positive feedback between the division of labour, mechanization, productivity growth, and demand growth. Issues of coordination are only discussed later on, building on such a dynamic background. Similarly, Karl Marx builds upon a long discussion of the relationships between a theory of production and labour relations, centred around the theory of value, capital accumulation, and technological progress. 'Coordination', if one can call it that, comes much later, taking for granted the intrinsically dynamic nature of capitalists' interactions. Keynes, too, never dreamt of separating 'what keeps the system together' from 'what keeps it going': indeed, the properties of shorter-term coordination—as revealed so prominently by involuntary unemployment—were derived from the properties of capital accumulation and the 'animal spirits' driving it.

By contrast, the current dominant theoretical creed in economics is the analytical opposite. It builds on the separation between 'coordination' and 'dynamics'. Moreover, notwithstanding his understanding of technological innovation as the driver of long-term change, even Schumpeter subscribed to this 'epistemological separation', building on the Walrasian approach to coordination. Nowadays, one begins with a *general equilibrium*, grounded on well specified *fundamentals* in terms of technologies, endowment, and preferences. Then comes a 'shock': in the Schumpeterian story, the entrepreneurial innovator introduces an *unexpected* innovation, yielding disequilibrium profits, changing relative prices, and bringing about 'creative destruction'. Thereafter, the economic system adapts via technological imitation and diffusion of the innovation. This is the 'transient' phase, until the system converges once more to a new (equilibrium) *circular flow* characterized by a new ensemble of fundamentals of the economy.

[2] See Dosi and Orsenigo (1988) for a more detailed discussion.

Indeed, this is a central tenet of the intellectual compromise on which the economics discipline has operated since the 1950s, with a rough division of labour between (i) 'micro-founded' general equilibrium models; (ii) 'short-run' macroeconomics; and (iii) growth theories. The last 30 years have also seen the emergence of new growth theories, bringing advances compared to the original Solow model but also significant drawbacks. The big plus is that innovation is endogenized into economic dynamics as either a learning externality or the outcome of purposeful efforts by profit-maximizing agents (compare Aghion and Howitt, 1997). However, endogenization comes at the cost of reducing innovative activities to an *equilibrium* outcome of the optimal inter-temporal allocation of resources. Hence, one loses the Schumpeterian notion of innovation as a *disequilibrium* phenomenon—*or at least as a transient*. Indeed, innovative activities undertaken by private actors are ultimately reduced to another instance of optimal inter-temporal resource allocation, with or without (probabilizable) uncertainty.

The key point is that innovation and knowledge accumulation are precisely the domains where the principles of scarcity and conservation are fundamentally violated: one can systematically get more from less, while dynamic increasing returns are the rule rather than the exception. Yet, we have experienced a major financial crisis, and its very appearance and its magnitude surely constitute a falsifying 'crucial experiment' and a *systemic failure of the economic profession* (Colander et al., 2009).[3] Can the mainstream paradigm be saved by appropriate modifications? I doubt it can because its fundamental interpretative failure is intrinsically linked to its core building blocks (forward-looking rationality, equilibrium, etc.).

5.3. Towards an Alternative Interpretation: The Economy as a Complex Evolving System

The community of evolutionary economists (including Bengt-Åke Lundvall) can take some pride in having worked on an alternative research programme well before the crisis itself (see e.g. Dosi, 2000), a programme that stands in opposition to the 'new classic economic paradigm' sketched earlier. Indeed, it starts by acknowledging that the object of study is the *economy viewed as a complex evolving system*.[4] Note that one starts here with a minimalist notion of 'complexity', capturing the fact that the economy is composed of multiple

---

[3] Stiglitz (2011) expresses related concerns about the state of macroeconomics.

[4] A series of conferences and books on this theme sponsored by the Santa Fe Institute yielded interesting insights, even if what was delivered was rather less than promised (compare Anderson, Arrow, and Pines, 1988; and Arthur, Durlauf, and Lane, 1997).

interacting actors—hence the illegitimacy of its 'anthropomorphization'.[5] Moreover, 'evolution' means that any assumption about 'the fundamentals' being 'given' (including technologies and preferences) represents a fundamental misrepresentation of the object of study.

In any analysis of a complex evolving economy, one has to go well beyond the Schumpeter/Samuelson separation between coordination and change. The (imperfect) coordinating features of the system are fundamentally shaped by its evolving nature. Just as it is relatively easy to stand up on a bicycle when cycling (only a few *virtuosos* are able to remain upright while standing still), so the relatively orderly properties of capitalist economies derive from their being in motion. This is the relative order of 'restless capitalism' (Metcalfe, 1998; Metcalfe and Ramlogan, 2006). Hence, prices move roughly in line with the average costs of production, which in turn depend on the underlying (technology-specific and sector-specific) rates of process innovation. Demand patterns are shaped by the ensuing prices and by the 'trajectories' in product innovation. Gross and net labour demand is affected by the two-sided nature of technical progress as a 'labour saver' and as a 'demand creator'.

These are all features of *imperfect coordination* and *relative order* in the distributional properties of whatever statistics on economic variables, stemming from the fact that the system is continuously changing in its process and product technologies, consumption patterns, and organizational forms. The evolutionary paradigm specifically addresses the properties of such endogenously changing multi-agent systems.

Let us next consider a few general features of such an interpretation.

Methodology

'DYNAMICS FIRST!'
The emphasis on dynamics and change is in tune with a more general methodological prescription common to the evolutionary research programme, namely Sid Winter's dictum *'dynamics first!'* In other words, the explanation for why something exists, or why a variable takes the value it does, should rest on an account of the process by which it came to be what it is. That broadly corresponds to the theoretical imperative: provide the process story either by formally writing down or simulating some dynamical system, or by providing a good qualitative historical reconstruction (or, if possible, *both*). Alternatively, be extremely wary of any interpretation of what is observed that consists entirely of *ex-post* equilibrium rationalizations ('it has to be like

---

[5] On 'complex dynamics', see Kirman (2010), whose views are close to those expressed here (and who is an important source of inspiration), and Rosser (2011).

that, given rationality'). Notwithstanding the widespread practice in economics, never take as a good 'explanation' either an existence theorem or a purely functionalist claim ('entity x exists because it performs function y').

REALISM
Realism is a virtue and in certain respects a necessity. Theories are necessarily abstract and generally incorporate less of reality than they omit: indeed, 'the map is not the territory', as Kay (2011) puts it (compare Korzybski, 1933). Yet there are some features of reality that are omitted at the theorist's peril, in that the resulting conclusions are unreliable guides to the interpretation of reality, though perhaps instructive regarding important mechanisms. More broadly, the 'prediction-centred' justification for modelling—'it does not matter the assumptions you make, what counts is the quality of your prediction'—is simply bad epistemology.

Some Substantive Building Blocks

Given these general epistemological prescriptions, let me now outline a number of substantive building blocks for a fully-fledged evolutionary research programme.[6]

MICRO-FOUNDATIONS
Theories ought to be *micro-founded* in the sense that they ought to be grounded explicitly (though perhaps indirectly) in a plausible account of what agents do and why they do it.[7] (Note that the proposition does *not* imply, however, that agents' objectives are in general achieved or their expectations fulfilled. In other words, to equate 'micro-foundations' with rational expectations would represent a fundamental misunderstanding.)

'BOUNDED RATIONALITY'—*SENSU LATO*
Among the fundamental micro-features is the fact that agents have an imperfect understanding of the environment in which they operate, and in particular of what the future will deliver. Thus, even the term 'bounded rationality' is misleading here as it implies a full 'Olympian' rationality, with the distance from actual behaviour corresponding to how much agents are actually

---

[6] More on the substance of the evolutionary research programme can be found in Nelson and Winter (1982); Dosi et al. (1988); Dosi and Nelson (1994); Coriat and Dosi (1998); Metcalfe (1998); the introduction to Dosi (2000); Dopfer (2005); and Dosi and Winter (2002), upon which I draw in this section.

[7] Quite a few 'aggregate' (i.e. non-micro-founded) dynamic models are nonetheless consistent with an evolutionary interpretation (some of them are surveyed in Coriat and Dosi, 1998, and in Silverberg and Verspagen, 2005). The point is also discussed in the introduction to Dosi (2000).

'bounded'. Yet in changing and highly complex environments, such 'perfect' rationality might not be definable, even in principle (Dosi, Marengo, and Fagiolo, 2005).

Instead, one has to adopt a very expansive notion of 'bounded rationality', related to limitations in (i) access to information; (ii) memory; and (iii) computational abilities; but also (more fundamentally) to (iv) intrinsically imperfect *representations* of the environment in which agents operate; (v) ubiquitous limitations in the agents' abilities to master physical and 'social' technologies;[8] and (vi) an intrinsic fuzziness, potential incoherence, and instability in the very perception of one's own preferences.

HETEROGENEITY

Imperfect understanding and imperfect, path-dependent learning entail persistent heterogeneity among agents. Agents are heterogeneous in (i) their preferences and endowments (well acknowledged by standard models in their full GE version, but less so by most current macro-models!). However, agents are also heterogeneous with respect to (ii) the *models of the world* they hold, even when faced with identical information; (iii) their technological repertoires; and (iv) (possibly) their learning processes. Capturing heterogeneity is crucial to the representation of aggregate dynamics: indeed, the lack of it underpins the pitiful state of contemporary macroeconomics.

PERSISTENT INNOVATIVE OPPORTUNITIES

Knowledge boundaries are always in flux: agents are potentially capable of discovering new technologies, new ways of organizing, and new behavioural patterns. Allowing for *ubiquity of novelty* is a major theoretical and modelling challenge. Evolutionary scholars of technological and organizational change have opened up a new field addressing the structure and dynamics of technological knowledge,[9] including major contributions by Lundvall.

INTERACTIONS, COORDINATION, AND SELECTION

While (imperfect) adaptation and persistent discovery generate variety, collective interactions within and outside markets operate, first, as mechanisms of *information exchange and coordination* and, second, as *selection mechanisms*, giving rise to differential growth (and survival probabilities) of different entities that are the 'carriers' of diverse technologies, routines, strategies, and so on. There are crucial issues here regarding (i) the coordinating power of whatever 'invisible (or visible) hand' oversees decentralized interactions;

---

[8] On the latter notion, which is related to the nature of institutions and behaviours therein, see Nelson and Sampat (2001).

[9] For a review of the state of the art, see Dosi and Nelson (2010).

(ii) the drivers, powers, and efficiency of selection mechanisms; and (iii) the interactions between the foregoing two processes. (Under a 'dynamics first' rule, demonstrations of the existence of a purported equilibrium, followed by some 'hand-waving theorem' based on casual anecdotes and assertions such as 'the system must get there in the end', do not count as serious arguments.)

AGGREGATE REGULARITIES AS EMERGENT PROPERTIES

Given all this, collective aggregate phenomena (e.g. regularities at different levels of aggregation, in growth processes, in industrial structures and dynamics) ought to be captured theoretically as *emergent properties*: the collective and largely unintentional outcome of *far-from-equilibrium micro-interactions* and heterogeneous learning. Thus, they are the relatively orderly properties of processes of *self-organization* (what Stan Metcalfe calls a 'self-transforming market order') but without any equilibrium connotation either in terms of market clearing of all markets or in terms of fulfilling the underlying expectations of individual agents. Note that such properties are often metastable; while persisting on a time-scale longer than the processes generating them, the probability that they will ultimately disappear is 1.[10]

ORGANIZATIONAL FORMS

A similar style of representation and interpretation should apply to the emergence and self-maintenance of *organizational forms* and institutions: they are partly the result of directed (purposeful) actions by agents but also, partly, the unintentional outcome of collective interactions and the interplay of agents' learning. I will return to the organizational domain later.

COEVOLUTIONARY DYNAMICS

The relation of 'higher level' regularities manifest in institutions, rules, and organizational forms to 'lower level' evolutionary processes is a complex one of coevolution across different *levels of analysis* and *time-scales*, and one that should be properly understood and possibly modelled as such. While the former are emergent properties of the latter, they may be considered as relatively invariant structures that constrain and shape the latter on shorter time-scales. Modelling approaches that take these higher levels as quasi-invariants have the same provisional legitimacy granted more generally to models that exclude significant forms of novelty, and which generally arrive at a much slower pace (e.g. for major institutional changes).

This is the 'grand programme', as Sid Winter (with whom I developed the above list of paradigmatic building blocks) and I see it. It is impossible to

---

[10] On the notions of the 'emergence' and 'metastability', see Lane (1993).

review here the rapidly growing literature that shares parts or all of it. Some discussion and a brief review of the achievements up to a decade ago can be found in Dosi and Winter (2002), and a more detailed summary specifically addressing technological change and industrial dynamics is in Dosi and Nelson (2010). Instead, let me highlight some crucial domains of research within such a 'grand programme' from the very micro to the macro.

5.4. The Structure of Technological Knowledge and the Process of Technological Innovation

The analysis of innovation as an evolutionary process and of the underlying characteristics of technological knowledge has long been a core component of the evolutionary research programme. Very briefly, significant advances have been made with respect to the following:

- The nature of technological search and learning, and their location within the economic system.
- The structure of technological knowledge (organized within 'paradigms') and the regularities in the trajectories of innovation.
- Inter-technological or inter-sectoral differences in patterns of innovation, emerging from quite robust taxonomies.
- The *procedural* nature of technological knowledge and its embeddedness within organizational routines and 'dynamic capabilities'.
- The role of innovation, imitation, and diffusion in corporate growth and industrial evolution.
- The characteristics and revealed performances of sectoral and national systems of production and innovation.

Indeed, the understanding of technological and organizational knowledge and innovation constitutes the basic 'glue' binding together the evolutionary community, although well short of offering a fully-fledged paradigm.

Let me turn to other equally important facets of the latter.

5.5. Micro-Foundations: Cognition, Behaviours, and Learning in Complex Evolving Environments

The notion of 'micro-foundations' corresponds to providing an account of the actual behaviour of agents. I have criticized elsewhere stories of the type 'let us start by assuming that agents maximize (something) and build some theory from there', with some dubious epistemological claims such as 'this is just a useful yardstick', or 'this is the outcome of an "as...if" process, even if I am unable to formally write it down'.[11] Critiques can also be found in Simon (e.g. 1957 and 1969), Winter (1964), and Nelson and Winter (1982). In most economic circumstances featuring change and innovation, maximizing rationality cannot be characterized *even in principle*, let alone as an attribute of actual behaviour.

But what then do people and organizations do? In order to answer this question—involving behaviour and learning—we must borrow from cognitive and social psychology, even if what we get from these is a far cry from the behavioural assumptions of mainstream economics:

> Psychological theories [...] cannot match the elegance and precision of formal normative models of belief and choice, but this is another way of saying that rational models are psychologically unrealistic [...] Psychology offers integrative concepts and mid-level generalizations, which gain credibility from their ability to explain ostensibly different phenomena in diverse domains. (Kahneman, 2003, p. 1449)

Recently, considerable progress has been made in several directions. One is *neuroeconomics*. That this can be a fruitful approach is not so much related to the reductionist flavour that some exercises convey (e.g. 'map greediness in this part of the brain and generosity in that part...'), but rather because neuroeconomics can help in identifying and classifying different drivers and processes underlying evaluations and decisions (for a comprehensive review, see Camerer, 2007 and Rangel et al., 2008). A second area of progress has been the exploration and refinement of the conjecture that humans operate on the basis of two distinct systems of. Following Kahneman (2003), we may call them *System 1* (driven by intuition—fast, parallel, automatic, effortless, associative, slow-learning, emotional); and *System 2* (driven by reasoning—slow, serial, controlled, requiring effort, rule-governed, flexible, neutral) (Kahneman, 2003, p. 1451; see also Schneider and Shriffin, 1977a, 1977b).

Most contemporary developments are somewhat *Simonesque* in spirit, although they move further away from any notion of rationality (even of a *procedural* kind) than Simon would have been prepared to go. Indeed, the research bordering on economics, psychology, and cognitive studies is increasingly contributing to a 'model of humans' that should ultimately include (i) the cognitive attributes of both 'System 1' and 'System 2', most likely based on imperfect and evolving *categorizations* and *mental models*; (ii) ubiquitous valuation and decision *heuristics*; (iii) *context-dependence* and

---

[11] One such discussion can be found in the introduction to Dosi (2000).

social-embeddedness of both interpretative models and decision rules; and (iv) evolving (and possibly inconsistent) goals and preferences.

Organizations: Behaviours and Learning Patterns

An isomorphic question concerns *organizations*. What do they actually do? And how do they change their behaviours and their internal functioning— that is, how do they learn? One familiar answer is that firms maximize something (plausibly profits) and are subject to technological constraints (their 'production function'), while their behaviour is conditional on the information they access. If so, as Herb Simon argued long ago, one does not need to open-up the 'organizational black-box'. It is sufficient to know what the firm maximizes, since the production function and the information set are able to account for what the firm will do without looking into its interior.

To be fair, mainstream theory has moved some way from such black-boxing. The recognition that organizations are made up of several people with interests that may not be perfectly aligned calls for the opening up of the box, because what the organization does and ultimately how it performs depend on intra-organizational relations among its members. This is what *Agency Theories* have been doing, more so than Transaction Cost Economics (TCE), the primary focus of which has been the Coasian question of the boundaries between organizations and markets.

However, the agency-inspired opening-up of the box had little to do with any inquiry about how organizations *actually behave*, and even less with their *actual internal set-ups*. Rather, efforts have focused on offering models of firms as microcosms composed of asymmetrically informed, self-seeking, sophisticatedly rational individuals linked by equilibrium contracts. What the members of the organization do, and how it ultimately performs, depends on the characteristics of such contracts together with conditions that are partly 'technological' and partly 'social'—including the distribution of information, the degree of observability of efforts and outputs, and so on.

In essence, the aim is to substitute the maximizing 'organizational black-box' with an ensemble of many, ever more sophisticated, contractually linked, *individual black-boxes*, in which the key word is *incentives*. The perspective outlined here entails advances in the *opposite* direction. As was argued in Dosi (2000) and Marengo and Dosi (2005), we may clear the way by assuming, to begin with, a *weak incentive compatibility*—that no one will be required to undertake actions that benefit the organization while substantially damaging the individual undertaking them.

Given this, our perspective offers, to a *first order*, a view of organizations as *complex problem-solving institutional arrangements*, where 'problem-solving' stands for production problems (e.g. how to build a car) and search problems (e.g. finding a vaccine for malaria) that are typically *complex* in the sense that (i) they might not be perfectly decomposable (so that whatever 'solution' is put forward to a sub-problem influences other sub-problems as well); and, (ii) several classes of such problems might be computationally 'hard', so that a full exploration of the problem-solving tree might take an amount of time that grows faster than at a polynomial rate (indeed at an exponential rate) with the number of the problem's arguments.[12]

While problem-complexity and decomposability, and the mapping into a distinct *intra-* (and *inter-*) organizational division of labour, have little to do with incentive governance (even if they influence the latter), they do impinge on the characteristics of organizational knowledge and its distribution. That, in turn, has much to do with the characteristics of *organizational routines*[13] and, relatedly, of *organizational memory* (see e.g. Dosi et al., 2012).

There is now an emerging *knowledge-based, and capability-based*, theory of the firm, grounded on a *procedural* view of distributed organizational knowledge.[14] In this, capabilities are seen as sets of interrelated routines and 'other quasi-genetic traits of the firm...' (Winter in Cohen et al., 1996)—inertial and path-dependent in nature, quite opaque to environmental feedbacks: in the short-term, representing *state-variables* as opposed to *control-variables of the firm*, as Winter (1988)put it. And they are resilient, *primarily because they are learned, knowledge-rich, responses to external or intra-organizational signals* grounded in cognitive and habit-related factors. Their *nature* is far from being from the outcome of some maximization exercise subject to certain constraints.

The Challenging Facts of Industrial Dynamics

A typical evolutionary story about the relationship between firm-specific characteristics and performance goes as follows. Different productivities, organizational setups, propensities to innovate, and corporate strategies make up the distinct corporate identities, which in turn influence firm performance. More productive firms are able to charge lower prices for the same quality goods and thus increase their market share; more innovative firms are able to sell products that are 'better' in certain respects, likewise increasing their

---

[12] On problem-solving in general, see the classic work by Simon (1969, 1983); a discussion can also be found in Dosi and Egidi (1991).

[13] On this notion, based on the seminal work by Nelson and Winter (1982), see for example Cohen et al. (1996), Becker et al. (2005), Becker (2005), and the literature reviewed there.

[14] For a review of formal models attempting to grasp procedural knowledge, routines, and their dynamics, see Dosi et al. (2011). Important contributions include Levinthal (1997), Gavetti and Levinthal (2000), Ethiraj and Levinthal (2004), and Siggelkow and Rivkin (2005).

shares; and, finally, more efficient and profitable firms are able to grow more because they are able to invest more, given less than perfect capital markets.

On theoretical grounds, the formal account of such a story is in terms of some Fisher–Price or other *replicator dynamics*, such as described in Silverberg et al. (1988) and Metcalfe (1998), or in terms of some implicit efficiency-related replication as implied by a Nelson–Winter type of investment dynamics. But how does this story stack up against the evidence?

Let us consider first the impact of different productivities upon profitability, growth, and survival probabilities. The basic idea is that productivity distributions change as a result of learning by incumbent entities; differential growth (a form of selection) of incumbent entities; death (a different and more radical form of selection); and the entry of new entities. Given the availability of micro longitudinal panel data, an emerging line of research (e.g. Olley and Pakes, 1996; Foster et al., 2001; Bottazzi et al., 2010; see also the discussion in Bartelsman and Doms, 2000) investigates the properties of such decompositions, identifying the contribution to productivity growth of (i) firm-specific changes while holding shares constant (sometimes called the '*within*' component); (ii) changes in the shares themselves, holding initial firm productivity levels constant (also known as the '*between*' component); (iii) some interaction term; along with (iv) exit; and (v) entry.

Although there is a considerable variation in the evidence depending on countries, industries, and methods of analysis, certain patterns emerge. First, the *within* component generally is significantly larger than the *between* one: that is, improvement of productivity by existing firms dominates over selection across firms as a mode of industry advancement, at least with regard to productivity (both labour and total factor productivities). Second, relative efficiencies do influence survival probabilities, and it may be that selective mechanisms across the population of firms operate more effectively in the medium/long term at this level rather than in terms of varying shares over the total industry output. Third, the evidence reveals little or no link between the profitability and firm growth of incumbents. However, other evidence suggests a systematic effect of profitability upon survival probabilities (compare Bartelsman and Doms, 2000; Foster et al., 2008).

The implications of the empirical regularities identified so far are far-reaching. The recurrent evidence at all levels of observation of inter-firm heterogeneity is consistent with an evolutionary notion of idiosyncratic learning, innovation (or lack of it), and adaptation. Heterogeneous firms compete with one another and, given (possibly firm-specific or location-specific) input and output prices, obtain different returns. In other words, they obtain different quasi-rents (or losses) above or below the notional 'pure competition' profit rates. Many firms enter, and a roughly equivalent number exit. In all this, the evidence increasingly reveals a rich structure in the processes of learning, competition, and growth.

At the same time, market selection among firms—the other central mechanism along with firm-specific learning in evolutionary interpretations of economic change—does not seem to be particularly powerful, at least on the yearly or multi-yearly time-scale at which statistics are generally reported. Diverse degrees of efficiency yield relatively persistent profitability differentials, but the latter do *not* in turn spur differential growth. That is, contemporary markets do not appear to be very effective selectors delivering rewards and punishments in terms of relative sizes or shares according to differential efficiencies. Moreover, the absence of any strong relationship between profitability and growth militates against the naive Schumpeterian notion that profits feed growth (e.g. by feeding investments).

Selection among different variants of a technology, different vintages of equipment, and different production lines does occur and is a major driver of industrial dynamics. However, it occurs largely *within* firms, driven by the implementation of better production processes and the dropping of less productive ones. The apparent market 'selection weakness' may be rooted in several possible explanations—from the sheer statistical to the genuinely interpretative.

First, one measures productivity very imperfectly: one ought to disentangle the price component of value-added (and price effects upon competitiveness) from physical efficiency to which productivity strictly refers, but only rarely can one do so, particularly when products differ in their characteristics and performance. As product innovation and product differentiation are often fundamental to competition in modern industries, one should explicitly account for the impact of the latter upon revealed selection processes.

Second, the assumption of clear boundaries between industries and generalized competition within them is unrealistic. It is more fruitful in many industries to think of different submarkets as the locus of competition (see Sutton, 1998). The characteristics and size of such submarkets also offer different constraints and opportunities for corporate growth.

Third, growing micro-level evidence reveals the interplay of technological and organizational factors as determinants of Schumpeterian competition. Bresnahan et al. (2012) illustrate this in the case of IBM and Microsoft confronting the introduction of the PC and the browser, respectively. Both firms faced organizational dis-economies precisely in those corporate activities where they were stronger, due to a mismatch between technological trajectories, internal organizational set-ups, and market requirements.

Fourth, the links between efficiency and innovation, on the one hand, and corporate growth, on the other, are mediated by large degrees of behavioural freedom, for example, in terms of propensities to invest, export, and expand abroad; pricing strategies; and patterns of diversification.

The evidence on the apparent weakness of selection processes requires that evolutionary theories rethink their account of *selection landscapes*—that is, the space in which competitive interactions are represented—possibly increasing the number of arguments (e.g. to include not only production efficiencies and prices but also product characteristics) and allowing for non-linear effects (so that competitive forces operate solely in favour of the very 'best' and against the very 'worst'). Indeed, important challenges lie ahead for the theory.

5.6. Towards a Soundly Micro-Founded Evolutionary Macroeconomics

The 'Grand Evolutionary Project', as outlined here, explicitly builds upon the foregoing properties of agents' behaviours, patterns of innovative search, and competitive interactions, trying to address 'head on' the issue of macroeconomic dynamics. Macroeconomic dynamics as generated in the class of models advocated here are the outcome of interactions among multiple individual behaviours. Non-linearities induced by heterogeneity and far-from-equilibrium interactions are the rule, including the coupled dynamics between aggregate variables (employment, output, etc.). The statistical properties exhibited by aggregate variables can be interpreted as *emergent properties* grounded in persistent micro-disequilibria. The observed stable relations among those aggregate variables may emerge from turbulent, disequilibrium, microeconomic interactions.

Let us illustrate the genre with reference to Dosi, Fagiolo, and Roventini (2010), who study an agent-based model (ABM) that bridges Keynesian theories of demand generation and Schumpeterian theories of technology-fuelled economic growth. Agents continually face opportunities for innovation and imitation, which they try to tap with expensive search efforts, under conditions of genuine uncertainty (so they unable to form any reliable judgements on the relation between search investment and the probability of a successful outcome). Hence (endogenous) technological shocks (the innovations themselves) are unpredictable and idiosyncratic.

The model builds on evolutionary roots, while also being in tune with 'good New Keynesian' insights (Stiglitz, 1994). It explores the feedback between factors influencing aggregate demand and those driving technological change in an effort to develop a unified framework accounting for long-term dynamics and higher-frequency fluctuations. It forms part of a growing literature on agent-based computational economics (Tesfatsion and Judd, 2006; LeBaron and Tesfatsion, 2008), responding to the pleas of evolutionary economists but also of Solow (2008) for micro-heterogeneity, with a multiplicity of agents interacting without any *ex-ante* commitment to the reciprocal consistency of their actions.[15]

Furthermore, the model—like most evolutionary ABMs—is 'structural' in that it explicitly builds on a representation of what agents do, how they adjust, and so on. The commitment is to 'phenomenologically' describe behaviours as close as one can get to the available micro-evidence. Akerlof's (2002) advocacy of a 'behavioural microeconomics' builds on that notion. Indeed, this is perhaps our first fundamental disciplining device.

A second, complementary discipline involves the ability of the model to jointly account for an ensemble of stylized facts regarding both 'micro' and 'meso' phenomena with genuinely macro 'stylized facts'. For the model given, they include (i) endogenous growth; (ii) persistent fluctuations; (iii) recurrent involuntary unemployment; (iv) pro-cyclical consumption, investment, productivity, employment, and changes in inventories; (v) fat-tailed distributions of aggregate growth rates, together with (persistent) asymmetries in productivity across firms; (vi) 'spiky' investment patterns; and (vii) skewed firm-size distributions. Using the model to investigate the properties of macroeconomic dynamics and the impact of public policies on supply, demand, and the 'fundamentals' of the economy, one finds that the complementarities between factors influencing aggregate demand and drivers of technological change affect both 'short-run' fluctuations and long-term growth patterns.

The simulations also show a complementarity between 'Keynesian' and 'Schumpeterian' policies, a result with far-reaching implications in terms of theory and policy. Both types of policies seem to be necessary to restore the economy to long-run sustained growth. Schumpeterian policies potentially foster an economic path but do not appear to be able alone to yield sustained long-run growth. In a broad parameter region, 'fundamental' (indeed, endogenously generated) changes in technology are unable to fully propagate in terms of demand generation and ultimately output growth. By the same token, complementary demand shocks (in the simplest case, induced by government fiscal policies) have persistent effects upon output levels, rates of growth, and rates of innovations. Hence, Keynesian policies not only have a strong impact on output volatility and unemployment but also seem to be necessary for long-run economic growth.

---

[15] For relevant agent-based models, see Delli Gatti et al. (2005), (2010), and (2011), Russo et al. (2007), Dawid et al. (2008, 2011), and Ashraf, Gershman, and Howitt (2011); for models with both Keynesian and Schumpeterian elements, see Verspagen (2002), the discussion in Silverberg and Verspagen (2005), Saviotti and Pyka (2008), and Ciarli et al. (2010).

Indeed, the results suggest that the matching (or mismatching) between innovative exploration of new technologies and the conditions of demand generation yields two distinct 'regimes' or 'phases' of growth, characterized by different short-run fluctuations and unemployment levels. Even when Keynesian policies allow for sustained growth, their tuning affects the amplitude of fluctuations and long-term levels of unemployment and output. Fluctuations and unemployment rates are also affected by 'Schumpeterian policies', holding constant macro-demand management rules.

The model seems to offer an encouraging template to be modified and refined in order to explore further domains of economic analysis. As such, it represents an important advance vis-à-vis the first generation of evolutionary models pioneered by Nelson and Winter, which arguably contain too much Schumpeter and too little Keynes. With their path-breaking merits in formalizing endogenous uncertainty-ridden technological search, the Nelson–Winter models are, from the macroeconomic point of view, equilibrium models: the labour market clears and so does the product market. A central reference for them is Solow's growth model and the related quest is for more reasonable (indeed, evolutionary!) foundations to the macro patterns of growth Solow identified. However, they fall short of Keynesian economics, which—as Paul Krugman puts it—is 'essentially about the refutation of Say's Law, about the possibility of a general shortfall in demand'. Under that perspective, one finds 'it easiest to think about demand failures in terms of quasi-equilibrium models in which some things, including wages and the state of long-term expectations in Keynes's sense, are held fixed, while others adjust toward a conditional equilibrium of sorts' (Krugman 2011, p. 3).

Furthermore, this has a crucial link with macroeconomic coordination issues and in particular unemployment rates. To quote Keynes (1943) as cited in Kaldor (1983):

> ...unemployment is not a mere accidental blemish in a private enterprise economy. On the contrary, it is a part of the essential mechanism of the system and has a definite function to fulfil. The first function of unemployment [...] is that it maintains the authority of masters over men. The master has usually been in a position to say: 'If you do not want the job, there are plenty of others who do'. When the men say 'If you do not want to employ me, there are plenty of others who will', the situation is radically changed.

5.7. Conclusions

The foregoing discussion of the major building blocks and achievements of the evolutionary research programme, as I see it, also highlights a long list of tall challenges ahead, all the way from micro-foundations to the interpretation of long-term development. Let me mention a few starting from the former.

If agents' behaviour is not driven by any exercise of maximization, what do they actually do? Here is where it is urgent to identify—in dialogue with cognitive and social psychology and organizational studies—cognitive and behavioural regularities, both at the level of individuals and organizations. A lot has been done in the analysis of both the processes of innovation and of organizational routines, but the work is far from completed. Moreover, economic activities go well beyond the search for innovation: for example, how are prices set? What are the rules determining investment and scrapping? What determines the amount of resources invested in research? Are there regularities in determinants of the consumption patterns and the allocation of income to consumption and savings? Without answering these questions one can hardly build robust macro-models with sound empirically grounded micro-foundations.

Second, both at micro and aggregate levels, relatively little attention has been devoted so far to all issues concerning income distribution and, relatedly, social conflict. Sometimes—possibly worse than sheer neglect!—some evolutionary economists seem content with a naively Schumpeterian view according to which profits are just innovation-related rents. On the contrary, I believe it is urgent to reassess the institutional drivers of income distributions, which are at least as important as technological ones. At last, evolutionary interpretations ought to acknowledge that the economic world is populated by workers, capitalists, banks, financial sharks, and the like! Indeed, as noted earlier, the evolutionary community is arguably too 'Schumpeterian' and too little 'Keynesian'. Too many of our 'invisible college' have the same interest in labour market dynamics, unemployment, and income distribution as Schumpeter did: that is, near zero!

Third, and relatedly, the importance attributed to the 'creative destruction' originated by innovation processes typically puts the emphasis on the 'creative' part, largely neglecting the social and ecological destruction often accompanying them. The time has come to address these issues.

Fourth, we live an international economy that is 'globalized'. Agent-based, evolutionary models ought at least to recognize this. Unfortunately, most models so far have been closed economy ones. The latter are bound to be a necessary first approximation, but we need to move on. To be fair, quite a few within the 'institutionalist/evolutionary family' address the issue, but there seems little urgency to offer reasonable formal accounts of interacting, and technologically and organizationally asymmetric, economies. Yes, there are many insightful hints, but the community is at fault in not linking up more with policy battles such as Paul Krugman's on the macro side or Dani Rodrick's stress on the internal incompatibility between globalization, national sovereignty, and democracy (Rodrick, 2011).

In this chapter, I have placed much stress on *formal* theories. This is not because other forms of analysis are less important. On the contrary, other approaches—from historically grounded 'appreciative' theorizing, to bottom-up statistical analyses, all the way to case studies—are important complements. The point is that much of the interpretation of economic phenomena and an overwhelming part of economic policy today is informed by *theory*—indeed, in my view a *very bad theory*, and one with *pernicious policy implications.*

Take the diagnosis of the current crisis. Leave aside the *pasdarans* who believe that it was the outcome of an aggregate supply shock and hence presumably there is no voluntary unemployment (or, if there is, it is just due to 'adjustment frictions'). Even neglecting them, many economists, after their initial surprise, are reconverging on propositions and policy advocacies derived from their old theoretical perspectives, and offering familiar advice such as: 'in order to increase employment, labour markets in general and wage-setting in particular have to be made more flexible...' (as if unemployment were not a consequence of a worldwide aggregate demand); 'the priority now is to balance the budget because only then growth will start again...' (as if there were any evidence of crowding out between private investment and public expenditure); 'one should stop pumping liquidity into the economy because this will fuel a hike in long-term interest rates and inflation...' (when, net of imported inflation associated with primary commodities, OECD countries are in the midst of a price *deflation*); and so on.

Indeed, establishing a sound *theoretical* alternative is probably a necessary, even if not a sufficient, condition for an alternative menu of policies. In short, one might call this a programme of *innovation-centred, environment-friendly, heavily redistributive, Keynesianism.*

The ambition, shared, one hopes, by many, is to 'better understand the world in order to contribute to making it better'. Needless to say, there is a vast gap between elements of an alternative understanding of how the economic system really works (or does not work) and a coherent ensemble of appropriate policy prescriptions. Filling this gap will require a huge collective enterprise. Let me end by flagging the utmost urgency of the task, at a historical moment when the scourge of misleading orthodoxies—much like in the early 1930s—carries the threat of dire impact on the management of a crisis that they contributed to generating in the first place.

Acknowledgements

Comments on previous versions by Pietro Dindo, Bill Janeway, Francisco Louçã, Stan Metcalfe, Dick Nelson, Alessandro Nuvolari, Evita Paraskevopoulou,

Andrea Roventini, and Sid Winter all helped considerably in preparing this chapter. Support from INET, the Institute for New Economic Thinking (grant IN01100022) is gratefully acknowledged.

References

Aghion, P. and Howitt, P. (1997). *Endogenous Growth Theory*. Cambridge, MA: MIT Press.

Akerlof, G. A. (2002). 'Behavioral Macroeconomics and Macroeconomic Behavior', *American Economic Review, 92*: 411–33.

Anderson, P. W., Arrow, K. J., and Pines, D. (eds) (1988). *The Economy as an Evolving Complex System I*. Redwood City, CA: Addison-Wesley.

Arthur, W. B., Durlauf, S., and Lane, D. (1997). *The Economy as an Evolving Complex System II*. Redwood City, CA: Addison-Wesley.

Ashraf, Q., Gershman, B., and Howitt, P. (2011). 'Banks, Market Organization, and Macroeconomic Performance: An Agent-Based Computational Analysis', NBER Working Paper, 17102.

Bartelsman, E. J. and Doms, M. (2000). 'Understanding Productivity, Lessons from Longitudinal Microdata', *Journal of Economic Literature, 38*: 569–94.

Becker, M. C. (2005). 'A Framework for Applying Organizational Routines in Empirical Research: Linking Antecedents, Characteristics and Performance Outcomes of Recurrent Interaction Patterns', *Industrial and Corporate Change, 14*: 817–46.

Becker, M. C., Lazaric, N., Nelson, R. R., and Winter, S. G. (2005). 'Applying Organizational Routines in Understanding Organizational Change', *Industrial and Corporate Change, 14*: 775–91.

Bottazzi, G., Dosi, G., Jacoby, N., Secchi, A., and Tamagni, F. (2010). 'Corporate Performances and Market Selection: Some Comparative Evidence', *Industrial and Corporate Change, 19*: 1953–96.

Bresnahan, T., Greenstein, S., and Henderson, R. (2012), 'Schumpeterian Competition and Diseconomies of Scope: Illustrations from the Histories of Microsoft and IBM', in J. Lerner, and S. Stern (eds), *The Rate and Direction of Inventive Activity Revisited*. Chicago: University of Chicago Press, 203–76.

Camerer, C. F. (2007). 'Neuroeconomics: Using Neuroscience to Make Economic Predictions', *Economic Journal, 117*: C26–C42.

Ciarli, T., Lorentz, A., Savona, M., and Valente, M. (2010). 'The Effect of Consumption and Production Structure on Growth and Distribution: A Micro to Macro Model', *Metroeconomica, 61*: 180–218.

Cohen, M., Burkhart, R., Dosi, G., Egidi, M., Marengo, L., Warglien, M., and Winter, S. (1996). 'Routines and Other Recurring Action Patterns of Organizations: Contemporary Research Issues', *Industrial and Corporate Change, 5*: 653–99.

Colander, D., Foellmer, H., Haas, A., Goldberg, M., Juselius, K., Kirman, A., Lux, T., and Sloth, B. (2009). 'The Financial Crisis and the Systemic Failure of Academic Economics', Kiel Institute for the World Economy Working Papers, 1489.

Coriat, B. and Dosi, G. (1998). 'The Institutional Embeddedness of Economic Change. An Appraisal of the 'Evolutionary' and the 'Regulationist' Research Programme', in K.

Nielsen and B. Johnson (eds), *Institutions and Economic Change*. Cheltenham: Edward Elgar, 3–32.

Dawid, H., Gemkow, S., Harting, P., Kabus, K., Wersching, K., and Neugart, M. (2008). 'Skills, Innovation, and Growth: An Agent-Based Policy Analysis', *Journal of Economics and Statistics*, 228: 251–75.

Dawid, H., Gemkow, S., Harting, P., van der Hoog, S., and Neugart, M. (2011), 'The Eurace@Unibi Model: An Agent-Based Macroeconomic Model for Economic Policy Analysis', Department of Business Administration and Economics, Bielefeld University (downloaded May 2013 from <http://www.wiwi.uni-bielefeld.de/vpl1/research/eurace-unibi.html>).

Delli Gatti, D., Desiderio, S., Gaffeo, E., Cirillo, P., and Gallegati, M. (2011). *Macroeconomics from the Bottom-up*. Milan: Springer.

Delli Gatti, D., Di Guilmi, C., Gaffeo, E., Giulioni, G., Gallegati, M., and Palestrini, A. (2005). 'A New Approach to Business Fluctuations: Heterogeneous Interacting Agents, Scaling Laws and Financial Fragility', *Journal of Economic Behavior and Organization*, 56: 489–512.

Delli Gatti, D., Gallegati, M., Greenwald, B., Russo, A., and Stiglitz, J. E. (2010). 'The Financial Accelerator in an Evolving Credit Network', *Journal of Economic Dynamics and Control*, 34: 1627–50.

Dopfer, K. (ed.) (2005). *The Evolutionary Foundations of Economics*. Cambridge: Cambridge University Press.

Dosi, G. (2000). *Innovation, Organization and Economic Dynamics. Selected Essays*. Cheltenham: Edward Elgar.

Dosi, G. (2011), 'A Response to John Kay: Elements of an Evolutionary Paradigm', INET (Institute for New Economic Thinking) blog (downloaded May 2013 from <http://ineteconomics.org/blog/inet/giovanni-dosi-response-john-kay-elements-evolutionary-paradigm>).

Dosi, G. (2013). *Further Essays on Economic Organization, Industrial Dynamics and Development*. Cheltenham: Edward Elgar.

Dosi, G. and Egidi, M. (1991). 'Substantive and Procedural Uncertainty: An Exploration of Economic Behaviours in Changing Environments', *Journal of Evolutionary Economics*, 1: 145–68.

Dosi, G. and Nelson, R. R. (1994). 'An Introduction to Evolutionary Theories in Economics', *Journal of Evolutionary Economics*, 4: 153–72.

Dosi, G. and Nelson, R. R. (2010). 'Technical Change and Industrial Dynamics as Evolutionary Processes', in B. H. Hall and N. Rosenberg (eds), *Handbook of the Economics of Innovation*. Burlington: Academic Press, Vol. I, 51–128.

Dosi, G. and Orsenigo, L. (1988). 'Coordination and Transformation: An Overview of Structures, Behaviours and Change in Evolutionary Environments', in G. Dosi, C. Freeman, R. Nelson, G. Silverberg, and L. Soete (eds), *Technical Change and Economic Theory*. London: Francis Pinter and New York: Columbia University Press.

Dosi, G. and Winter, S. G. (2002). 'Interpreting Economic Change: Evolution, Structures and Games', in M. Augier and J. March (eds), *The Economics of Choice, Change and Organization*. Cheltenham: Edward Elgar, 337–53.

Dosi, G., Fagiolo, G., and Roventini, A. (2010). 'Schumpeter Meeting Keynes: A Policy-Friendly Model of Endogenous Growth and Business Cycles', *Journal of Economic Dynamics and Control*, 34: 1748–67.

Dosi, G., Faillo, M., Marengo, L., and Moschella, D. (2011). 'Modeling Routines and Organizational Learning: A Discussion of the State-of-the-Art', *Seoul Journal of Economics*, 24: 247–86.

Dosi, G., Freeman, C., Nelson, R., Silverberg, G., and Soete, L. (eds) (1988). *Technical Change and Economic Theory*. London and New York: Francis Pinter/Columbia University Press.

Dosi, G., Marengo, L., and Fagiolo, G. (2005). 'Learning in Evolutionary Environments', in K. Dopfer (ed.), *The Evolutionary Foundations of Economics*. Cambridge: Cambridge University Press, 255–328.

Dosi, G., Marengo, L., Paraskevopoulou, E., and Valente, M. (2012). 'The Value and Dangers of Remembrance in Changing Worlds: A Model of Cognitive and Operational Memory of Organizations', LEM Working Paper, forthcoming.

Ethiraj, S. and Levinthal, D. (2004). 'Bounded Rationality and the Search for Organizational Architecture: An Evolutionary Perspective on the Design of Organizations and Their Evolvability', *Administrative Science Quarterly*, 49: 404–37.

Foster, L., Haltiwanger, J. C., and Krizan, C. J. (2001). 'Aggregate Productivity Growth, Lessons from Microeconomic Evidence', in C. R. Hulten, E. R. Dean, and M. J. Harper (eds), *New Developments in Productivity Analysis*. Chicago: University of Chicago Press, 303–72.

Foster, L., Haltiwanger, J. C., and Syverson, C. (2008). 'Reallocation, Firm Turnover and Efficiency, Selection on Productivity or Profitability?', *American Economic Review*, 98: 394–425.

Gavetti, G. and Levinthal, D. (2000). 'Looking Forward and Looking Backward: Cognitive and Experimental Search', *Administrative Science Quarterly*, 45: 113–37.

Kahneman, D. (2003). 'A Perspective on Judgment and Choice: Mapping Bounded Rationality', *American Psychologist*, 58: 697–720.

Kaldor, N. (1983). 'Keynesian Economics after Fifty Years', in J. Trevithick, and D. Worswick (eds), *Keynes and the Modern World*. Cambridge: Cambridge University Press, 1–48.

Kay, J. (2011). 'The Map is Not the Territory: An Essay on the State of Economics', INET (Institute for New Economic Thinking) blog (downloaded May 2013 from <http://ineteconomics.org/blog/inet/john-kay-map-not-territory-essay-state-economics>).

Keynes, J. M. (1943). 'Planning Full Employment: Alternative Solutions to a Dilemma', *The Times*, 23 January.

Kirman, A. (2010). *Complex Economics: Individual and Collective Rationality*. London: Routledge.

Korzybski, A. (1933). *Science and Sanity: An Introduction to Non-Aristotelian Systems and General Semantics*. Lancaster: Science Press.

Krugman, P. (2011). 'Mr Keynes and the Moderns', Prepared for the Cambridge conference commemorating the 75th anniversary of the publication of Keynes' *General Theory of Employment, Interest, and Money*.

Lane, D. (1993). 'Artificial Worlds and Economics', *Journal of Evolutionary Economics*, 3: 89–107 and 177–97.

LeBaron, B. and Tesfatsion, L. (2008). 'Modeling Macroeconomies as Open-Ended Dynamic Systems of Interacting Agents', *American Economic Review*, 98: 246–50.

Levinthal, D. (1997). 'Adaptation on Rugged Landscapes', *Management Science*, 43: 934–50.

Marengo, L. and Dosi, G. (2005). 'Division of Labor, Organizational Coordination and Market Mechanisms in Collective Problem-Solving', *Journal of Economic Behavior and Organization*, 58: 303–26.

Metcalfe, J. S. (1998). *Evolutionary Economics and Creative Destruction*. London: Routledge.

Metcalfe, J. S. and Ramlogan, R. (2006), 'Restless Capitalism: A Complexity Perspective on Modern Capitalist Economies', in E. Garnsey and J. McGlade (eds), *Complexity and Evolution*. Cheltenham: Edward Elgar, 115–46.

Nelson, R. R. and Sampat, B. (2001). 'Making Sense of Institutions as a Factor Shaping Economic Performance', *Journal of Economic Behaviour and Organization*, 44: 31–54.

Nelson, R. R. and Winter, S. G. (1982). *An Evolutionary Theory of Economic Change*. Cambridge, MA: The Belknap Press of Harvard University Press.

Olley, G. S. and Pakes, A. (1996). 'The Dynamics of Productivity in the Telecommunications Equipment Industry', *Econometrica*, 64: 1263–97.

Rangel, A., Camerer, C., and Read Montague, P. (2008). 'A Framework for Studying the Neurobiology of Value-Based Decision Making', *Nature-Neuroscience*, 9: 545–59.

Rodrick, D. (2011). *The Globalization Paradox: Democracy and the Future of the World Economy*. New York and London: W.W. Norton.

Rosser, B. J. (2011). *Complex Evolutionary Dynamics in Urban-Regional and Ecologic-Economic Systems: From Catastrophe to Chaos and Beyond*. New York: Springer.

Russo, A., Catalano, M., Gaffeo, E., Gallegati, M., and Napoletano, M. (2007). 'Industrial Dynamics, Fiscal Policy and R&D: Evidence From a Computational Experiment', *Journal of Economic Behavior and Organization*, 64: 426–47.

Saviotti, P. P. and Pyka, A. (2008). 'Micro and Macro Dynamics: Industry Life Cycles, Inter-Sector Coordination and Aggregate Growth', *Journal of Evolutionary Economics*, 18: 167–82.

Schneider, W. and Shiffrin, R. M. (1977a). 'Controlled and Automatic Human Information Processing: I. Detection, Search, and Attention', *Psychological Review*, 84: 1–66.

Schneider, W. and Shiffrin, R. M. (1977b). 'Controlled and Automatic Human Information Processing: II. Perceptual Learning, Automatic Attending and a General Theory', *Psychological Review*, 84: 127–90.

Siggelkow, N. and Rivkin, J. W. (2005). 'Speed and Search: Designing Organizations for Turbulence and Complexity', *Organization Science*, 16: 101–22.

Silverberg, G. and Verspagen, B. (2005), 'Evolutionary Theorizing on Economic Growth', in K. Dopfer (ed.) *The Evolutionary Foundations of Economics*. Cambridge: Cambridge University Press, 506–39.

Silverberg, G., Dosi, G., and Orsenigo, L. (1988). 'Innovation, Diversity and Diffusion: A Self-Organising Model', *Economic Journal*, 98: 1032–54, reprinted in Dosi (2000).

Simon, H. A. (1957). *Models of Man: Social and Rational*. New York: John Wiley and Sons.

Simon, H. A. (1969). *The Sciences of the Artificial*. Cambridge, MA: MIT Press.

Simon, H. A. (1983). *Reason in Human Affairs*. Stanford: Stanford University Press.

Solow, R. M. (2008). 'The State of Macroeconomics', *Journal of Economic Perspectives*, 22: 243–6.

Stiglitz, J. E. (1994), 'Endogenous Growth and Cycles', in Y. Shionoya and M. Perlman (eds), *Innovation in Technology, Industries, and Institutions: Studies in Schumpeterian Perspectives*. Ann Arbor, MI: The University of Michigan Press, 121–56.

Stiglitz, J. E. (2011). 'Rethinking Macroeconomics: What Failed, and How to Repair It', *Journal of the European Economic Association*, 9: 591–645.

Sutton, J. (1998). *Technology and Market Structure: Theory and Evidence*. Cambridge, MA: MIT Press.

Tesfatsion, L. and Judd, K. L. (2006). *Handbook of Computational Economics: Agent-Based Computational Economics*. Amsterdam and Oxford: Elsevier.

Verspagen, B. (2002). 'Evolutionary Macroeconomics: A Synthesis between Neo-Schumpeterian and Post-Keynesian Lines of Thought', *Electronic Journal of Evolutionary Modeling and Economic Dynamics*, IFReDE—Université Montesquieu Bordeaux IV, 1007, <http://www.e-jemed.org/1007/index.php>.

Winter, S. G. (1964). 'Economic 'Natural Selection' and the Theory of the Firm', *Yale Economic Essays*, 4: 225–72 (available at <http://www.lem.sssup.it/books.html>).

Winter, S. G. (1988). 'On Coase, Competence, and the Corporation', *Journal of Law, Economics, and Organization*, 4: 163–80.

6

Is Innovation Always Good?

Luc Soete

6.1. Introduction

Just like the old Guinness advert, *'innovation is good for you'* appears to be the common feature of most science, technology, and innovation studies over the last decades. In the Guinness case though, this was actually correct. A pint of Guinness a day compares to an aspirin a day in the prevention of blood clots and the risk of heart attack. Unlike other beers, Guinness contains antioxidants like those found in red wine and dark chocolate.[1] In its wisdom, however, Guinness decided to stop its *'good for you'* marketing campaign in Ireland, which had primarily consisted of offering free beer to blood donors in blood donor clinics.[2] The company did not want to be identified as a health company!

Maybe innovation scholars should do the same thing. The slogan 'innovation is good for you' appears to have been underlying most business and policy analyses, which seems surprising given the fact that innovation failure rather than innovation success appears the most common feature of innovation studies. Hence the simple, but straightforward, question that I would like to address in this chapter: could it be that innovation is *not* always good for you? My claim is that at the broader societal level, innovation does not always represent a Schumpeterian process of *'creative destruction'*, renewing society's dynamics and hence leading to higher levels of economic development and welfare—destroying a few incumbents to the benefit of many newcomers—but rather represents now and then the exact opposite pattern: a process of what I will call here *'destructive creation'*—in other words, innovation

---

[1] See Mann and Folts (2004).   [2] *Irish Times*, 22 March 2010.

benefiting a few at the expense of many with, as a result, the opposite pattern of a long-term reduction in overall welfare or productivity growth. As I will try to illustrate, a common feature of '*destructive creation*' innovation appears to be its short-termism, its easy free-rider nature, and its dependency on networks in which the regulatory framework governing the network sometimes provides the major source for innovation.

The second claim I will make here is that the core reason why such patterns of '*destructive creation*' appear to have blossomed over the last 10 to 20 years is closely related to the advent and widespread diffusion and use of new, digital Information and Communication Technologies (ICT). ICT has allowed for a dramatic growth in opportunities for the fragmentation of service delivery: what has become known as the 'long tail' of product and service delivery differentiation (Anderson, 2006). There is little doubt that, in doing so, ICT has had major growth and welfare-increasing effects. It has allowed for the satisfaction of consumers' wants practically along the full demand curve. As a result, many consumers who before could not afford a particular service, can now consume a particular cheap version of such services at a much lower price—think of cheap air flights. New 'versions' of services have emerged in many sectors and have been behind the rapid growth of many new varieties of services satisfying a much broader spectrum of consumer desires.

However, in many areas, and in particular network services, the emergence of such service differentiation has also led to opportunities for cherry-picking: for selecting those segments of demand for profitable delivery at the expense of other less profitable segments, undermining as a consequence 'full' service delivery. As a result, many features of 'universal service' delivery associated with previous network service delivery have come under pressure. Their quality of delivery has become of lower quality, or in the worst case has even been discontinued. In network services, it has increasingly become expensive to be poor.

At the same time, existing network regulators were neither well-prepared nor informed about the many new digital opportunities. On the contrary, deregulation and/or liberalization led to new products or service delivery inspired by changes in regulation and exploiting more fully the new digital opportunities for product differentiation with, in some cases, negative societal externalities or even systemic failures.

Economists, and social scientists more generally, seem to have not been sufficiently forthcoming in highlighting the limits of innovation in sectors where such forms of '*destructive creation*' appear much more common than the usual well-known Schumpeterian forms of creative destruction. By contrast, colleagues in the Science and Technology Studies community did, of course, have a well-documented framework in which they explicitly looked at some of the possible negative externalities of technical inventions. But, over time, these technology assessment analyses developed further outside of the economics profession, and innovation assessment never emerged.[3]

In this chapter I limit myself to two examples of such patterns of 'destructive creation': first, our ecologically unsustainable, innovation-led consumerism growth path (dealt with in the next two sections); and, second, financial innovations as the exemplar *par excellence* of 'destructive creation' (in Section 6.4). In both cases, the solution will have to be found in strengthening society's capacity to develop innovations of the welfare-enhancing 'creative destruction' type.

6.2. Innovation, Planned Obsolescence, and Unsustainable Consumption Growth

Of course, we know from the large literature on the economics of innovation that there are plenty of cases of technological failure: the long term 'locking in', for example, of producers and consumers in technologically inferior trajectories, as highlighted by Paul David (1985, 2001) and Brian Arthur (1989) amongst others. And we also know that at the policy level there are numerous conflicts in the design of innovation policy between innovation support and the speed of diffusion as highlighted by Paul Stoneman (2001) and Paul David (2012).

Here, though, I would like to look more closely at the way innovation in consumer goods might have led our societies to a conspicuous consumption path of innovation-led 'destructive creation' growth. In most modern growth models, the decision to invest in research and development is driven by the prospect of monopoly profits on the incremental value that new vintages of products or services provide. In short, innovation goes hand-in-hand with value creation.

Yet one can also imagine exactly the opposite pattern: a process of destructive creation in which innovation actually destroys the usage value of the existing stock of durable goods and as a result induces consumers to repeat their purchase. Emilio Calvano from Igier-Bocconi University developed a formal model illustrating the widespread nature of such a phenomenon. Let me briefly quote from his paper:

> By allowing innovation to affect the value of the existing stock of durable goods, we highlight the role of destruction rather than creation in driving innovative activity.

[3] As Paul David put it in a set of provocative comments that run in a very similar direction to those presented here, but which are more directed towards the 'economics of innovation' profession: 'The optimum rate of innovation for an economy, or a social organization is a notion that rarely is discussed, except by implication, which has left it poorly defined. Yet, unless this concept somehow was implemented and thereby operationally defined, how could one claim to judge whether the pace of innovation currently prevailing in a given branch of industry or sector of the economy was too slow, rather than just right or too fast? By contrast, the optimal rate of Harrod-neutral technical change and hence the optimal steady-state rate of labour productivity growth is nicely defined, at least for certain familiar classes of growth models; and, in the literature on the economics of R&D, the question whether we have too much or too little (R&D) input into the

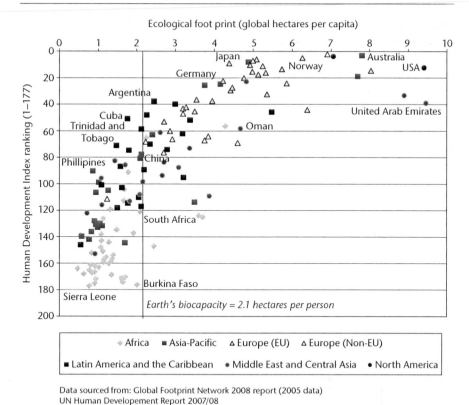

Figure 6.1. Human welfare and economic footprints compared
Source: <http://en.wikipedia.org/wiki/File:Human_Development_vs_Ecological_Footprint.jpg>.

The formal analysis shows that destructive creation unambiguously leads to higher profits whatever the innovation costs. On second thought this shouldn't come as a surprise. If the 'problem' from a profit maximizing perspective, is the durability of the output then it follows that any (cheap enough) mechanism that reduces or eliminates it would put the monopolist in a stronger position (i.e. 'closer' to the rental outcome). The power to 'wreck' the value of old versions of a product ends up serving much the same purpose and hence the profit restoral. (Calvano, 2010, p. 1)

Of course, this destruction of others' monopolies may happen to the destructive creator later, but the point is that there is no mechanism to take into account the optimal timing of innovations with regard to the destruction costs of all sorts of affected capital. The analysis presented by Calvano highlights the fact that the phenomenon of 'destructive creation' is rather widespread and has been very much induced by the emergence of new ICT consumer goods.

processes of research and invention is frequently asked and answered empirically. Why should not excessive innovation be acknowledged to be just as much a possibility as is excessive investment in scientific research, or in industrial R&D?' (David, 2012, p. 511–12).

Easy and cheap ways in which existing usage value can be destroyed are, for example, through product design and restrictive aftermarket practices, and in the extreme case through so-called 'planned obsolescence' purposely limiting the life-span of particular consumer goods.[4] We will not go into the conspiracy versions of such theories here, but rather follow the internal economic logic of innovations destroying old product versions as highlighted by Calvano. Probably the most extreme and widespread case would be new product design, for instance in fashion clothing or shoes,[5] destroying existing output, but there are of course many other forms and sorts of restrictive aftermarket practices that can be found in many ICT-related sectors, such as software writers limiting backward compatibility, or electronic goods manufacturers ceasing to supply essential after-sales services or spare parts for older products, not to mention smart phones, mobiles, iPods, or iPads. It is actually surprising in how many areas processes of 'destructive creation' exist that hinder prolonged usage and induce customers to migrate continuously to newer models.

Elsewhere (Soete, 2010), I have argued how this 'conspicuous innovation' consumption growth path, which in its environmental impact and ecological footprint will be unsustainable in the developed world and increasingly so in the rapidly emerging country world, ultimately warrants a shift in the process of research and innovation (see Figure 6.1).

6.3. From Innovation for the Tip to the Bottom of the Income Pyramid

In many ways, and as highlighted in the Calvano model, the focus of industrial research and innovation has been on continuous quality improvements of existing and new consumer goods, enlarging continuously the demand for such improved quality or new consumer goods. It formed the basis of the growth model as it emerged over the post-war period in the USA, Europe, and Japan, which then generated its own infinite demand for more material consumer goods—a continuous growth path of rising income with increasing consumer goods' production *and* consumption (Pasinetti, 1981). The continuously rising industrial R&D efforts in high-income countries appeared to match perfectly the continuously rising incomes of the citizens of those countries, leading to a continuous enlargement of their consumption basket with new, better designed, or better performing, products. The initial demand for such quality improvements often arose from extreme professional, sometimes

---

[4] See for example the legal case brought against Apple in 2003 with respect to the planned obsolescence of the battery life of the batteries in the iPod.

[5] The Imelda Marco syndrome as Paul David (2012, p. 511) put it: 'The near pathological impulse to push the rate of innovation to be ever-faster needs a medical psychiatric designation, and I propose to refer to it as the innovation fetish's "Imelda Marco syndrome"—in memory of a famous instance of the uncontrollable, obsessive accumulation of more and more pairs of women' shoes (another, richly documented fetish object).'

military, circumstances, but thanks to the media—which typically would emphasize the prestige image of such professional use through symbolic figures such as sport athletes or movie actors—the average, non-professional consumer could easily become convinced that he or she was also in need of new goods with such technologically sophisticated and professional quality characteristics, even though those characteristics might ultimately add only marginally to one's utility. In certain respects, the highest income groups in society, the '*tip*' of the income pyramid, acted often as the first, 'guinea pig', group in society, contributing happily to the innovation monopoly rents of the innovating firm. So a continuous circle of research was set in motion, centring on the search for new qualitative features[6] to be added to existing goods.

As highlighted earlier, in Calvano's model, this '*professional-use driven*' innovation circle has been the main source for extracting innovation rents from consumer goods—ranging from consumer electronics, sport goods, shoe wear, household equipment, and computers to mobile telephony, medical diagnostics, sleeping comfort, and so on—with an inconveniently long *physical* lifetime.[7]

The need for a shift in research on innovation in private businesses away from such conspicuous innovation has been popularized by C. K. Prahalad (2005) in his famous book: *The Fortune at the Bottom of the Pyramid* with the provocative subtitle 'Eradicating Poverty Through Profits'. One of the best-known Prahalad examples of a Bottom of the Pyramid (BoP) innovation is the multiple-fuel stove innovation developed for the rural poor, in which cow dung and biomass (sticks and grass) can be used as cooking fuels. Traditionally, these fuels are used in an extremely inefficient way and are dangerous to use, due to the smoke inhaled from indoor fires. Since Prahalad's book, there has been a flood of similar examples of BoP innovations being primarily introduced by foreign, large, multinational corporations from developed countries in developing countries, sometimes in poor rural villages, sometimes in urban slums.[8] This is where BoP innovation takes on, in my view, a new meaning in line with its creative destruction nature.

---

[6] One may think of improved sound, vision and clarity, miniaturization and mobility, weight and shock/water resistance, feeling and ergonomiticity, and so on.

[7] The worldwide risks of this relatively straightforward professional-use driven innovation strategy for existing global multinational corporations have increased significantly, not least because of globalization. While the world market for new innovative goods appears at first sight gigantic, and without any doubt sufficient to recoup investments relatively quickly, the huge research, development, prototype, and global marketing costs, coupled with ever-increasing numbers of competing international players, means that the length of time that a company can enjoy its innovation rents is diminishing very rapidly. Hence, despite the growing high-income classes in the large emerging BRIC economies, the new generation of goods being sold to the emerging high-income classes in those countries will be insufficient in actual earning opportunities to fund both the shift towards mass production and the development of the next technology generation of the good in question. Having developed incredibly technologically sophisticated new goods, many firms are encountering global sales problems over a much contracted product life cycle with increased competition and rapidly saturated markets.

[8] For some examples in the sanitation area, see Ramani (2008). For an overview of the BoP literature, see Weehuizen (2008).

In this sense, the notion of *'grassroot innovation'* developed by Anil Gupta, one of our close colleagues at Ahmadabad, can be considered as the endogenous, intrinsic version of Prahalad's external, top-down version of BoP innovation. The innovation process is now in the true destructive creation sense likely to be reversed, starting with the design phase that will be confronted directly with the need to find functional solutions to some of the particular BoP users' framework conditions. This will involve not just the need to bring the product onto the market at a substantially lower price than existing goods, as Prahalad emphasized, but also a clear adaptation to the sometimes poor local infrastructure facilities with respect to energy delivery systems, water access, transport infrastructure, digital access, and so on. *Autonomy* is the key word here. It is no surprise that the most rapidly spreading technology in developing countries has been mobile communication, with currently more than three billion users worldwide. Freedom from the need for high-quality energy, water, or broadband networks is undoubtedly one of the most pervasive drivers for BoP innovation. Another might well be *'cradle to cradle'* sustainable innovation. The lack of high-quality logistic infrastructure facilities in rural development settings might well imply that once goods are sold, the repair and/or central recollection of obsolete goods or their parts would be expensive. By contrast, local re-use along the principles of cradle-to-cradle might well be a new form of sustainable grassroot innovation. It is in this sense that one might talk about *'appropriate innovation'*, and there seems to be some analytical similarity with the old notion of 'appropriate technology'.[9]

The feedback from BoP users and from design developers upstream towards more applied research assistance, even fundamental research in some of the core research labs of Western firms, might well become one of the most interesting examples of the reverse transfer of technology (from the South to the North), reinvigorating and motivating the research community in our highly developed world increasingly 'in search of relevance'. Not surprisingly, the main focus within the developed world at the moment is on BoP innovations in the health area, a sector where applied medical research is increasingly dominated by access to new technologically sophisticated equipment and much less by more down-to-earth research questions about such matters (and the list is non-exhaustive) as antibiotic resistance, infectious diseases, or resistant tuberculosis. Not surprisingly, health is the sector most in need for what could be called a 'bottom of the pyramid' research reprioritization.

---

[9] The notion of appropriate technology was, of course, much more formalized in terms of a rational set of economically determined 'choices of technique' (Sen, 1968), depending very much on capital-labour substitution possibilities. The term 'appropriate innovation', by contrast, is much more open.

6.4. From Financial Innovations to Systemic Failure

I now turn to my second case of 'destructive creation': the archetypal case of financial innovations. The latter have actually been described as a 'destructive creation' type of innovation[10] and have by now been well covered in the popular economics literature.[11]

Personally, I disagree with economists claiming that the financial product innovations of the last 10 to 20 years (broadly since the advent of digital information technologies) like Credit Default Swaps (CDS) or securitization were just 'wind-making' innovations or illustrations of the lack of knowledge about risk management exhibited by financial experts. These new financial products were, at the time they were introduced, truly innovations in the real sense of the term. Back in 2005, Alan Greenspan observed that:

Deregulation and the newer information technologies have joined, in the United States and elsewhere, to advance flexibility in the financial sector. Financial stability may turn out to have been the most important contributor to the evident significant gains in economic stability over the past two decades. Historically, banks have been at the forefront of financial intermediation, in part because their ability to leverage offers an efficient source of funding. But in periods of severe financial stress, such leverage too often brought down banking institutions and, in some cases, precipitated financial crises that led to recession or worse. But recent regulatory reform, coupled with innovative technologies, has stimulated the development of financial products, such as asset-backed securities, collateral loan obligations, and credit default swaps that facilitate the dispersion of risk...These increasingly complex financial instruments have contributed to the development of a far more flexible, efficient, and hence resilient financial system than the one that existed just a quarter-century ago. (Greenspan, 2005)

Clearly the systemic impact of such global 'dispersion of risk' tools combined with the deregulation[12] of the banking system was incorrectly assessed by the US Fed Chairman. Regulators did not pay attention or were unaware of the systemic risks stemming from those new innovative opportunities. This was even more the case after the sceptics in the Basel I process were ignored,

[10] For example, the common definition found on the Internet: 'destructive creation was popularized during the financial crisis of 2007–9, when large banks and insurance companies ceased to exist as a result of financial innovations' (see <http://www.investopedia.com/terms/d/destructive-creation.asp#ixzz1cHoBVswo>).

[11] See, for instance, the debate on whether 'financial innovation boosts economic growth' between Ross Levine (in favour) and Joe Stiglitz (against) reported in *The Economist* (see <http://www.economist.com/debate/overview/166>), or the article by Bruce Nussbaum on 'The Culture of Finance—Why Financial Innovation Failed', *Business Week*, 13 January 2010 (see <http://www.businessweek.com/innovate/NussbaumOnDesign/archives/2010/01/the_culture_of.html>).

[12] There is today probably a broad consensus that the repeal of the so-called Glass–Steagel Act in the USA in 1999 opened the door for calamitous 'destructive creation' innovations.

instead giving way to the lobbyists of banks engaged in creating various balance-sheet tricks. In short, society sorely missed an appropriate innovation assessment tool.

The result is that the current stock market value of banks, on the basis of Datastream's bank index, is (at the time of writing) at a level broadly similar to that at the end of December 1985, over a quarter of a century ago. As the Dutch economic journalist, Maarten Schinkel, recently put it in a Dutch newspaper (the NRC) in his column entitled *A quarter century of money thrown away*:

> Imagine all those mergers, demergers, strategic plans. All this bragging of investment bankers, of the buying up of very expensive teams from competitors. The payment to personnel that apparently possessed supernatural talents with ever more bonuses. The explorations into unknown territories with financial derivatives, structured finance, or the financing through South Korea of a motorway in Pakistan. All these measures, enterprises and strategic plans have always been defended with the ultimate argument of the banking CEOs: shareholder's value. So...where is it? (Schinkel, 2011)

Our liberalized, deregulated financial sector represents in many ways the perfect example of destructive creation based on short-term opportunities—yesterday and today. What, then, is the solution to financial innovations? The answers are actually well known to specialists.[13] Unfortunately, the specialists are paid best by those who create the damage by making money using financial innovations.

6.5. Conclusions

The two examples given here of innovation through a process of 'destructive creation' leading to long-term systemic risks both require a highly sophisticated regulatory framework that is flexible enough to respond to those perverse 'innovative opportunities'. In each case, as I have tried to argue, this calls for expertise with public agencies adequately staffed with high quality personnel and sufficiently independent to be able to resist the pressures of firms seeking new, short-term innovative opportunities driven more by planned obsolescence than by true innovation, as highlighted in the first case; or the financial interests of sectoral and individual traders, as in the case

---

[13] They include: the return of transparency into accountancy; forbidding destabilizing "'naked"' short sales; banning the hiding of information through various off-balance-sheet constructs; responsibility on the part of the selling agent for the veracity and completeness of the information given; dropping sales provisions not in favour of pricing of advice but rather in favour of payment of agents in proportion to the stock of contract values; clear personal responsibility for the screening of purchased packages; and so on-the list is by no means exhaustive.

of fast, destructive financial innovations described in the second example. In short, the innovation processes described here do not call for 'less public sector', but rather for a more qualified, independent public sector attracting people with advanced qualifications who are at the service of the public interest and who will try to make the best out of the continuous flow of innovative challenges that society is continuously throwing up.

Acknowledgements

In writing this chapter I have greatly benefited from comments from a large number of people, and in particular Esben Sloth Andersen, Paul David, Jan Fagerberg, Bengt-Åke Lundvall, Ben Martin, Pari Patel, and Bart Verspagen. A first version of this chapter was presented on the occasion of the Marie Jahoda Lecture 2011 held at SPRU at Sussex University in October 2011, and a second version on the occasion of the Tans Lecture 2011 held at Maastricht University in November 2011. A third version was presented at the Lundvall Symposium in Aalborg in February 2012.

References

Anderson, C. (2006). *The Long Tail: Why the Future of Business Is Selling Less of More*. New York: Hyperion Books.

Arthur, B. (1989). 'Competing Technologies, Increasing Returns and Lock-In by Historical Events', *Economic Journal*, 99: 106–31.

Calvano, E. (2010), 'Destructive Creation', SSE/EFI Working Paper Series in Economics and Finance, No. 653, December, mimeo.

David, P. A. (1985). 'Clio and the Economics of QWERTY', *American Economic Review*, 75: 332–7.

David, P. A. (2001), 'Path Dependence, Its Critics and the Quest for Historical Economics', in P. Garrouste and S. Ionnides (eds), *Evolution and Path Dependence in Economic Ideas: Past and Present*. Cheltenham: Elgar, 15–40.

David, P. A. (2012), 'The Innovation Fetish among the *Economoi*: Introduction to the Panel on Innovation Incentives, Institutions, and Economic Growth', in J. Lerner, and S. Stern (eds), *The Rate and Direction of Inventive Activity Revisited*. Chicago: University of Chicago Press, 509–14.

Greenspan, A. (2005), 'Economic Flexibility, Remarks by Chairman Alan Greenspan Before the National Italian American Foundation', Washington, DC, 12 October (downloaded May 2013 from <http://www.federalreserve.gov/boarddocs/speeches/2005/20051012/default.htm>).

Mann, L. B. and Folts, J. D. (2004). 'Effects of Ethanol and Other Constituents of Alcoholic Beverages on Coronary Heart Disease: A Review', *Pathophysiology*, 10: 105–12.

O'Brien, T. (2010). 'Guinness Ends "Good for You" Promotion', *The Irish Times*, 3 March 2010.

Pasinetti, L. (1981). *Structural Change and Economic Growth: A Theoretical Essay on the Dynamics of the Wealth of Nations*. Cambridge: Cambridge University Press.

Prahalad, C. K. (2005). *The Fortune at the Bottom of the Pyramid*. Upper Saddle River, NJ: Wharton School Publishing.

Ramani, S. V. (2008), 'Playing in Invisible Markets: Innovations in the Market for Toilets to Harness the Economic Power of the Poor', UNU-MERIT Working Paper 2008-012 (downloaded May 2013 from <http://www.merit.unu.edu/publications/wppdf/2008/wp2008-012.pdf>).

Schinkel, M. (2011), 'Een kwart eeuw van weggegooid geld', *NRC*, 28 October: p. 26.

Sen, A. K. (1968). *Choice of Techniques: An Aspect of the Theory of Planned Economic Development* (third edition). Oxford: Blackwell.

Soete, L. (2010). 'From Science and Technology to Innovation for Development', *African Technology Development Forum Journal*, 6(3/4): 9–14.

Stoneman, P. (2001). *The Economics of Technological Diffusion*. Oxford: Wiley-Blackwell.

Weehuizen, R. (2008), 'Innovation for the Bottom of the Pyramid', March, UNU-MERIT, mimeo.

Part II

Challenges for Innovation Studies in the Years Ahead

7

Innovation Studies at Maturity

W. Edward Steinmueller

7.1. Introduction[1]

We hear much discussion today that our field of study[2] has reached a state of maturity. It is certainly true that many of the names we associate with its mid-twentieth century origins are no longer with us and we cherish those who remain. The experience of individuals' lives shapes their perception and often expression. In our role as teachers and mentors, we are consistently confronted by the challenges of rebuilding the foundations of understanding with new students. Student often begin with a mix of pre-conceptions (often misconceptions) and prototypical novelties of understanding that can contribute to new insights and advance understanding. Working with students and younger professionals in our field provides us with opportunities to reflect on how people absorb the existing corpus of knowledge and also the ways in which new phenomenon in the world fit into existing frameworks or require modifying or extending those frameworks.

My thesis is that the field of innovation is beginning to have the features of a Kuhnian paradigm where it will be appropriate to characterize some of the existing corpus of knowledge as 'normal science'. To the extent this is

[1] With many thanks to my discussants at the symposium, Patrick Llerena and Bart Verspagen, as well as the other participants, to Robin Mansell, and to the editors of this volume, all of whom contributed to this work, often with trenchant criticism.

[2] Our field is variously referred to as innovation studies, the economics of technological change, or science, technology, and innovation (STI) studies, with the usage governed in part by where scholars and programmes are situated in universities—for example business schools, economics departments, or inter-disciplinary centres or departments respectively. As I note later, I also include scholars of science, technology, and society, and science and technology studies (both fields sharing the STS acronym) in the community that I will be considering in this chapter.

true, the field may be said to have a degree if maturity at which it is appropriate to consider the desirability of developing and strengthening the learning resources and some of the institutions conventionally associated with normal science. This chapter has three aims: first to assess the claim regarding maturity, second to trace the implications of maturity for professional practice including education in the field, and third to examine the robustness of existing understanding in face of new challenges that the field faces in this century. In examining the claim to maturity, principal questions are whether (i) the foundations have been constructed for arriving at a consensus on elementary theory and empirical findings; and (ii) whether it is possible to distinguish between research that is principally an elaboration of these foundations and research that seeks to extend the existing foundations. It seems likely that the very dynamism of science, technology, and innovation processes will present a continuing stream of new issues that requires the revision and even the possible rejection of established understandings. In pursuing this investigation, I begin by examining the state of our field and the supporting pedagogical and existing institutional structures we have constructed.

7.2. The Argument for Innovation Studies as Normal Science

In a work that has been particularly influential in the study of science and related bodies of knowledge,[3] Thomas Kuhn argues for the existence of scientific paradigms that are defined by a theory which accounts for phenomena using a particular language and around which experimental evidence and theoretical elaboration occurs until interrupted by a discontinuity that initiates a 'revolutionary' period in which a new paradigm may emerge. Thus, for Kuhn, science generally begins with phenomenology, the identification and delineation of a set of phenomena that come to define the field of study. In the case of our field, three phenomena have been central: (i) the incidence and prevalence of innovation; (ii) the organization and support of scientific and technological development; and (iii) the relation between science, technology, and society. I will not belabour the nature of these phenomena, which will already be familiar to most readers. Instead, I will focus on the challenges that these phenomena present in the education of young researchers. Each of these areas has been an 'attractor' for individuals to enter our field as well as providing a framework for research.

---

[3] Kuhn (1996); Kuhn first expressed these ideas in 1962.

The Incidence and Prevalence of Innovation

The circumstances of human lives are obviously, and sometimes very force-fully, influenced by capacities and developments that previous generations did not experience. In making sense of the world, it would be hard to avoid considering the role of technological change—including both new outputs and improvements in productivity. Until the middle of the twentieth century, however, economists took the history of economic growth to be primarily the consequence of the accumulation of the inputs of capital and labour with the recognition that productivity improvements would add an extra boost to the accumulation process. Changes in productivity were, however, recognized as uneven over the business cycle and only tenuously linked to 'technical change' affecting how these inputs could be used to produce outputs.

In demonstrating that productivity change rather than capital and labour accumulation dominated the twentieth century growth experience, Solow (1956) launched a revolution that had far greater impact in stimulating interest in the nature of technological change than it had (at least initially) on economics. Solow referred to 'technical change' as the factor respon-sible for productivity growth while Abramovitz (1956, p. 11) referred to the increase in output not explained by accumulation as a 'measure of our ignorance', noting how little was actually known about the determinants of productivity change. As Solow admitted, his use of the term 'technical change' was very broad, involving not only the improvement of production techniques but also the effects of new products and changes in organiza-tional arrangements and routines.[4] Nonetheless, technical change was gen-erally taken by economists to be a factor affecting the 'supply side' of the market and, in particular, the commercialization of invention (novel ideas and artefacts). The broader term, innovation, has emerged as the more com-prehensive (and in some cases, less precise) term to refer to all phenomena associated with novelty and change, including the economic idea of techni-cal change.[5]

Although Solow suggested the relative importance of technical change and innovation, he did not provide an explanation of the origins of these changes nor how they might be linked to changes in productivity. Investigation of these issues required a better explanation of 'the rate and direction of inven-tive activity', which was to be a part of the title of a 1962 conference with that title (Nelson, 1962). In the lead article of the conference, Kuznets (1962, p. 32) suggests the need for the professional study of human capacities for invention

[4] He was arguing that technical change was anything that might shift the aggregate production function rather than representing a movement along it (through accumulation).

[5] This broad use of the term is ironic given its initial use to differentiate the processes of inven-tion from the (later) process of commercializing invention (see Freeman, 1974).

and the population of inventors.[6] A key contribution in this early period was the idea of diffusion—that is considering how, once an innovation existed, it spread within society—which was addressed from the viewpoints of economics by Griliches (1958) and of sociology by Rogers (1962).

Despite these early contributions to the conceptual framing of ideas about invention and innovation, the issue of their incidence and prevalence remained for some time an abstraction which, although influenced by Schumpeter's (1947) views on entrepreneurs as the agents of creative destruction, lacked a specific focus in studies of the organization of innovation processes (also a theme of Schumpeter). This situation was improved by a renewed attention to the nature of industrial innovation by the Sappho project at SPRU during the period 1967–70 (see Curnow and Moring, 1968), and by two other landmark empirical studies, namely Jewkes et al. (1969), and Langrish et al. (1972). Combined with his own work, this allowed Chris Freeman to write a pioneering summary and synthesis of the state of knowledge regarding industrial innovation (Freeman, 1974).

Is there a basis for characterizing the developments in understanding of the relation between invention, innovation, and productivity that began towards the end of the 1950s and continued for the next three decades as a 'Kuhnian revolution'? Reasons favouring an affirmative answer include the increased focus on phenomena that had previously been viewed as incidental or ancillary to economic life, the articulation of a specific language for considering these phenomena, and a growing community of researchers engaged in their empirical study using a variety of models that were, to a degree, standardized. The extent of standardization of concepts and methods was, of course, initially limited, but included the distinction between invention and innovation, the role of diffusion, and the observation of the uneven industrial distribution of innovative activity. The resulting knowledge base and research agenda is a complex and systemic body of knowledge, more akin to the biological and ecological sciences than physics—but it is one that can be conveyed at various levels of granularity. It feeds and is fed by quantitative measures and indicators, such as patent and authorship counts, R&D investment levels, and employment of individuals in roles supporting invention and the commercialization of invention. It may be debated whether the result is sufficiently broadly accepted to mark the end of a Kuhnian shift of paradigm, but many of the elements of normal science are present.

The incidence and prevalence of innovation is, of course, not a closed subject. The landscape and associated factors co-shaping innovation are not only

---

[6] Some years later, a work addressing these issues was published by Neumeyer and Stedman (1971).

changing but so are the ways in which knowledge is exchanged, the relationships between supporting bodies of knowledge and innovative activity, and the nature of demand for innovations, both intermediate and final. If we are to compare this field with those on which Kuhn focused, such as physics, there is an absence of 'closure', in large measure because the processes that are being examined are subject to evolution and transformation by experimentation and experience.

The Organization and Support for Scientific and Technological Development

In the same year as Solow's article, Nelson (1959) opened up to investigation the economic logic of scientific research and began to consider the interplay between public and private rationales, that is between market failure and the adequacy of the profit incentive. He was joined by Arrow (1962) and together their works provided a coherent economic rationale for advancing Vannevar Bush's *Endless Frontier* (Bush, 1945), in other words, the public support for scientific research in return for the prospect of social return. Nonetheless, efforts to measure the economic returns from science funding have remained mixed.[7] In addition, the deterministic model by which greater science funding is expected to lead inexorably to a wider range of commercial application, referred to as the linear model, has been partially abandoned in favour of more interactive and recursive understandings of the relation between science and innovation, such as that put forward by Kline and Rosenberg (1986). A more expansive set of roles for collective purpose and action in fostering connections between science, technology, and development has been developed with an abandonment of the earlier generation's faith in the certainties of technology transfer and R&D portfolio management. Nonetheless, it is still claimed that these connections can be enhanced by appropriate policies designed and implemented by governmental authority.

The tools and rationales for these interventions continue to expand. For example, increasing recognition that 'technology transfer' is so problematic that the term verges on being an oxymoron has led to policies for fostering new scientific networks and encouraging researcher mobility. The related idea that 'knowledge is sticky' (i.e. it is difficult to transfer or exchange over longer geographical and cultural distances) has led to research seeking early detection of the emergence of new sites of specialization and policies that

---

[7] Illustrations of these efforts include National Science Foundation (1969), Office of the Director of Defense Research and Engineering (1969), Mansfield (1980), and David, Mowery, et al. (1992). These and other studies are compared in Steinmueller (1994).

would encourage 'cluster' or regional development to take advantage of the greater efficiency of localized knowledge exchange. Some of these interventions have a rather slender evidence base to support their application and suffer from the opportunistic capture of the purposes or funding of these interventions by their recipients. Efforts to learn from the experience with interventions has fostered a literature in policy evaluation, again with some of the features of 'normal' science regarding the standardization of methods and the growth of both literature and research communities.

Innovation management has outgrown the narrow confines of engineering and R&D management where it originated in the 1950s and 1960s, and perhaps is the most expansive branch of our field. It provides a distillation of the vast array of experience in stimulating, moderating, and directing the changes associated with technological development. Whilst studies of innovation management often obscure or ignore the connections between science and technology, they nonetheless offer some guide to those who might attempt to overcome organizational inertia in order to establish something new. I admit to some scepticism about the scientific nature of management studies, where publication often seems to involve little more than new catchphrases or demonstrating, once again, that doing everything well is an advantage. Nonetheless, innovation management has also matured in its deployment of a growing array of standardized concepts and language.

Our field of study shares some of the historical burden of political economics. We lived through most of the twentieth century with two diametrically opposed ideologies with regard to social organization—state socialism and unrestrained 'free market' capitalism—but also the practical reality of the mixed economy in Western Europe and elsewhere. In our era, market triumphalism, at its peak, seemed to offer the prospect of an end to the history of major social and political movements and a future involving only incremental adjustment in the ways in which the pursuit of profit might be bounded or regulated. In the last couple of decades, few voices in academia have been offering or even acknowledging alternatives to the centrality of the market as the way in which human affairs can and should be organized. During this time, our field has been deeply engaged with the practical education of those who would seek to improve regulation and exert greater social control over processes of technological change. This may be a matter of some concern if the maturity of our field means that the tools and techniques it offers are seen as having their principal value in making marginal improvements to the existing range of systems rather than in challenging the organization and carrying out innovation with the aim of more fundamental societal transformation.

The Relation between Science, Technology, and Society

The previous two sections have considered phenomena with direct ties to economic and policy analysis. Research in these areas is principally concerned with the role of innovation in influencing growth, employment, and productivity. However, science, technology, and innovation are human pursuits with values that are not denominated only in monetary terms. The social and cultural values of science, and its precursor, natural philosophy, have provoked study and reflection since ancient times. Fields of study such as the history of science and technology are antecedent to two more recent fields of study, both bearing the STS acronym—science, technology, and society, and science and technology studies. Both of these fields originate from the late 1960s and were first motivated by a concern for preserving and extending the values of science for future generations. According to Roy (1999), the precursors to science, technology, and society studies were largely located in history and philosophy. Those motivated to depart from these traditions sought to raise questions about the 'adequacy of typical college curricula in preparing students to understand, serve, or lead our technology-dominated culture'.[8]

The more critical tone of science and technology studies is reflected by Edge (1995, p. 5) who depicts the field as standing in opposition to the received view of 'science and technology as asocial, impersonal activities—a positivistic, even mechanistic, picture of an endeavour that defines its own logic and momentum, and legitimates its progress by appealing to the assumption that the authority of nature is independent of, and prior to, the authority of society'. There are gulfs between these perspectives as well as between the more instrumental political and economic viewpoints discussed in the previous two sections. While I do not see these gulfs as having been bridged, there is at least a more frequent ferry service connecting their respective shores. Even as we consider issues of science and technology policy in terms of promoting the best use of human knowledge, we are also living in a world where the precautionary principle and the democratization of technology assessment now play an increasingly central and progressive role. The view that science is a social enterprise that may be directed towards social purposes, while controversial, is another of the ways in which the prior authority of nature has been practically contested.

The subjects that have recently provoked the greatest impetus to critical perspectives of science and technology studies and the more instrumental approaches of economic and policy studies are climate change and sustainability. The fact that environmental externalities span national boundaries as

---

[8] Roy (1999, p. 461).

well as sectoral systems of innovation has invigorated the study and practice of regulation in these areas. Policy interventions in areas such as niche management and participatory governance have provided opportunities to combine social and technological insights (e.g. regarding behavioural change, engineering constraints and opportunities, and the foundations of production and consumption). Indeed, the scale of technological change required to make a difference has revived thinking about the sustainability of mass production and consumption in the wealthier countries and the prospects for reproducing these patterns as other nations achieve higher levels of income.[9] In this respect, we have come full circle from the origins where the certainties of the Atomic Age foundered on the spectres of nuclear winter and silent spring, and propelled critics like Carson (1962), Mumford (1964), or Ellul (1977) to question where our journey was leading.

While often explicitly hostile to economic rationales or theories, the STS community has had no shortage of theories of its own concerning these phenomena. Some of these theories remind us that human agency can be mobilized for darker or more misguided purposes as well as in the Promethean tradition. It would be inappropriate to conclude that either of the STS traditions has reached the maturity associated with normal science. However, if again we consider the field as having emerged from distinct voices like Ellul or Mumford, we find more recent scholars such as Winner (1977), Jasanoff (1990, 2005), or Beck (1992) setting a path for another generation of scholars. These views are becoming more intertwined and the communities that engage with their work have become more interactive (although sometimes engaging in sectarian strife), a process resembling that characterizing at least the early stages of the emergence of normal science. In terms of professional organization, STS is well-represented by professional associations and journals.[10]

In terms of the maturation of the broad field of studies spanning science, technology, and innovation studies, as well as STS, it is reasonable to conclude that a development of maturation has occurred in the process of development. Whether this constitutes normal science as compared to physics or chemistry, or indeed social sciences such as economics or behavioural psychology, depends upon what one might expect from normal science in the case of social sciences. Several of the basic features of normal science might be taken to be: (i) the emergence of a body of knowledge that is considered a foundation for further investigation; (ii) a vocabulary of terms of art that

---

[9] For example, see Warde and Southerton (2012).

[10] For example, the Society for Social Studies of Science, the European Association for the Study of Science and Technology (EASST), and Japanese Society for Science and Technology Studies. Some of the journals published from this community include *Science as Culture*, *Technology and Culture*, *Science and Public Policy*, *Social Studies of Science*, and *Science, Technology and Human Values*.

serve to define a set of views on the phenomena relevant for investigation; and (iii) a capacity to distinguish novel and path-breaking research from research that is primarily confirmatory or supportive of an existing body of results. In this sense, the earlier discussion has illustrated the emergence of a normal science of science, technology, and innovation studies and some steps towards this status in the case of the two fields bearing the initials STS. Alternatively, if the expectation is that normal science should represent a level of standardization that supports the replication of experimental results or, indeed, the establishment of physical constants that are invariant over time within a frame of theoretical reference, very little, if any, social science can be described as having reached this level of maturity.[11]

There are two larger aims of discussing the Kuhnian framework. First, considered in the next section, is to consider what the progress towards normal science might mean for the development of pedagogy and for the intellectual institutions of this research community. Second is to question the robustness of the current paradigm of understanding in the face of immanent challenges, and this aim is pursued in the penultimate section of this chapter.

7.3. Pedagogical and Institutional Implications of our Field as Normal Science

If one accepts the principal conclusion of the foregoing discussion, then it follows that the education of new entrants to our field is increasingly one that requires a structure and organization that is characteristic of other areas of human knowledge in which a paradigm has become normalized. Such a structure would involve commensurate vocabularies and standardized measures and indicators for studying recognized phenomena. It would also be organized so that there was a clear ladder leading from common elementary understandings and observations to an intermediate level of theory and findings that are applicable and transferable (with reservations) across contexts, and finally to advanced levels at which contradictions and contestations of the intermediate or 'received' level of theory and observation are entertained.

Constituted in this way, it would be possible to regard the field as 'free standing', even if some elements continued to draw heavily upon disciplinary specializations and methods. To be 'free standing' is to deny the exclusive priority of any existing discipline in addressing the range of phenomena considered by the field as relevant issues and problems, and instead accords

---

[11] Exceptions may exist in cognitive behavioural psychology and some areas of behavioural economics, both of which have adopted experimental methods supporting the replication and standardization of results.

priority to a collective, networked, and inter-disciplinary approach to these phenomenon and problems (Klein, 2010). Alternatively, one might argue for a multi-disciplinary programme that emphasizes the discourse between different bodies of knowledge developed and maintained within disciplinary boundaries. I will argue that the current state of affairs falls short of either of these objectives with regard to pedagogical tools, professional institutions, and communicative presence. Thus, unlike the body of knowledge, which I have argued is approaching and, in some cases, attaining the features of normal science, the means for reproducing, sustaining, and recruiting researchers to participate in this field are underdeveloped.

My thesis is that it would be a desirable aim to provide new and basic pedagogical aids (what might be called introductory texts, even if this may unduly particularize the nature of that particular aid) for students to master a range of ideas forming the foundations of our field. To sustain this thesis, it is important to address several questions. First, in pursuing this aim, is there a particular pedagogical or epistemic value in rejecting the primacy of a disciplinary position, such as economic or management studies? Taking the view that knowledge of the field is best comprehended in an inter-disciplinary way, that is by an active synthesis of disciplinary approaches, this question suggests an immediate affirmative answer. If, instead, comprehension is best achieved by proceeding from a well-established disciplinary base, it will be better to begin by first mastering a particular discipline. Even in a discipline-based approach to pedagogy, it seems desirable to signal the existence of links and interactions between the separate strands of our field. Second, even if it is preferable on epistemic or pedagogical grounds to pursue a more inter-disciplinary agenda, is such an aim practical in the modern academy? That is, where in the modern university would the use of such learning aids be likely to occur? I am less certain about this. Much of the value of the university stems from its capacity to maintain and build upon the past, a feature that creates a conservative bias that is most apparent in the dynamics of the disciplines. This bias is often antithetical to inter-disciplinary or multi-disciplinary inquiry and instruction. Moreover, in many countries, universities are being asked to produce 'qualified' graduates in established disciplines that, in theory, prepare them to make an immediate contribution to society. Third, and in partial response to this pressure for qualifications, might the pedagogical aids developed for an inter-disciplinary or multi-disciplinary approach provide a better defined quality of graduate education and thereby provide a more coherent rationale for recruitment and professional identification? My answer to this question is 'yes', an answer that also indicates the possibility that our field might more rapidly advance its maturity, and better establish its identity, by reducing its reliance on a particular discipline (such as economics). A more complete argument for this conclusion involves considering current research and education challenges, the subject of the penultimate section of this chapter.

The generally affirmative answers to the questions posed in the previous paragraph nevertheless require an important qualification. Although I have argued that all of the specific areas within our field have matured to some degree, this maturity is uneven. For example, one might say that particular issues in the economics of technological change have, for some time, been investigated in a normal science framework. A case in point would be the economics of technological adoption (or diffusion studies) of innovations, where a steady stream of work (e.g. Griliches, 1958; David, 1966, 1971) has created the foundation for a vast body of research.[12] It is worth noting, however, that the economics literature on the diffusion of innovations largely ignores an equally vast literature stemming from Rogers (1962), an example of the impact of disciplinary 'silos' on the study of innovation. Whether differences in the maturity of specific areas could lead towards a multi-disciplinary approach favouring economics, but not excluding other disciplines, may be a question of authorship.[13]

Viewed from a disciplinary perspective, the argument for the inadequacy of pedagogical guides is less supportable. For example, in the area of the economics of innovation, Freeman and Soete (1997) continue to offer a powerful template for understanding the phenomenology of innovation as well as touching upon some of the issues of economic policy (although largely excluding issues of institutional frameworks or regulation). More evocative of the need for reform of economic theory is the aging but still relevant collection edited by Dosi et al. (1988) and the continuing appeal of Nelson and Winter (1982) on evolutionary economics. Perhaps of equal didactic value is a new generation of handbooks, some of which—such as Fagerberg et al. (2005) for innovation studies, Stoneman (1995) and Hall and Rosenberg (2010) for economics, Moed et al. (2004) for the phenomenology of informational outputs of invention and innovation processes, and the authoritative handbooks in STS edited by Jasanoff et al. (1995) and Hackett et al. (2007)—can greatly accelerate a student's progress in entering our field. Some of the gaps in the works mentioned here are filled by additional works: for example, in the area of development by Ruttan (2001), in the area of science policy advice by Jasanoff (1990), in the case of intellectual property by Jaffe and Lerner (2006) or Carrier (2009), and in the area of management by Tidd and Bessant (2009). This abbreviated account illustrates two facts: first, that

---

[12] Similar claims may be made for other areas of the economics of technological change, summaries for many of which can be found in Fagerberg et al. (2005) or Hall and Rosenberg (2010).

[13] For example, Davis et al. (1972), a text that helped modernize instruction in American economic history, relied on no less than 12 editors, each of whom had distinct expertise in different facets of the field.

there is a wealth of resources for specific facets of our field; and second, that a broader view revealing how these related literatures are related is missing. In practice, building the contextual knowledge to support this broader viewpoint is currently a rather 'hit and miss' affair, dependent upon the breadth of knowledge embodied in individual scholars. Arguably, a more synthetic work cast in the form of a textbook is both feasible and desirable.

One of the reasons that we have been able to approach normal science without creating advanced textbooks is because of our 'broad church' tradition. A consequence of the 'broad church' is that ecumenical gatherings are a challenge. The Schumpeter Society and DRUID are vitally important gathering places but are dominated by economists and business scholars. Other gatherings, such as the European Association of Evolutionary Political Economics or the Triple Helix conferences also exhibit sectarian tendencies. We have not done very well in including the fields of practice from further afield such as the history or sociology of science and technology, policy sciences, or innovation management.

Efforts to organize and deliver advanced training to PhD students have become more challenging over the years. Summer school efforts were vitally important from the 1990s through to the first years of this century, when such programmes would attract individuals pursuing graduate studies in their own universities with one or two senior colleagues but with few others at their university sympathetic to or even capable of comprehending their research agenda. These summer school programmes have become less common in Europe as the result of funding pressures. A more limited collection of doctoral student conferences organized in the USA by the Consortium on Competitiveness and Cooperation (University of California, Berkeley), in Europe by the Danish Research Unit on Industrial Dynamics (DRUID) of the Universities of Aalborg and Copenhagen, and on a global basis by Globelics, as well as student organized conferences such as SPRU's DPhil Day, offer young researchers the opportunity to meet and learn from one another. Considering the role of such programmes and activities in the future is part of the debate between the inter-disciplinary and multi-disciplinary programmes. Whatever future such summer schools and graduate student conferences may have, ways to augment the circulation of young researchers among institutions seem essential to forge the professional and personal associations that foster a closer knit community.

In the Information Age, we are far behind many other fields and disciplines. Although there are some very accomplished websites promoting specific research institutes or confederations, particularly MERIT and the DRUID/IKE, some useful project websites (such DIME or PRIME), and some interesting personal webpages, our field is relatively poorly represented on the Internet. This has significant implications for the next generation. The opportunity that young scholars have to learn about our field is severely constrained by this lack of a strong Internet presence. It is ironic that the scholars of technological change should be so reticent in joining the Information Age.

The uneven translation of the normal science features of our field into the usual pedagogical and community tools—whether in the form of texts, conferences, training programmes, or a digital presence—is clearly an impediment to recruitment and cohesion. We can no longer justify these shortcomings by claiming that we are new or small.

7.4. Contemporary Issues and the Challenges to our Field

Turning to the question of our field's capacity to address specific contemporary issues, my argument is that there is a need for a renewed consideration of the debate between inter-disciplinary and multi-disciplinary approaches because of three features of the contemporary policy and research landscape that are likely to persist for some time to come. First, the most productive and fertile areas for advance are at the interstices or juncture points between various disciplines and bodies of knowledge that are pertinent to our field of study, as I will illustrate in this section. Second, the most powerful and sustained motivation for pursuing our field of study stems from the desire to make a difference in the larger world in which academia is embedded. Third, a fundamental understanding of the nature of specific sciences and technologies is a vital, and often underappreciated, force for stabilizing and directing the development of our field of study. These features are conspicuously present in the three examples of challenges that I will now consider. They illustrate the need, at the very least, for greater attention to multi-disciplinary issues and suggest possible gains from an even stronger programme of inter-disciplinary integration.

The Epistemology of Systems: Productive, Labour, and Technological

The analysis of innovation reveals shortcomings in the mainstream or competitive equilibrium economic approach. Nowhere are these more apparent than in the efforts to narrow the global division between rich and poor. Our efforts to reify the past experiences of successful development in a series of lessons that might be applicable to the present have only been partially successful. Recognizing that there is a societal challenge in creating institutions for supporting learning the acquisition of capabilities—what Abramovitz (1989) called social capabilities—means more than wiring up innovation systems into better functioning networks, as scholars like Bengt-Åke Lundvall have long realized and frequently expressed (for example, Lundvall, 1992;

159

Lundvall and Maskell, 2000; and Lundvall et al., 2011). The field of study that we have developed clearly points to important features of this process—the lack of equivalence between information and knowledge, the cumulative process involved in those forms of knowledge that we could call capabilities, and the significance of aligning organizational incentives and cultures to pursue aims that are correctly timed and proportional to needs.

Nonetheless, we do not actually have a very convincing model of how organizations, let alone societies, learn. This is an open space in the landscape of our field, perhaps one that might best be filled by greater interaction with those in the development studies field who have emphasized community participation and interaction. However, these are more often directed at the underemployed and impoverished rather than the working poor or those who are able to achieve a measure of social and economic mobility during their lifetimes. It is an important space because, without it being filled, we do not have a workable baseline for improving on ad hoc approaches to development activities—either in under- or over-developed contexts.

One of the difficulties that we face in filling this space is assembling the empirical knowledge needed. In this task, normal science is our enemy. We encourage young scholars, intent on demonstrating their competence, to seize upon concepts that already exist 'in the literature' to guide their investigations. Many of these concepts are now historically venerable—the historical experience represented by the USA, the experience of catching up undertaken by the late industrializers in Europe and then later in Asia (e.g. Toyota and the Japanese system of manufacturing). These may be relevant guides for some contexts. However, they fail to address systems in which the dominant value added comes about through service innovation, the application of information and communication technologies, or the exploitation of a global information and transport infrastructure comprised of containerized shipping and air freight transport. In this respect, the third feature of the research landscape mentioned at beginning of this section, the need for a more fundamental understanding of the nature of specific sciences and technologies, can serve as a vitally important guide to our investigations.

A fundamental problem that this situation creates for training young researchers is the tension between the essentially conservative processes of creating academic works, which need to be grounded in an established discourse, and the shortcomings of this discourse as perceived by many of those students. This applies not only to the range of tools offered from mainstream economics and the various heterodox departures from it. It also applies to the broader issues surrounding innovation systems, knowledge exchange, and organizational dynamics, particularly as these concepts are applied to a more complex world in which we may wish to question the sustainability (in any meaning of that word) of 'following the leaders'. This amounts to a plea for greater topical heterodoxy to accompany the methodological heterodoxy that many of us have championed over the years.

Tensions Between Convergence and Divergence

The best prospects for the future may lie in a departure from the lessons of the past. Advocating bold departures is neither a new endeavour nor one that should be taken lightly. In the many cases where such departures fail, the boldness of the departure is often correlated with the magnitude of loss. Nonetheless, the depth of the current economic crisis is generating a deeper questioning of the aims of economic growth and the purposes of development. So far, the primary outputs of this discourse are re-examinations of the issues of distributional equity and social justice, and the social and political polarization that is the nearly inevitable consequence of such discussions.

A consequence of the success of our field is that we now think that we have something to say to policy-makers about the course of action that they should pursue. It is worthwhile, however, to ask how often these messages involve implicit or explicit reproduction of policies derived from previous experience and whether that experience is still relevant to the contemporary world. Implicitly, we often are arguing that future paths to higher levels of economic and social development will involve a recapitulation of past paths—we may speak of acceleration, leapfrogging, and other ideas about the possibility of speeding the processes of convergence, but it is an open question what results such actions will produce.

It must be said that this line of thought is one that involves going against the flow. Many countries throughout the world are attempting in a self-conscious way to emulate familiar policies. These tendencies are further amplified by the doctrine of market triumphalism which shapes policies towards liberalization and privatization. However, the market is neither the problem nor the solution. The impact of economic liberalism is the discrediting of public purpose and public administration, which is supported and accompanied by the discrediting of political purposes and processes.

Our field has an uneasy relationship with public administration as well as politics. No doubt this is partially the consequence of the fact that so many of us are economists, a tribe that paradoxically dominates public administration while at the same time harbouring severe doubts about public purposes. This is reflected in our programmes of research and training—we rarely engage with scholars of law, public administration, social policy, or education, and even less often with political theory, ethics, or philosophy. A consequence is that our young researchers who then enter public administration require a lot of on-the-job training to become effective. We are even less likely to be linked to community activism, those people in NGOs and other organizations that are attempting to engage 'civil society' with a series of challenges and opportunities and whose activities constitute a fertile source of organizational and conceptual innovations.

Again, there are specific problems suggested by this line of analysis for the training of young researchers. In examining nascent organizations and experiments, it is difficult to achieve the 'substantiality' typically required of doctoral theses. Comprehending the nature of truly novel social or organizational innovations such as open source software communities or social enterprise requires substantial effort to be devoted to ethnographic and 'descriptive' activities, activities which, often, are disparaged. In either the multi-disciplinary or more integrative inter-disciplinary models for our field's future development, the question is how to legitimize such investigations. One way forward would be to establish awards or prizes for path-breaking work, where the award criteria focused on novelty and originality rather than conventional criteria of excellence.

The Nature of Globalization

Aside from the urgency arising from the current financial crisis, which continues to pose the risk of a decade-long economic depression (with all the consequent issues this raises for inter-generational equity), we are also living during a remarkable era marked by the re-emergence of China as a global force, the beginnings of sustained growth in India, and fragile but encouraging signs of progress in other middle-income countries. Arguably, scientific and technological progress have played a smaller role in these countries' progress than the sustained application of trade liberalization and the infrastructures of communication and transport. Nonetheless, in a European context, the progress of globalization has produced severe disquiet and the rise of a populist conservatism, the fervour of which is only slightly less than the disquieting levels evident in the United States. An important appeal from the right is the promise, however unrealistic, of self-reliance, a message that may yet unite people with very disparate beliefs on social issues.

Our field can make an important contribution to this situation by critically examining both our affections and our distastes. With regard to our affections, we would like to believe that scientific and technological advances provide the foundations for a sustainable economic future for citizens educated to ever higher standards. However, we continue to de-industrialize and to improve labour productivity in ways that make job creation and employment recovery more difficult. This faith is embodied in our aspirations with regard to R&D investment, education, and support for sunrise industries. If instead we took our primary measure of social and economic health to be full employment, would we be able to offer confident assurances about our ability to reach this target in the future? As for distastes, we are often sceptical of the claims of neo-liberalism and of neo-classical dogma, and this leads us to be critical of the simplistic arguments regarding the universality of trade benefits and 'trickle down' theories of economic progress. However, what economic prospects would we face if the liberal economic order were to unravel, as it did so dramatically in other periods of grave economic crisis?

I suggest that both with regard to our faith in scientific and technological progress and our scepticism regarding ideas like factor price equalization and comparative advantage, we have a role to play in making forward-looking assessments—assessments that are informed by realistic assessment of potential developments and options. Here, again, I would suggest that the specific knowledge of scientific and technological opportunity must play a larger role in making such assessments—otherwise we have little to fall back upon other than an appeal to 'it was ever thus' or the nostrums of general competitive analysis.

However, although we need more specific knowledge of scientific and technological issues and the means to achieve this literacy and thereby improve our appeal to individuals considering whether to enter our field, I suspect that the normalization of our paradigm may again be an enemy. Normalized paradigms involve larger 'getting started' costs and also tend to punish deviance. As our field of study becomes a career foundation for people interested in policy studies, including regulation, and management studies in the context of rapid technological change, the risk is that we will be appealing to those people whose priority is the acquisition of the tools of these trades rather than the challenge of building new monuments and entirely new neighbourhoods for our community.

7.5. Summary

I have argued, somewhat provocatively, that a substantial degree of maturity, verging on the assembly of the apparatus of a Kuhnian 'normal science' is present in much of the field of science, technology, and innovation studies, and that related fields such as STS are also maturing. My intent is to focus attention on the future of this field of studies. From a multi-disciplinary perspective, it is a field where particular disciplines, such as economics, have become a frequent point of entry and a continuing reference standard for new researchers. Those who continue their work in the field are often drawn to a more synthetic inter-disciplinary perspective, at the very least acknowledging the value of contributions in areas other than their own to the advance of the field. These observations about the entry and maturation of researchers in the field suggest the value of building a broader foundation from the outset in the form of texts and other resources available to those commencing professional studies in this field.

In considering several of the major contemporary challenges that societies face, I have contended that a broader and more synthetic approach to both research and education is urgently needed. Our field is enriched and renewed by people seeking to make a difference in the world. What I have said concerning the need for a broader perspective should not be taken as an argument in favour of closure when we do not yet have answers to vitally important questions. Such a closure would have the effect of raising entry barriers at precisely the time when we have even greater needs for diversity than in the past. Instead, I have proposed that we need to retain and renew our commitment to arriving at a fundamental understanding of the processes of research, the specific nature of sciences and technologies, and their social connections. One potential way forward is placing a greater premium on the pursuit of truly path-breaking and creative work that deepens our insights into contemporary science and technology.

Among the most promising and potentially rewarding areas of study for the future might be a renewed and more sincere engagement with innovation as it affects individuals and groups in society—in the first instance, through their work and the skills and competences that this work entails, but also in the connections between these skills and the educational and recreational activities that individuals pursue. I have also suggested that what we know about the experience of economic growth, technological change, and social development from the past may not be an entirely reliable guide for addressing the challenges of this century. In particular, I have suggested that a deeper understanding of the differences between modern technologies and those that created the 'industrialized' countries is needed to understand the contemporary phenomenon of globalization in all of its manifestations.

In addressing these research and educational challenges, there continues to be a need to forge alliances with neighbouring research fields and to maintain a broad church, one that not only resists closure, but which also maintains a candle at the window to attract those who share our interests and passions in understanding the roles of science, technology, and innovation, regardless of their prior training or disciplinary traditions.

References

Abramovitz, M. (1956). 'Resource and Output Trends in the United States Since 1870', *American Economic Review*, 46(2): 5–23.

Abramovitz, M. (1989). *Thinking About Growth and Other Essays on Economic Growth and Welfare*. Cambridge: Cambridge University Press.

Arrow, K. J. (1962). 'Economic Welfare and the Allocation of Resources for Invention', in R. Nelson (ed.), *The Rate and Direction of Inventive Activity*. Princeton: National Bureau of Economic Research and Princeton University Press, 609–25.

Beck, U. (1992). *Risk Society: Towards a New Modernity*. London: Sage.

Bush, V. (1945). *Science: The Endless Frontier: A Report to the President on a Program for Postwar Scientific Research*. Washington, DC: United States Office of Scientific Research and Development (1945), National Science Foundation (reprinted 1960).

Carrier, M. A. (2009). *Innovation for the 21st Century: Harnessing the Power of Intellectual Property and Antitrust Law*. Oxford: Oxford University Press.

Carson, R. (1962). *Silent Spring*. New York: Houghton Mifflin.

Curnow, R. C. and Moring, G. G. (1968). ' "Project Sappho": A Study in Industrial Innovation', *Futures* 1(2): 82–90.

David, P. A. (1966). 'The Mechanization of Reaping in the Ante-Bellum Midwest', in H. Rosovsky (ed.), *Industrialization in Two Systems: Essays in Honor of Alexander Gerschenkron*. New York: John Wiley and Sons, 3–39.

David, P. A. (1971). 'The Landscape and the Machine: Technical Interrelatedness, Land Tenure and the Mechanization of the Corn Harvest in Victorian Britain', in D. N. McCloskey (ed.), *Essays on a Mature Economy: Britain after 1840*. Princeton NJ: Princeton University Press, 145–205.

David, P. A., Mowery, D., et al. (1992). 'Analysing the Economic Payoffs from Basic Research', *Economics of Innovation and New Technology*, 2: 73–90.

Davis, L. E., Easterlin, R. A., et al. (eds) (1972). *American Economic Growth: An Economist's History of the United States*. New York: Harper and Row.

Dosi, G., Freeman, C., et al. (eds) (1988). *Technical Change and Economic Theory*. London: Pinter Publishers.

Edge, D. (1995). 'Reinventing the Wheel', in S. Jasanoff, G. E. Markle, J. C. Petersen, and T. Pinch (eds), *Handbook of Science and Technology Studies*. London: Sage Publications, 3–23.

Ellul, J. (1977). *Le système technicien* (*The Technological System*, trans. Joachim Neugroschel). Paris: Calmann-Lévy (New York: Continuum, 1980).

Fagerberg, J., Mowery, D., et al. (2005). *The Oxford Handbook of Innovation*. Oxford: Oxford University Press.

Freeman, C. (1974). *The Economics of Industrial Innovation*. London: Penguin.

Freeman, C. and Soete, L. (1997). *The Economics of Industrial Innovation (third edition)*. London and Washington, DC: Pinter.

Griliches, Z. (1958). 'Research Costs and Social Returns: Hybrid Corn and Related Innovations', *Journal of Political Economy*, 66 (October): 419–431.

Hackett, E. J., Amsterdamska, O., et al. (2007). *The Handbook of Science and Technology Studies (third edition)* Cambridge, MA: MIT Press.

Hall, B. and Rosenberg, N. (eds) (2010). *Handbook of the Economics of Innovation*. Amsterdam: Elsevier.

Jaffe, A. B. and Lerner, J. (2006). *Innovation and Its Discontents: How Our Broken Patent System is Endangering Innovation and Progress, and What to Do About It*. Princeton, NJ: Princeton University Press.

Jasanoff, S. (1990). *The Fifth Branch: Science Advisors as Policymakers*. Cambridge, MA: Harvard University Press.

Jasanoff, S. (2005). *Designs on Nature: Science and Democracy in Europe and the United States*. Princeton, NJ: Princeton University Press.

Jasanoff, S., Markle, G. E., et al. (1995). *Handbook of Science and Technology Studies*. Thousand Oaks, CA/London/New Delhi: Sage.

Jewkes, J., Sawers, D., et al. (1969). *The Sources of Innovation*. London: Macmillan.

Klein, J. T. (2010). *Creating Interdisciplinary Campus Cultures: A Model for Strength and Sustainability*. San Francisco, CA: John Wiley & Sons.

Kline, S. J. and Rosenberg, N. (1986). 'An Overview of Innovation', in R. Landau and N. Rosenberg (eds), *The Positive Sum Strategy: Harnessing Technology for Economic Growth*. Washington, DC: National Academic Press, 275–305.

Kuhn, T. S. (1996). *The Structure of Scientific Revolutions (3rd edition)*. Chicago: University of Chicago Press.

Kuznets, S. (1962). 'Inventive Activity: Problems of Definition and Measurement', in R. Nelson (ed.), *The Rate and Direction of Inventive Activity*. Princeton, NJ: Princeton University Press, 19–51.

Langrish, J., Gibbons, M., et al. (1972). *Wealth from Knowledge: A Study of Innovation in Industry*. New York: Halsted Press Division, John Wiley and Sons.

Lundvall, B.-Å. (ed.) (1992). *National Systems of Innovation: Towards a Theory of Innovation and Interactive Learning*. London: Pinter.

Lundvall, B.-Å., Joseph, K. J., et al. (eds) (2011). *Handbook of Innovation Systems and Developing Countries: Building Domestic Capabilities in a Global Setting*. Cheltenham, UK: Edward Elgar.

Lundvall, B.-Å. and Maskell, P. (2000). 'Nation States and Economic Development—From National Systems of Production to National Systems of Knowledge Creation and Learning', in M. S. Gertler (ed.), *The Oxford Handbook of Economic Geography*. Oxford: Oxford University Press, 353–72.

Mansfield, E. (1980). 'Basic Research and Productivity Increase in Manufacturing', *American Economic Review*, 70(5): 863–873.

Moed, H. F., Glänzel, W., et al. (2004). *Handbook of Quantitative Scence and Technology Research: The Use of Publication and Patent Statistics in Studies of S&T Systems*. Dordrecht/Boston/London: Kluwer Academic Publishers.

Mumford, L. (1964). *The Pentagon of Power*. New York: Harcourt Brace and Javanovich.

National Science Foundation (1969). *Technology in Retrospect and Critical Events in Science (TRACES)*. Washington, DC: National Science Foundation.

Nelson, R. R. (1959). 'The Simple Economics of Basic Scientific Research', *Journal of Political Economy*, 67 (June): 297–306.

Nelson, R. R. (ed.) (1962). *The Rate and Direction of Inventive Activity: Economic and Social Factors*. Princeton, NJ: Princeton University Press.

Nelson, R.R. and Winter, S. (1982). *An Evolutionary Theory of Economic Change*. Cambridge, MA: Harvard University Press.

Neumeyer, F. and Stedman, J. C. (1971). *The Employed Inventor in the United States*. Cambridge, MA: MIT Press.

Office of the Director of Defense Research and Engineering (1969). *Project Hindsight: Final Report*. Washington, DC: USGPO.

Rogers, E. M. (1962). *Diffusion of Innovations*. Glencoe, IL: Free Press.

Roy, R. (1999). 'STS and the BSTS: Retrospect and Prospect, 2000 C.E.', *Bulletin of Science, Technology and Society, 19*(6): 461–464.

Ruttan, V. W. (2001). *Technology, Growth and Development*. Oxford: Oxford University Press.

Schumpeter, J. (1947). *Capitalism, Socialism and Democracy* (Second Edition). New York: Harper and Row.

Solow, R. M. (1956). 'A Contribution to the Theory of Economic Growth', *Quartely Journal of Economics, 70* (February): 65–94.

Steinmueller, W. E. (1994). 'Basic Science and Industrial Innovation', in M. Dodgson and R. Rothwell (eds), *Handbook of Industrial Innovation*. London: Edward Elgar, 54–66.

Stoneman, P. (1995). *Handbook of the Economics of Innovation and Technological Change*. Oxford: Blackwell.

Tidd, J. and Bessant, J. (2009). *Managing Innovation* (4th Edition). Chichester UK: John Wiley and Sons.

Warde, A. and Southerton, D., (eds) (2012). 'The Habits of Consumption', COLLeGIUM of Studies Across Disciplines in the Humanities and Social Sciences (Volume 12). Helsinki, Helsinki Collegium for Advanced Studies (Open Access: downloaded from <http://www.helsinki.fi/collegium/e-series/volumes/volume_12/index.htm>).

Winner, L. (1977). *Autonomous Technology: Technics-out-of-Control as a Theme in Political Thought*. Cambridge, MA: MIT Press.

8

Innovation Studies: An Emerging Agenda

Ben R. Martin

8.1. Introduction

The field of innovation studies is now approximately 50 years old. The occasion has been marked by several studies looking back to identify the main contributions made over that period. In this chapter, starting from a list of 20 major advances over the field's history, I set out to identify a number of challenges for coming decades. The intention is not so much to come up with a definitive list as to provoke a fruitful debate among the innovation scholars on what the key challenges we face are and on what sort of field we aspire to be. I have therefore deliberatively phrased the challenges and underlying arguments in a blunt and sometimes critical manner to jolt readers from the cosy assumptions of conventional wisdom, encouraging them to apply the critical lens that we normally apply to others instead to ourselves.

At the International Congress of Mathematicians in Paris in 1900, David Hilbert set out a number of major mathematical problems as challenges to the mathematics community (Hilbert, 1902). These challenges were to spur the efforts of mathematicians for decades to come. Can one similarly identify a number of major challenges for scholars of innovation studies to address over coming decades? In some respects, this attempt to look into the future in our field is more complex than that confronting Hilbert, in that the field of innovation studies (IS) is more subject to external influences, the unpredictability of which renders our task more difficult. Another reason why the task might be harder is that, once a mathematical problem has been set, it is relatively straightforward to say when a solution or proof has been found. In IS, by contrast, there is no such simple delineation of when a challenge has been met. This highlights the need to formulate the challenges in such a way that there is a relatively clear target. In addition, I take as a boundary condition

168

that a challenge must be such that overcoming it will result in significant benefits extending well beyond the field of IS.

To peer into the future to identify the challenges, we first need to build a robust viewing platform. Given the strong element of continuity and path-dependence involved, the foundations for this are probably best constructed from the major achievements of previous decades. It is therefore helpful to begin by reminding ourselves what have been the main advances over the lifetime of IS. I then set out a series of 15 challenges for the field before ending with some more general conclusions.

8.2. What have been the Main Achievements of Innovation Studies over Previous Decades?

Let me first define my focus. The field I am focusing on comprises economic, management, organizational and policy studies of science, technology, and innovation, with a view to providing useful inputs for decision-makers concerned with policies for, and the management of, science, technology, and innovation (Martin, 2012a). Originally known as 'science policy research', over the last decade or so it has come to be known as 'innovation studies'. Science policy research began in a recognizable form in the late 1950s, when just a handful of people were interested in the subject (Martin, 2012a). Now, there are several thousand researchers around the world making up the innovation studies community (Fagerberg and Verspagen, 2009).

In previous work, I identified the most important contributions over the last 50 years in science policy and innovation studies (Martin, 2012a). Many of these can be synthesized into a list of 20 major advances in understanding (Martin, 2010), as summarized in Table 8.1.

Of these 20 advances, which have had an impact on the management of, or policies for, science, technology, and innovation? There are around eight (numbers 1, 3, 4, 7, 13, 16, 18, and 20 in Table 8.1) for which one could make a convincing case that they have had a significant impact on technology and innovation *management* in industry. Which have had a major impact on science, technology, and innovation *policy*? Here the list is shorter, perhaps four or so (numbers 1, 2, 13, and 14). It is not my task here to explore the possible explanations for this somewhat disappointing record in terms of impact on policy-making.[1] I will instead merely note that we clearly need to develop a more sophisticated model of the interaction between policy research and policy-making. As I have suggested elsewhere (Martin, 2012a), this might

---

[1] For a preliminary attempt at this, see Martin (2010).

Table 8.1. Twenty advances in science policy

1	From individual entrepreneur to corporate innovators
2	From *laissez faire* to government intervention
3	From two factors of production to three
4	From single division to multidivisional effects
5	From technology adoption to innovation diffusion
6	From science push to demand pull?
7	From single factor to multifactor explanations of innovation
8	From a static to a dynamic model of innovation
9	From the linear model to an interactive 'chain-link' model
10	From one innovation process to several sector-specific types
11	From neo-classical to evolutionary economics
12	From neo-classical to new growth theory
13	From the optimizing firm to the resource-based view of the firm
14	From individual actors to systems of innovation
15	From market failure to system failure
16	From one to two 'faces' of R&D
17	From 'Mode 1' to 'Mode 2'
18	From single technology to multitechnology firms
19	From national to multilevel systems of innovation
20	From closed to open innovation

Source: Martin (2010), which also explains in more detail what each of these advances involved and lists key references.

resemble our model of the innovation process following Kline and Rosenberg (1986)—in other words, a chain-linked interactive model.

8.3. The Challenges

As noted earlier, it is hard to be as precise in the formulation of challenges confronting IS as in mathematics. The first ten are expressed in similar terms to the advances or major shifts identified over previous decades—that is 'from X to Y'. The remaining five represent more general challenges for the field of IS and its practitioners. Thus in total, I have identified 15 challenges.

From Visible Innovation To 'Dark Innovation'

Organizations and institutions often reflect the environment in which they were formed. With the IS field now being some 50 years old, 'innovation' tends to be conceptualized, defined, and measured in terms of the dominant forms of innovation from several decades earlier. During the 1960s, manufacturing along with primary industries still predominated. In that era, innovations were mostly: (i) technology based; (ii) involved prior R&D; (iii) developed by large manufacturing companies, often on the basis of internal R&D; and (iv) frequently involved patenting. All this encouraged the development of tools to 'measure' innovative activity through indicators such as R&D funding, numbers of researchers, and patents. Today, however, these indicators are in danger of 'missing' much innovative activity that is: (i) incremental; (ii) not in the form of manufactured product innovations; (iii) involves little or no formal R&D; and (iv) is not patented.

Over the years, most empirical IS studies have tended to focus on product and process innovations rather than other types, and more on radical than incremental innovations. Other types of innovations have often been ignored or are essentially 'invisible' in terms of conventional indicators—for example, innovations based more on design, branding, software, or other intangible investments rather than R&D. Yet it is apparent that a huge amount of innovative activity is going on 'beneath the radar', which does not involve R&D or work by 'scientists' or patents, and hence is invisible—for example, incremental process innovations in the factories of China and other developing economies.

Other examples relate to innovation in services. While manufacturing was still dominant in the early years of IS, now the manufacturing sector has fallen below 20 per cent of GDP in many advanced countries and is dwarfed by services. Yet empirical studies in IS still tend to focus predominantly on manufacturing (Martin, 2012c, table 2), although there has been some shift over the last decade.[2] In financial services in particular, there have been crucially important innovations over the last couple of decades, especially credit derivatives. The development of these involved substantial 'research', often conducted by former scientists (so-called 'rocket scientists'), but it was almost invisible as far as IS was concerned. Like generals who continue to fight the last war, or like politicians in thrall to a long-dead economist, we seem to be devoting a disproportionate level of effort to addressing yesterday's problems. If innovation is fairly evenly spread across manufacturing and services (and there is little reason to think it is not), then the challenge for IS scholars is to distribute their empirical efforts more evenly in line with the large and growing share of services in GDP.

Organizational innovations such as business reorganization are likewise too often 'invisible'.[3] So, too, institutional innovations. The 2008 financial crisis was partly caused by changes in the regulatory framework, in other words, by institutional innovations. Again, these are often 'invisible' to existing innovation measurement tools. And the same is true for many innovations resulting in profound social change, such as those associated with

---

[2] Recent high-impact studies of innovation in services include Evangelista (2000), Jansen et al. (2006), and Castellacci (2008).

[3] The work by authors such as Lorenz (see Chapter 3) is the exception rather than the rule.

Facebook or Twitter, or 'grass-roots innovations' in India (Gupta et al., 2003), or micro-finance (Morduch, 1999), or the innovative use of mobile phones by farmers in Africa (Bailard, 2010). All these are generally not captured in conventional innovation indicators.

There is an analogy here with cosmology. Astronomers' observations reveal only a small proportion of the universe—the majority lies unseen in the form of 'dark matter' and 'dark energy'. We know it's there but we cannot measure it with existing instruments. Likewise, we are aware of the growing amount of innovative activity that is going on around the world but it is just not visible using existing indicators—that is, it is what might be described as 'dark innovation'.[4] The challenge to the next generation of IS researchers is to resist the lure that entraps the drunk into looking for his keys under the lamp-post simply because that's where the light is, and instead to conceptualize, define, and come up with improved methods for measuring, analysing, and understanding 'dark innovation'.

From 'Boy's Toys' to Mundane but Liberating Innovations

Many of the current leaders of IS made their names in the 1980s or 1990s, when the focus was on competition between the USA, Europe, and Japan, and on high-tech manufacturing. Analysis of the empirical subject matter of studies published in *Research Policy* reveals a clear tendency to focus on what might be characterized as 'boy's toys' (e.g. computers, cars, TVs—see Martin (2012c), table 3). This may reflect the fact that: (i) a high proportion of researchers in the field are men; and (ii) researchers are likely to focus their empirical work on an area they feel passionate about. Yet there are other, more mundane, innovations that have done at least as much to improve human lives over the last 50 years, in particular those that have freed women from the domestic drudgery of being 'housewives', but which have received relatively little attention from the IS community. This focus on high-tech innovations may well have skewed our search for a better understanding of the innovative process with respect to methodological tools, concepts, analytical frameworks, and models. Those we have developed may consequently be less relevant for other forms of innovations. The challenge for the next generation of IS researchers is to give more equal treatment to often more mundane innovations that have done (or could potentially do) as much to improve the lot of humanity, for example, in terms of liberating the poor from grinding poverty.

---

[4] No pejorative sense is intended here—the term has simply been adopted by analogy with cosmology.

From National and Regional to Global Systems of Innovation

The notion of a 'national system of innovation' (NSI) is one of the most important conceptual developments to emerge from IS in the last 25 years. We have been aware from the start that not all innovative activity is national in scope, but this focus was originally justified in terms of most R&D being nationally focused, and most companies conducting the bulk of their R&D in their home country. Over time, these assumptions have become less true, with multinational corporations increasingly operating on a global scale with regard to innovation and R&D. In so doing, they have begun to forge links between previously separate national systems of innovation, with the emergence of a *global* system in some sectors. The challenge for IS researchers is to analyse these global systems of innovation, and to understand their interactions with national systems. This will surely yield important policy implications, just as the development of the NSI concept originally did, not least as we are confronted by ever more urgent global challenges and attempt to respond to these. Here, the proposal by Lundvall (see Chapter 11) for the establishment of a Norwegian Observatory for Global Governance Innovation could provide an institutional environment in which IS scholars might address this challenge.

From Innovation for Economic Productivity to 'Green Innovation'

During the 1980s and 1990s, the political and economic agenda was dominated by concerns with economic competition, growth, wealth creation, and productivity, and with shifts in these between Europe, the USA, and Asia. Innovation was seen as key to achieving these goals, and policies were shaped to stimulate such innovations. There was relatively little concern with sustainability or environmental impact. Hence, the cognitive resources developed within IS were oriented primarily to innovation for economic productivity, as analysis of the empirical focus of IS papers reveals (Martin, 2012c, table 4). The late 1990s, however, saw increasing concern with environmental damage and global warming. This led a few IS scholars, particularly in the Netherlands, to become more interested in innovation for sustainability. They drew substantially upon inputs from Science and Technology Studies (STS), one of the few occasions where this has occurred over recent decades. It resulted in work on regime shifts, niche formation, and socio-technical transitions by authors such as René Kemp, Johan Schot, and Frank Geels. The work is now beginning to have a significant impact (e.g. Geels, 2002), but much remains to be done before we complete the transition to 'green' innovation.

From Innovation for Economic Growth to Innovation for Sustainable Development[5]

Despite the achievements of recent decades in removing hundreds of millions in China and elsewhere from poverty and shifting them into a more affluent urban lifestyle, large parts the world are still afflicted by poverty and stunted development. This is not the place to rehearse the arguments here, nor what challenges these pose for the IS community—they are set out eloquently in Lundvall (Chapters 2 and 11—see in particular his ideas on linking innovation systems research to development economics), and Perez (Chapter 4). Yet even after all the work by Lundvall and the GLOBELICS network in recent years, there is still a long way to go. The challenge for IS scholars is to respond to the pressing world need for more equitable development, and to ensure we have the conceptual, methodological, and analytical tools needed to facilitate this shift towards innovation for sustainable development through appropriate policies.

From Risky Innovation to Socially Responsible Innovation[6]

Science, technology, and innovation have been major contributors to the historical improvement in economic and social conditions, not least in dramatically extending our life expectancy. However, they have also brought risks and unintended consequences, whether in terms of damage to the environment or other adverse effects on the quality of life (see Perez in Chapter 4). Over the last 50 years, concern with risks has brought about fierce debates over such issues as nuclear energy, insecticides, and GM crops. The assessment of the potential adverse consequences of technology underpinned elements of previous work in IS such as that on technology assessment and appropriate technology. This is also an area where there has been a major contribution from the STS community, stressing that a more open and democratic approach to decision-making is needed to enable all stakeholders to have their say. The research has been carried out under such labels as constructive technology assessment, the public understanding of science, the ethical, legal, and social implications of research, and the precautionary principle, as well as through mechanisms such as consensus conferences, citizen juries, and other approaches for 'opening up' decision-making processes (Stirling, 2008, 2012). It has given rise to a call for 'responsible innovation' (e.g. Hellström, 2003). Although some have begun to respond to this challenge (e.g. Owen

---

[5] I am indebted to Lundvall (Chapter 2) for this particular challenge.
[6] Others refer to the related concept of 'inclusive innovation' (e.g. Utz and Dahlman, 2007).

and Goldberg, 2010; von Schomberg, 2011), there is still much to be done in coming decades.

From Innovation for Wealth Creation to Innovation for Wellbeing (or from 'More is Better' to 'Enough is Enough')

For several centuries, 'progress' has been seen essentially in terms of 'more is better'. The political agenda has been driven largely by economic growth. We have become victims of the tyranny of GDP, assuming that more wealth and more 'stuff' will result in improved wellbeing. And that was probably true for most of human history. However, some research on wellbeing suggests that this assumption may be only true up to a particular point, a certain level of income—the so-called 'Easterlin paradox' (Easterlin, 1974; Easterlin et al., 2010). Moreover, it is clear that the world cannot sustain a population likely to plateau at around nine–ten billion, all with US living standards—it would need half a dozen worlds to sustain such a lifestyle. Therefore, the political and economic agenda and, more fundamentally, our very notion of progress all need to change. The IS community likewise needs to shift the focus of its empirical work from innovation for wealth (see the data in Martin, 2012c, table 5) to innovation for wellbeing (see also Lundvall in Chapter 2).[7] Such a transformation in our concept of progress and in societal goals will require fundamentally new policies, and these, in turn, require the development of appropriate empirical methods, indicators, analytical approaches, and conceptual frameworks. Work on such issues has been begun by a few, but the next generation of IS scholars needs to build on these foundations if the shift to innovation for wellbeing is to be achieved.

From 'Winner Takes All' to 'Fairness For All'?

As Lundvall (in Chapter 2) notes, polarization and growing inequality seem to be inherent in the globalizing economy. One apparent consequence of globalization is an increasing incidence of the 'winner takes all' phenomenon (Frank and Cook, 1995), in which one organization benefits from an innovation to a far greater extent than rivals with only slightly inferior products. This can be seen most obviously in the IT sector but also in others such as pharmaceuticals. Among the insidious effects of this phenomenon has been encouragement of a wider belief that extreme wealth for a few individuals is a necessary facet of free-market capitalism—that CEOs should be paid

---

[7] Also relevant here is Soete's discussion (in Chapter 6) of less than desirable innovations and the phenomenon of 'conspicuous innovation'.

hundreds of times the average salary of their staff, or that top bankers need multi-million pound bonuses if they are not to become demotivated.

Innovation studies is clearly not to blame for the 'winner takes all' phenomenon. But to what extent are we complicit in this? By contributing to improved understanding of the innovation process, to the development of more effective innovation policies, and to improved management of technology and innovation, IS has presumably helped to a certain extent in the development of innovations that triumph in the gladiatorial combat in which the winner takes all.[8] If so, can we simply sit back and say that the consequences are 'not our fault'—that *how* the knowledge, skills, and tools we have developed are used is nothing to do with us? Or do we, like doctors, have some higher moral responsibility for ensuring that we 'do no harm'? I would contend that we do indeed have a duty to explore whether we can say something about how corporations and others might generate innovations that, rather than turning a few fortunate individuals into billionaires, instead result in greater 'fairness for all' (see also Perez in Chapter 4 and Mazzucato in Chapter 10). Perhaps IS needs to adopt a more critical perspective (see Lundvall in Chapter 11). To achieve this, IS might benefit from forging closer links with STS, a community with a more established tradition of dealing with issues of fairness.

From Government as Fixer of Failures to the Entrepreneurial State[9]

Under *laissez faire* neo-liberalism, government has come to be seen as playing a restricted and largely passive role. Its task is to ensure the macroeconomic climate is right for free-market capitalism to operate without let or hindrance, and then to 'get out of the way'. The cheerleaders for neo-liberalism have often been drawn from prominent mainstream economists. Central to the neo-liberalism ideology is an almost religious belief in 'efficient markets', with Nobel prizes being awarded for economists claiming to prove that government intervention invariably results in inefficiency or other forms of harm (Lundvall in Chapter 2). The contrast between the public and the private sector is always drawn in unflattering terms—the former is seen as lumbering, bureaucratic, and inefficient, while the private sector is nimble, efficient, and above all 'entrepreneurial' (Mazzucato, 2013b). The government role, at least

---

[8] Besides the 'winner takes all' effect among producers, there is, as Soete (Chapter 6) points out, the parallel issue of who benefits among the users, with many innovations primarily benefiting those at the 'top' of the economic pyramid rather than those at the bottom. The term 'frugal innovation' has been used to describe innovations that, by contrast, provide ' "good-enough", affordable products that meet the needs of resource- constrained consumers' (Zeschky et al., 2011, p. 38).

[9] I am indebted to my SPRU colleague, Mariana Mazzucato, for this challenge.

in liberal market economies[10] such as the USA and UK, is viewed as largely confined to fixing 'market failures', such as those encountered in the area of defence, health, education, research, and more recently banks.

The caricature just outlined grossly underplays the entrepreneurial role of the state with regard to many crucial innovations of the last 50 years, including pharmaceuticals, airliners, micro-chips, PCs, Internet, the World Wide Web, cell-phones, and GPS (Mazzucato, 2013b). Yes, there is also a long list of government failures, such as nuclear fusion, supersonic transport, and synthetic fuels. Yet surely it is unrealistic to assume that *all* government policies will be successful. In the case of research, we do not assume that all research will be successful. And in the case of entrepreneurial initiatives, we know the vast majority will fail. Surely similar considerations of fallibility should apply with regard to our expectations concerning government policies? If governments do not take risks in their policies, they may not have failures but they won't have any great successes either. Today's pressing need for green innovation to tackle climate change will not be solved by 'the market' or by taxation or even by 'nudging', such is the power of established vested interests and the path-dependent nature of the trajectories pursued over many decades. Instead, the state will need to play an entrepreneurial role—not just as coordinator or fixer of market failures, but as strategist, lead investor, and risk-taker, until technology has reached a sufficiently mature stage where venture capital and industry are willing to take over (Mazzucato, 2013b).

From Faith-Based Policy (and Policy-Based Evidence) To Evidence-Based Policy?[11]

The driving philosophy of the founders of IS was premised on the assumption that science, technology, and innovation are fundamental to economic and social progress, but that one needs effective policies to ensure the potential benefits are actually achieved. It was further assumed that STI policy research could provide data, methods, analytical tools, and conceptual frameworks that would help ensure better policies, and that the resulting evidence-based policies would, in turn, lead to greater benefits for humanity. Over the years, there has certainly been some progress with regard to providing relevant data, methods, and conceptual frameworks (Martin, 2012a). Some advances in IS have had an impact on policy although, as noted earlier, that impact has been rather infrequent. Those attempting to provide systematic evidence

---

[10] As the 'varieties of capitalism' literature has shown, besides liberal market economies, there are other distinct types, in particular coordinated market economies and state-influenced market economies, in which the state plays a rather different role. However, for reasons of space, I am unable to deal with these here.

[11] The formulation of this challenge was prompted by Steinmueller (Chapter 7).

in support of a particular policy option have often found that policy-makers may resist their overtures, being already politically wedded to a particular policy (i.e. ideology- or faith-based policy), and only willing to take on board evidence supporting that position (i.e. they seek 'policy-based evidence') rather than evidence which might point towards a different policy (i.e. evidence-based policy). Thus far, we have little evidence that our efforts have resulted in better policies. And as for whether those policies have resulted in the world becoming a better place, the evidence 'locker' is essentially bare! Providing such evidence and encouraging a shift to evidence-based policy represents another crucial challenge to IS researchers.[12]

Pricking Academic Bubbles

As Perez (2002) has observed, economic history has been punctuated by periods of unbridled optimism, giving rise to a rapidly expanding 'bubble' that eventually bursts with disastrous consequences. Examples include speculation in exotic tulips in seventeenth-century Holland, the canal building 'mania' in the late eighteenth century, the railway mania in nineteenth-century Britain, and the US stock market bubble in the 1920s. Scientists do not seem immune to such herd instincts. In physics, there are thousands of 'string theorists' devoted to a theory for which there is no direct scientific evidence. A few years ago, among scientists and social scientists there was a dramatic upsurge of research on 'chaos' and then 'complexity', although the outcome in terms of testable predictions has been disappointing. At first sight, it might seem puzzling that researchers, as rational and reasonably intelligent individuals, should be just as vulnerable to being swept along in a wave of 'irrational exuberance'. However, closer inspection of the psychological makeup of the researcher suggests an explanation. What drives them is a passionate belief that what they are studying is important—indeed, that their research is *more* important than that of other researchers. To justify the large personal commitment required, they must first convince themselves that they are on the right track to some fundamental new advance in knowledge. Hence, their strong if not over-riding self-belief.

Do we, the IS community, sometimes fall prey to similar manias or bubbles? With the benefit of hindsight, can one identify topics where perhaps rather too much attention was given? For example, was too great an emphasis given in the past to total factor productivity and 'the residual', or in the 1980s to Japanese production processes (e.g. total quality management)? Have we on occasions been guilty of contributing to the hype over biotechnology, or of exaggerating the potential benefits of clusters or networks, or the innovative

[12] As noted earlier, we also need to develop a better understanding of the complex interaction between policy researchers and policy-makers.

potential of SMEs? The challenge to younger (and even some older) IS scholars is to maintain the ability to look objectively and to decide if a particular line of research is in danger of becoming a fad or whether it still represents the most promising line of enquiry. In short, we need a few 'contrarians' willing to risk ridicule by suggesting that the new emperor has no clothes!

Avoiding Disciplinary Sclerosis

Initially, the emerging field of IS was populated by 'immigrants' from other disciplines. It thus became intrinsically inter-disciplinary—an intellectual 'melting pot' characterized by diversity and eclectic borrowing of cognitive resources from others (Fagerberg et al., 2012a; Martin, 2012a). The research was mainly explorative and qualitative, with case-studies featuring prominently (Nelson, 2012, p. 37; see also Chapter 1). It was driven primarily by policy issues (Lundvall in Chapter 2), not least those arising from Cold War tensions and later the growing economic competition between the USA, Europe, and Japan. Over time, IS matured as a research field (Morlacchi and Martin, 2009; Martin, 2012a). There are dozens of dedicated research centres on innovation, and IS now trains a large proportion of its own PhD students rather than recruiting them from other disciplines. It boasts its own journals and conferences, and has developed rigorous methodologies, often quantitative in nature. In short, it is beginning to exhibit certain disciplinary characteristics (Martin, 2012a), perhaps even being in the throes of a Kuhnian transformation (see Steinmueller in Chapter 7).

Yet while becoming more discipline-like is testament to the field's growing academic standing, it also has various consequences that give pause for thought. One is an increasing homogeneity in terms of researchers (most with a PhD in the field, with the attendant danger of intellectual 'inbreeding'), the studies they carry out (an increasing proportion of which are econometric), and the papers published (a growing number taking a fairly standard form). Peer review can give 'non-conventional' studies a rough ride, damning them for a lack of theory or hypotheses even when the exploratory nature of the paper's theme makes that unrealistic. With the emergence of a possible proto-paradigm in the form of the 'Stanford–Yale–Sussex synthesis' (Dosi et al., 2006), there are signs that IS may be becoming more theory-driven and less policy-driven (Martin, 2012a), more 'normal science' (Kuhn, 1962) and less adventurous (see Steinmueller in Chapter 7). Now is the time for a debate as to what sort of field we aspire to be. Do we want to become a more academic discipline, or a field that continues to respond to challenges encountered by decision-makers in government, industry, and elsewhere, even if that means operating as an inter-disciplinary 'mongrel' of lower academic status rather than a disciplinary 'pedigree'? Resolving this issue represents another challenge for the next generation of IS leaders.

Identifying the Causes of the Current Economic Crisis

The economic crisis now confronting us is arguably the most serious since the 1930s. Just as that earlier crash spawned a vast literature on its causes, so we need to understand the causes of this latest crisis. Earlier, we noted the often calamitous contributions of the economics profession to the crisis, but innovations also had a major part in this. Financial innovations such as collateralized debt obligations and credit default swaps played a central role, giving rise to a process of 'destructive creation' (see Soete in Chapter 6). Here, it is not that IS contributed to these innovations, but that we almost completely failed to provide any analysis of them, and hence were unable to offer any warnings. With a few honourable exceptions (e.g. participants in the recent FINNOV project),[13] the IS community has been strangely silent on the financial innovations emerging since the liberalization of banking. Even sociologists and anthropologists have had rather more to say (e.g. Beunza and Stark, 2004; Mackenzie, 2006; Tett, 2009).

How might we explain this 'curious incident of the dog that failed to bark'? Partly, it reflects the continuing fascination of IS researchers with innovation in manufacturing and high-tech industry. Related to this is a lack of data on innovative activity in financial services, and the large amount of effort needed to remedy this. There may also be a problem of access, in that banks tend to be less welcoming to academic researchers than industrial firms. In addition, many IS researchers are perhaps put off by the technical complexity of financial products such as derivatives. The challenge to younger IS researchers is to overcome these hurdles, and to provide us with an understanding of the role played by financial innovations in contributing to the current economic crisis, and the lessons one can draw in order to minimize the risk of such an event happening again.

Helping to Generate a New Paradigm for Economics[14]—From Ptolemaic Economics to ???

Lundvall (Chapter 2) and Dosi (Chapter 5) are in little doubt that economists, through the policy advice they provided, share a major responsibility for the current financial crisis. Nor does mainstream economics seem to have any credible ideas for getting us out of the mess. The current crisis is similar to

---

[13] See <http://www.finnov-fp7.eu/events/finnov-final-conference-2012> (downloaded on 7 November 2012).

[14] I am again indebted to Lundvall (Chapter 2) for this challenge, although the phrasing owes more to Dosi (2011).

the one in 1930s in the sense that there would appear to be a strong need for a paradigm shift in economics. Hence, we need to discuss how innovation scholars with roots in economics can contribute to such a paradigm shift. Lundvall (Chapter 2) and Dosi (Chapter 5) set out some ideas on what this might involve; so rather than repeat all this, I instead refer the reader to their chapters as well as that by Perez (Chapter 4).

Instead, let me offer an observation. Like Dosi (2011), I find economics today eerily reminiscent of Ptolemaic astronomy with its complicated epicycles. To Ancient Greeks and Romans, it was axiomatic that the heavenly bodies should move in perfect circles around the Earth. In order to explain why observations of planets suggested otherwise, an ever more complicated set of epicycles was invoked. Likewise, neo-classical economics seeks to protect its core beliefs in equilibrium, rational agents, perfect information, utility maximization, efficient markets, representative firms, and the like. But to do so in the face of accumulating inconvenient evidence to the contrary, not least from innovation studies, it has had to invoke an increasing panoply of ad hoc 'fixes' such as bounded rationality, imperfect information, information asymmetry, satisficing, prospect theory, and cognitive bias—in short, an embarrassing accumulation of 'epicycles'. As Kuhn (1962) observed, the accumulation of 'anomalies' is often the prelude to the end of a period of normal science and the onset of revolutionary science with the eventual transition to a new paradigm. If this is the case here, then IS scholars would seem well placed to respond to the challenge of helping to construct a new and more effective paradigm for economics, perhaps one incorporating substantial elements of neo-Schumpeterian or evolutionary economics (Dosi, 2011, and Chapter 5).

Maintaining our Research Integrity, Morality, and Collegiality

For most of its history, 'the Republic of Science' has operated on the basis of 'self-policing'. It was assumed that misconduct is rare, generally low-level and self-correcting, that any serious misconduct is quickly detected by peer review and stopped, and that the risk of being caught and the severe repercussions that follow are such that few researchers are tempted to err (Martin, 2012b). However, the growing incidence of plagiarism (Martin et al., 2007) and other forms of research misconduct (Martin, 2013) casts all this into doubt.

As a field, we were fortunate in our 'founding fathers'—individuals such as Chris Freeman and Richard Nelson—who, besides making immense intellectual contributions, also shaped the culture and norms under which we operate. In particular, these individuals personified a spirit of openness, integrity, and intellectual generosity. However, as competition for funds, tenure, and academic status intensifies, there are worrying signs that the culture of our field may be changing for the worse. As a journal editor, I have received complaints from referees about how their data have been used without permission by the authors of papers they were sent to review. Some researchers, fearful of their ideas being purloined, are apparently no longer willing to present early drafts of papers at conferences. Such behaviour risks weakening the 'invisible college', removing a key mechanism for improving the quality of papers and stimulating the cross-fertilization so essential to the future of the field.

Occasionally, perhaps because of the pressure of a deadline, individuals may succumb to the temptation to engage in outright plagiarism. Fortunately such cases appear to be rare. Rather more common, and certainly on the increase, is the phenomenon of 'salami publishing' (Martin, 2013). With the growing use of publications as a performance indicator comes escalating pressure to exploit one's research to the full with as many articles as possible. Hence, some authors 'slice the salami very thinly'. In the worst cases, this shades into self-plagiarism, where an author re-uses material from earlier publications without explicitly drawing the attention of the reader to the existence of earlier work (Martin, 2013). This raises the question: 'Where precisely is the boundary between acceptable and unacceptable research behaviour?' There is a challenge here for IS researchers not only to define that boundary in a universally agreed manner, but also to ensure that we maintain the norms, incentives, and sanctions to police that boundary, and hence ensure the continuing integrity of the field. This is the final of my 15 challenges for innovation studies over coming decades (see the summary in Table 8.2).

Table 8.2. Fifteen challenges for innovation studies

1	From visible innovation to 'dark innovation'
2	From 'boy's toys' to mundane but liberating innovations
3	From national and regional to global systems of innovation
4	From innovation for economic productivity to 'green innovation'
5	From innovation for economic growth to innovation for sustainable development
6	From risky innovation to socially responsible innovation
7	From innovation for wealth creation to innovation for wellbeing (or from 'more is better' to 'enough is enough')
8	From 'winner takes all' to 'fairness for all'?
9	From government as fixer of failures to the entrepreneurial state
10	From faith-based policy (and policy-based evidence) to evidence-based policy?
11	Pricking academic bubbles
12	Avoiding disciplinary sclerosis
13	Identifying the causes of the current economic crisis
14	Helping to generate a new paradigm for economics—from Ptolemaic economics to ???
15	Maintaining our research integrity, morality, and collegiality

8.4. Conclusions

Given that the field of innovation studies is half a century old, now is an appropriate time not only to look back and reflect on what has been achieved, but also to look forward and discuss the next major challenges to be tackled and, more generally, what sort of field we aspire to be. The Lundvall symposium in February 2012 provided a suitable occasion to begin this task. The field of innovation studies has come a long way in 50 years, establishing itself as a vibrant research community with a long and impressive list of achievements (Fagerberg et al., 2012a, b; Martin, 2012a). However, attaining academic respectability brings with it the risk of also becoming 'middle aged', of becoming set in our ways.

In this chapter, I have argued that the focus of our empirical studies has not always kept pace with the fast changing world and economy, in particular the shift from manufacturing to services and the growing need for sustainability as well as economic growth. Moreover, the very way we conceptualize, define, operationalize, and analyse 'innovation' may be too rooted in the past, leaving us less able to grapple with other less visible or 'dark' forms of innovation. The relative neglect of financial innovations has left us with little to contribute to the analysis of the current financial crisis and the growing polarity between rich and poor, and how economics needs to be fundamentally restructured or even shifted to a new paradigm if we are to avoid similar problems in the future.

Let me conclude by re-emphasizing that the list of 15 challenges presented here is not intended to be prescriptive. My purpose is to join with others, such as Bengt-Åke Lundvall and fellow contributors to this volume, in launching a debate. The hope is that, once started, such a debate might be pursued both through informal discussions but perhaps also formally at workshops or conference sessions and even through journal articles and other publications. Such a debate could shape the future of innovation studies for decades to come.

Acknowledgements

This chapter had its origins in a 2009 lecture setting out the 20 main advances made by IS over its 50 years, where a question from Frank Geels prompted me to begin thinking about future advances in the field. Later, work with Piera Morlacchi took this further (Morlacchi and Martin, 2009). However, it was the invitation to participate in the Lundvall symposium and reading the papers by Bengt-Åke Lundvall, Ed Steinmueller, and others that stimulated me to develop the ideas set out here. In doing so, I drew upon work by Mariana Mazzucato (2013b), on contributions to a 2012 OECD workshop on 'The changing geography of innovation', and on presentations at the final FINNOV conference (particularly those by Carlota Perez and Giovanni Dosi), all of which helped catalyse the ideas expounded here. I am grateful to all the above for their inputs. I may well have picked up further ideas along the way from reading or listening to others; if so, I apologize if I have not cited them directly. The paper has also benefited from comments on earlier drafts by Keld Laursen and others at the Lundvall symposium, and by Jan Fagerberg, Irwin Feller, Frank Geels, and Andy Stirling. A longer and more detailed version of this paper identifying 20 challenges (Martin, 2012c) is currently under preparation.

References

Bailard, C. S. (2010). 'Mobile Phone Diffusion and Corruption in Africa', Liberation Technologies Seminar Series, Stanford University, 14 October (downloaded on 6 December 2012 from <http://iis-db.stanford.edu/evnts/6254/Mobile_Phone_Diffusion_CB.pdf>).

Beunza, D. and Stark, D. (2004). 'Tools of the Trade: The Socio-Technology of Arbitrage in a Wall Street Trading Room', *Industrial and Corporate Change*, 13: 369–400.

Castellacci, F. (2008). 'Technological Paradigms, Regimes and Trajectories: Manufacturing and Service Industries in a New Taxonomy', *Research Policy*, 37: 978–94.

Dosi, G. (2011). 'Economic Coordination and Dynamics: Some Elements of an Alternative "Evolutionary" Paradigm', Institute for New Economic Thinking (downloaded on 9 November 2012 from <http://ineteconomics.org/blog/inet/giovanni-dosi-response-john-kay-elements-evolutionary-paradigm>).

Dosi, G., Llerena, P., and Labini, M. S. (2006). 'The Relationships between Science, Technologies and their Industrial Exploitation: An Illustration through the Myths and Realities of the So-Called "European Paradox"', *Research Policy*, 35: 1450–64.

Easterlin, R. A. (1974). 'Does Economic Growth Improve the Human Lot? Some Empirical Evidence', in P. A. David and M. W. Reder (eds), *Nations and Households in Economic Growth: Essays in Honor of Moses Abramovitz*. New York: Academic Press, 89–125.

Easterlin, R. A., McVey, L. A., Switek, M., Sawangfa, O., and Zweig, J. S. (2010). 'The Happiness–Income Paradox Revisited', *Proceedings of the National Academy of Sciences*, 107: 22463–68.

Evangelista, R. (2000). 'Sectoral Patterns of Technological Change in Services', *Economics of Innovation and New Technology*, 9: 183–221.

Fagerberg, J. and Verspagen, B. (2009). 'Innovation Studies—The Emerging Structure of a New Scientific Field', *Research Policy*, 38: 218–33.

Fagerberg, J., Fosaas, M., and Sapprasert, K. (2012a). 'Innovation: Exploring the Knowledge Base', *Research Policy*, *41*: 1132–53.

Fagerberg, J., Landström, H., and Martin, B. R. (2012b). 'Exploring the Emerging Knowledge Base of "the Knowledge Society"', *Research Policy*, *41*: 1121–31.

Frank, R. H. and Cook, P. L. (1995). *The Winner-Take-All Society: Why the Few at the Top Get so Much More than the Rest of Us.* New York: Free Press.

Geels, F. W. (2002). 'Technological Transitions as Evolutionary Reconfiguration Processes: a Multi-Level Perspective and a Case-Study', *Research Policy*, *31*: 1257–74.

Gupta, A. K., Sinha, R., Koradia, D., Patel, R., Parmar, M., Rohit, P., Patel, H., Patel, K., Chand, V. S., James, T. J., Chandan, A., Patel, M., Prakash, T. N., and Vivekanandan, P. (2003). 'Mobilizing Grassroots' Technological Innovations and Traditional Knowledge, Values and Institutions: Articulating Social and Ethical Capital', *Futures*, *35*: 975–87.

Hellström, T. (2003). 'Systemic Innovation and Risk: Technology Assessment and the Challenge of Responsible Innovation', *Technology in Society*, *25*: 369–84.

Hilbert, D. (1902). 'Mathematical Problems', *Bulletin of the American Mathematical Society*, *8*(10): 437–79 (previously published in German in *Göttinger Nachrichten* (1900): 253–97, and *Archiv der Mathematik und Physik*, 1 (3rd series, 1901): 44–63 and 213–37).

Jansen, J. J. P., Van Den Bosch, F. A. J., Volberda, H. W. (2006). 'Exploratory Innovation, Exploitative Innovation, and Performance: Effects of Organisational Antecedents and Environmental Moderators', *Management Science*, *52*: 1661–74.

Kline, S. J. and Rosenberg, N. (1986). 'An Overview of Innovation', in R. Landau and N. Rosenberg (eds), *The Positive Sum Strategy: Harnessing Technology for Economic Growth.* Washington, DC: National Academy of Sciences, 275–305.

Kuhn, T. S. (1962/70). *The Structure of Scientific Revolutions.* Chicago: University of Chicago Press.

MacKenzie, D. (2006). *An Engine, Not a Camera: How Financial Models Shape Markets.* Cambridge, MA: MIT Press.

Martin, B. R. (2010). 'Science Policy Research—Having an Impact on Policy?', *OHE Seminar Briefing*, No. 7, Office of Health Economics, London (downloaded on 6 December 2012 from <http://www.ohe.org/publications/article/science-policy-research-having-an-impact-on-policy-14.cfm>).

Martin, B. R. (2012a). 'The Evolution of Science Policy and Innovation Studies', *Research Policy*, *41*: 1219–39.

Martin, B. R. (2012b). 'Does Peer Review Work as a Self-Policing Mechanism in Preventing Misconduct: A Case Study of a Serial Plagiarist', in N. H. Steneck and A. Mayer (eds). *Promoting Research Integrity on a Global Basis.* London and Singapore: World Scientific Publishing/ Imperial College Press, 97–114.

Martin, B. R. (2012c). 'Twenty Challenges for Innovation Studies', working paper, SPRU, University of Sussex.

Martin, B. R. (2013). 'Whither Research Integrity? Plagiarism, Self-Plagiarism and Coercive Citation in an Age of Research Assessment', *Research Policy*, *42*: 1005–174.

Martin, B. R. et al. (2007). 'Keeping Plagiarism at Bay—a Salutary Tale', *Research Policy*, *36*: 905–11.

Mazzucato, M. (2013b). *The Entrepreneurial State*. London: Demos.

Morduch, J. (1999). 'The Microfinance Promise', *Journal of Economic Literature, 37*: 1569–614.

Morlacchi, P. and Martin, B. R. (2009). 'Emerging Challenges for Science, Technology and Innovation Policy Research: A Reflexive Overview', *Research Policy, 38*: 571–82.

Nelson, R. R. (2012). 'Some Features of Research by Economists on Technological Change Foreshadowed by *The Rate and Direction of Inventive Activity*', in J. Lerner and S. Stern (eds), *The Rate and Direction of Inventive Activity Revisited*. Chicago: University of Chicago Press, 35–41.

Owen, R. and Goldberg, N. (2010). 'Responsible Innovation: A Pilot Study with the U.K. Engineering and Physical Sciences Research Council', *Risk Analysis, 30*: 1699–707.

Perez, C. (2002). *Technological Revolutions and Financial Capital: The Dynamics of Bubbles and Golden Ages*. Cheltenham and Northampton, MA: Elgar.

Stirling, A. (2008). '"Opening Up" and "Closing Down"—Power, Participation, and Pluralism in the Social Appraisal of Technology', *Science, Technology, & Human Values, 33*: 262–94.

Stirling, A. (2012). 'Opening Up the Politics of Knowledge and Power in Bioscience', *PloS Biology, 19*: e1001233.

Tett, G. (2009). *Fool's Gold: How Unrestrained Greed Corrupted a Dream, Shattered Global Markets and Unleashed a Catastrophe*. London: Little, Brown.

Utz, A. and Dahlman, C. (2007). 'Promoting Inclusive Innovation in India', in M. A. Dutz (ed.), *Unleashing India's Innovation: Towards Sustainable and Inclusive Growth*. Washington, DC: World Bank, 105–28.

von Schomberg, R. (ed.) (2011). *Towards Responsible Research and Innovation in the Information and Communication Technologies and Security Technologies Field*, Luxembourg: European Commission (downloaded on 6 December 2012 from <http://ec.europa.eu/research/science-society/document_library/pdf_06/mep-rapport-2011_en.pdf>).

Zeschky, M., Widenmayer, B., Gassman, O. (2011). 'Frugal Innovation in Emerging Markets', *Research Technology Management, 54*(4): 38–45.

9

Reflections on the Study of Innovation and on Those Who Study It

Richard R. Nelson

I interpret my mandate as to reflect on the earlier chapters and add to the discussion of where the field of innovation studies presently is, and where it should be going.

I want to begin by noting that today there are several different communities of scholars studying various aspects of innovation. The group that put together this volume is probably the largest and most diverse of these. The broad agenda of the scholars writing here includes study of innovation as a process and the institutions supporting and moulding innovation, the effects of innovation on society as a whole but particularly on the economy, and issues of public policy regarding science, technology, and innovation. A significant fraction of this community has affiliation with centres and institutes expressly concerned with these topics.

There also are several other intellectual communities of scholars who study innovation, and the dynamics of science and technology, located in other regions of academia. The sociology of science is an important part of modern sociology. There is now a long tradition of research on the history of science, and a more recent one on the history of technology. A sizeable community of scholars in business schools study the management of innovation. And the economics of technological change is studied by at least a few scholars in economics departments.

I note that our community is much more inter-disciplinary than these others, and its research agenda is broader. At the same time it has, over the years, developed a set of shared concepts, and a language for talking about them, that holds us together. On the other hand, our academic place tends to be outside the mainstream university structure that is based around disciplinary departments and professional schools. I shall return to this matter later.

While the range of interests of our community is very broad, the agenda for future research laid out by the authors of this volume is strongly economics-oriented. This is not surprising. A number of our authors had their graduate training in economics. Others come from other backgrounds but have developed a strong interest in innovation as an economic activity and in the economic effects of innovation. The current economic malaise obviously has shaped the research orientation of these scholars, and many others in our community.

The chapters in this book include commentaries both on how modern economies are performing in various dimensions, and on the question of how one ought to theorize about the workings of modern economies. For the most part, the authors see modern economies as not performing very well in important aspects. And all of the authors see modern mainstream economic analysis as providing a very inadequate understanding of how modern economies work.

A central reason for this lack of enthusiasm for standard economics, of course, is the failure of the latter to recognize adequately the importance of innovation as a driver of economic activity and outcomes. Needless to say, I share this point of view. However, scholars in our camp may have a tendency to exaggerate the role that innovation plays in influencing what happens in an economy, and to credit or blame what is happening on the innovation front for economic phenomena the causes of which involve a wide range of factors.

Thus, a central theme of several of the chapters is that, in recent years in many countries, both high income and low, innovation-driven economic development has done almost nothing to reduce the incidence of poverty, and various forms of poverty undoubtedly have actually increased. This certainly is true, and disturbing. But several of the authors then go on to argue, partly explicitly but also sometimes implicitly, that this is largely a consequence of the kinds of innovations that are being made, and that dealing effectively with the problem will require a significant reorientation of the kinds of innovations that are generated. This argument makes me uneasy for several reasons.

I agree that it is likely that the kinds of innovations that have been driving economic development have been a factor behind the splitting income distribution that one sees in many countries. However, in my judgement the innovations that have been most important in this respect have been those that changed how firms were organized and managed, most prominently in the financial industry, but also in manufacturing and non-financial services, rather than technological innovation. And these are not the kinds of innovation that scholars in our camp have mostly been studying; I shall say more relating to this in a moment. In addition, there were many other things going on as well. In particular, in many countries government policies worked against the alleviation of poverty. I would argue that economic development could well have served to reduce poverty significantly, even given the kinds of innovations driving it, had policies been different. Relatedly, I would propose that we don't have to change the kind of innovating that is occurring to deal more effectively with the poverty problem. There are a variety of policies that almost surely can make headway there, and the problem is the political one of getting those policies in place.

I also want to remind my colleagues that changing the orientation of innovation in a reliable way is a very difficult thing to do, at least given what we know and don't know at present. In this particular case, it is not clear what kinds of innovation are particularly effective at poverty reduction. And even if we knew that, our knowledge, and ability, to change the kinds of innovations that are generated in society is limited. It well may be innately very difficult to do that. In any case, it is clear that at present we have little knowledge about how to do so.

This discussion leads me to three important areas where the innovation research community has a lot of work to do. One is study of innovations that involve 'Technology with a capital T' to only a limited degree. A second is the study of what factors affect the kinds of innovations that are generated, and how we can influence these. And third, we need to gain a better understanding of what determines whether the fruits of innovation are widely shared or accrue largely to particular groups and interests.

Most of the scholars who have put together this book have grown up with a central interest in science and technology policy. Their interest in innovation has come from that broad orientation, and this has meant that the innovations they have studied have almost exclusively been ones in which new technology has been central: the development of new chemical products and processes, pharmaceuticals, computers, electronic devices more generally, steel-making processes, and so on. Schumpeter, in the catalogue of different kinds of innovation that he developed 100 years ago, had new products and production processes at the top of his list. But he also included things like new modes of organizing work, new ways of operating on markets, and a variety of other departures from current practice that involved new technology to, at most, a limited degree. Our camp of innovation scholars has studied these hardly at all.

Our colleagues at business schools have done somewhat better. Chandler's wonderful studies have opened up the field of research on the evolution of business organization and management, and a few scholars have followed in his footsteps. But the general arena of innovation on modes of business organization and management practice remains little explored. If I am right that these have had an enormous influence on the nature and consequences flowing from economic development over the last half century, it is high time that scholars of innovation got more into this work.

I note that several of the earlier chapters in this book argued that we need to do more research on innovation in services. I am in accord. But what I am arguing is not the same thing. The kinds of organizational and managerial innovations to which I am calling attention go on across the spectrum of economic sectors, including manufacturing. On the other hand, the question of what kinds of such innovations occur in different sectors, and why, and the consequences, would seem very important to study.

Which leads me to my second proposal: that scholars of innovation need to do a lot more work on understanding the factors behind the kinds of innovations that are being generated, and the factors and policies that can influence the directions of innovation. As several of the earlier chapters have suggested, scholars of innovation today have a much more sophisticated understanding of the factors and institutions determining the kinds of innovations being generated in society than we had, say, a quarter century ago. We now recognize clearly that innovation is influenced by both demand-side factors— what customers are interested in buying, modified by how this is reflected in incentives for potential innovators—and supply-side factors—including the state of scientific knowledge and what available technological capabilities would seem to allow. The concepts of technological paradigms and trajectories involve both aspects. The now widespread use of the innovation systems concept involves a broadening of recognition of the kinds of actors involved in what is going on, to include firms at different places in the value chain, and their customers, universities, and government agencies, and the modes of interaction among the different actors. We recognize the considerable differences among the innovation systems operating in different sectors and technologies.

But while this body of theory certainly helps us to understand or rationalize, for example, the kinds of innovations that have led to the energy technologies and the industrial structures in those fields that we now have, we still are a long way from being able to provide informed advice regarding just how to change that regime in a way that will hold back global warming. We understand much better than many of our colleagues in economics departments that we need to do far more in this arena than simply 'getting the prices right'. But we are not in a position to propose with any confidence just what those other things are. There is a major challenge here for scholars of innovation.

As I have noted, and as their chapters reflect, an important source of the interest in innovation held by the scholars represented in this book is their conviction that innovation is the key driving force behind economic development (of both high- and low-income countries) and their normative beliefs that the benefits of economic development ought to be widely shared. Regarding their beliefs about the economic importance of innovation and some of the mechanisms involved, they are Schumpeterian in the broad sense of that term. Modern scholars of innovation have gone considerably beyond Schumpeter in recognizing in the concept of innovation systems the complex institutional structures of modern capitalism. But, while recognizing that innovation-driven economic development involves creative destruction, they have not gone much beyond Schumpeter in studying that process, and the harm it generates along with the benefits, and what might be done to avert the worst of the harm. More generally, there has been little careful study of how the pace and pattern of innovation affects different groups in the economy.

Thus, with only a few exceptions, scholars of innovation in this camp have done little in the way of 'diffusion' studies. There has been very little systematic research on how uses for new products and processes emerge and develop, or on how the community of users operates. While increasingly referring to development as a 'learning' process, most of the study of learning has been on how firms learn, rather than on how groups of people, whose modes of employment and skills have been eroded by innovation, learn to make productive new lives for themselves. As I noted earlier, there has been little study of government policies that have the promise of making innovation-driven economic development more inclusive. More generally, there needs to be much more study of the distributional effects of innovation-driven economic development, and the factors that influence distribution.

Our ability to make headway with this agenda may depend to some extent on our ability to enlist the interest of our colleagues in the other communities studying innovation, and to work with them. As I have noted, we have done little research on innovations that involve little in the way of 'technology'. If we broaden our scope to include innovations in organization and management, and there are good reasons to do so, there clearly would be strong advantages in working more closely with business school scholars who have been studying innovation in these areas. Presently, the communication between the two groups is generally open, but in my view rather limited— more collaboration here would surely be fruitful.

In contrast, research on the factors influencing the kinds of innovations that occur has long been a non-trivial part of our research portfolio. The problem is that we achieved broad understanding of the forces and variables influencing the kind of innovations that occur some time ago, and since that time there has been little sharpening up of that understanding. In my view, the route to sharper understanding almost certainly involves detailed historical research, and probably also gaining a better understanding of how members of the relevant innovation communities interact to develop shared views or technological paradigms. The advantages of working with historians strike me as considerable. Our present relationships with the historians and sociologists working on innovation has been perfectly amicable, but not particularly active.

In particular, the third area of research I have flagged—research aimed at understanding the distributional effects of innovation-driven economic progress—brings us more closely into the set of issues studied by economists, and we certainly would benefit from being able to draw on their knowledge and research cooperation. However, as scholars in our community know all too well, our relationships with mainstream economics over recent years have not been particularly amicable, much less cooperative.

In my view, how well our community fares in the coming years will be strongly affected by how our relationships with these potential partners evolve. Earlier in this chapter, I have focused on the gains from more interaction on the quality and quantity of research that is carried out in important areas. But the relationships between scholarly communities also strongly influence the flow of people. I believe we would benefit substantially from being able to attract and hire some of the best young scholars trained by the other camps. And our doctoral students certainly would benefit greatly if the potential market for them included business schools, history and sociology departments, economics departments, and research institutes. Today, these cross-community flows exist but only to a limited extent.

At present, our community is intellectually lively, highly inter-disciplinary, and diverse. There is a lot of good research going on, and several of our training programmes are excellent. However, our programmes tend to stand relatively separate from other scholarly communities with which we could be having more productive interchanges, and a large percentage of the new scholars we take aboard are home-grown. This is both because we have not been particularly effective at bringing in and integrating into our research groups top-flight young scholars trained elsewhere, and because the fine young scholars we train often do not have other places to go. We are in danger, therefore, of becoming parochial. It hasn't happened yet, but we need to be alert to this danger.

Finally, I also should confess to being uneasy about the ability of our kind of innovation research to hold its own in the face of the tight academic budgets that will be with us for some time to come, unless we forge stronger connections with the broader community of scholars studying innovation. We are the principal group of academic scholars studying issues of science and technology policy, and our expertise in this arena is recognized and valued. But our place within academic institutions tends to be outside the core that academic officials generally protect when times are hard. At present, few scholars in other parts of the university know much about what we are doing, and few are inclined actively to support us. Stronger connections with other groups of innovation scholars, located more in the core, could help to protect us. I am concerned that in the coming years we are going to need that help.

10

Smart and Inclusive Growth: Rethinking the State's Role and the Risk–Reward Relationship

Mariana Mazzucato

Recent periods of economic growth, at the national and transnational level (EC, 2011; OECD, 2012), have highlighted the need for innovation economists to better understand why periods that were characterized by high rates of spending on innovation—such as the 1990s with heavy investments in dot.com, nanotech, and biotech—were also decades in which inequality increased rapidly. It is argued below that the challenge requires bringing the study of innovation and inequality back together again—after a century of separation. I also argue that re-engaging with the inequality debate requires rethinking how investments in 'value creation' by the State (led by 'systems of innovation' type policies) can create a more direct reward for tax-payers, and reduced scope for 'value extraction' by a narrow group of actors.

10.1. Innovation and Inequality

The origin of economics as a discipline, separate from that of philosophy and political theory, coincides with the advent of the industrial revolution and its impact on distributional issues. Writers like Adam Smith, Karl Marx, and David Ricardo—the 'classical' economists—were fully aware that innovation and distribution were fundamentally connected. But over time, this relationship became fractured, with economists interested in innovation focusing on areas like technology, learning, and the dynamic of capabilities, leaving issues of distribution and inequality to be studied by economists mainly within a traditional neo-classical approach. In recent years, there has been increasing attention to the relationship between innovation and inequality, through so-called 'new' growth theory (Aghion et al., 1999; Acemoglu, 2002). According to this approach, the twentieth century should be understood as a period characterized by skill-biased technical change prompted by a rapid rise in the supply of skilled workers (reflecting higher returns to education), which induced skill-complementary technologies. However, in the USA, from 2000 to 2007, real incomes for the bottom 90 per cent of earners rose only about 4 per cent, while for the top 0.1 per cent, incomes climbed by 94 per cent (Atkinson et al., 2011). Is it realistic to explain this dramatic increase solely in terms of skills? Furthermore, while raising important empirical issues related to skills and technology, the approach is totally divorced from insights on how innovation actually happens.

It is this challenge that motivates Lazonick and Mazzucato (2012), where innovation and inequality are linked within a framework that focuses on the characteristics of innovation dynamics. We focus on the 'collective', 'uncertain', and 'cumulative' characteristics of innovation, which the innovation community has contributed to documenting (Dosi et al., 1997). We argue that when, across the collective actors, the distribution of financial rewards from the (uncertain) innovation process reflects the distribution of contributions to the process, innovation may reduce inequality. However, when some actors are able to reap shares of financial rewards from the innovation process that are disproportionate to their contributions to the process, innovation tends to increase inequality. Because innovation is 'cumulative', unless policies are in place to mitigate this process, the capture can be very large—essentially the entire integral under the cumulative (distribution) curve.

However, it should be stressed that this is just one approach—there are surely many other innovation-centred approaches that can contribute to our understanding of inequality.

10.2. Innovation and the State—Beyond Fixing Market Failures and Building Systems of Innovation

While it is clear that innovation can lead to growth, it is less obvious whether the profits that are generated from that growth are shared among those that have engaged in the investments. Part of the problem here is how the State's role is perceived. In particular, the role of the State in the innovation 'ecosystem' continues to be focused mainly around 'creating the conditions' for innovation, under-emphasizing its role in investing in areas of high risk and uncertainty where the private sector is too fearful to tread. This is because, despite the achievements of the 'systems of innovation' perspective (Lundvall, 1992; Nelson, 2007), the role of the state is still mainly understood in terms of traditional neo-classical 'market failure' theory. Yet the active government interventions both upstream and downstream in the most radical new technologies can hardly be explained via market failure theory (Mazzucato, 2013b).

Market failure theory discusses 'risk' in terms of the 'wedge' between private and social returns, which may arise from the 'public' nature of goods or different types of externalities (Laffont, 2008). This is the classical argument that is used to justify State spending on basic research. However, the *mission-oriented* investments, which make up about 75 per cent of public sector investments in innovation in many advanced economies, can hardly be justified in this way (Mowery, 2012; Mazzucato, 2013b). Such missions, from putting a 'man on the moon' to developing the Internet (which was done through DARPA, an agency of the US Department of Defense) are driven not by the dynamics of the private/social 'wedge' but by direct objectives of the government in question. Indeed, almost all general purpose technologies were fundamentally state funded. For every Internet, there are, of course, many failures. Yet without the willingness to fail, there would be no successes.

And it is not just about 'research'. While many associate risk capital with either business angels or venture capital (VC), in reality in many countries and regions, including in Silicon Valley, it has often been public not private funds that have filled the high-risk funding gap. For example, in those areas of green technology with high capital intensity and high market/technological risk, private VC is virtually absent. This is because venture capitalists prefer to fund lower risk areas that can generate returns within a three to five year time-period. Indeed, Pisano (2006) argues that the short-termism of venture capital makes it an *inappropriate* model to drive innovation in science-based sectors, such as nanotech, which require much longer time horizons.

Understanding the State as lead risk-taker raises the question of whether there is an appropriate risk–reward relationship in place. It can be argued that it is inappropriate to consider direct returns to the State because the State already earns a return from its investments *indirectly* via the taxation system. Yet the fact that tax evasion and avoidance are so common (and, realistically, will not disappear), and that global movements of capital are so easy, mean that the particular region funding the innovation may not reap the benefits in terms of local job creation, rendering this argument problematic.

Indeed, Apple Computers is a case in point. Apple received its early-stage funding from the US Government's SBIR programme, and all the technologies that make the iPhone 'smart' were likewise government-funded: the Internet, GPS, touchscreen display, and even the latest voice activated SIRI personal assistant (Roush, 2010; Breakthrough, 2012). Yet Apple has used common practices that have resulted in a much lower tax bill for the US government. According to a *New York Times* investigation, Apple formed a subsidiary in Reno, Nevada, where there is no corporate income or capital gain tax, in order to avoid paying State taxes in California, where its headquarters are located. Since 2006, Apple reportedly earned $2.5 billion in interest and dividends, but to avoid paying capital gain tax in California, these have been reported in Nevada (Duhigg and Kocieniewski, 2012). Arguably, California's State budget deficit would have been significantly reduced if companies such as Apple had fully reported their US revenues where the value (discovery, design, sales, marketing, etc.) was created.

What to do? Where technological breakthroughs have occurred as a result of targeted State interventions, there is potential for the State, over time, to reap some of the financial rewards, by retaining ownership over a small proportion of the intellectual property created (a 'golden share', as suggested by Burlamaqui, 2012). This is not to say the State should possess an exclusive license, nor hold a large proportion of the value of an innovation, which might deter its wider spread. But government should explore whether it is possible to retain a portion of the value it has helped to create, which over time could yield significant value and subsequently be reinvested into growth-generating investments. Furthermore, loans as well as grants could have conditions attached, like income contingent loans, similar to those of *student loans*. And of course there is the opportunity to retain some equity, as is done in countries like Finland, where SITRA, one of the main public funding agencies, retained equity in its early-stage investments in Nokia, thus generating profits that could then be used to fund other new companies. Equity retained by state investment banks is also important. Both the German State investment bank, KfW, and the Brazilian Development Bank, BNDES, have not only provided important counter-cyclical lending but also helped to guide investments in key new areas that the private sector was too fearful to fund, such as renewable energy (GWEC, 2012).

Thus, more thinking is needed about how to reward the winning investments—when they occur—so they can both cover some of the eventual losses (which are inevitable in the innovation game) and also raise funds for future investments. Had the public investments in the Internet earned even just 1 per cent return, there would be considerably more money today to fund green technology. While many fear this 'directed' view of government, in reality the issue is not so much whether the State should or should not play this role, but whether it has been adequately remunerated for doing so.

10.3. A Parasitic or Symbiotic Ecosystem?

Last, I would like to highlight another question that could be useful in guiding research by our innovation community: how can we be sure that the innovation ecosystem that results is a *symbiotic* one and not a *parasitic* one? That is, will increased investments by the State in the ecosystem cause the private sector to invest less, and focus its retained earnings on areas like boosting its stock prices rather than on human capital formation and R&D?

Usually a question like this might be framed in terms of 'crowding out'—a hypothesis that focuses on the danger of the State, in its active investment strategy, using up valuable resources on activities that the private sector would otherwise support through its own investment plans (Friedman, 1979). Keynesians have argued against the idea that State spending crowds out private investment, emphasizing that this would only hold in a period of full resource utilization. However, the issues here raise a further point: the areas that the State often invests in around innovation, including both upstream basic research and downstream company finance, are (if done correctly) precisely those that the private sector would not fund, even if it had the resources. Business investment is mainly limited not by savings but by its own lack of courage (or of Keynesian 'animal spirits'). But what if that potentially courageous aspect of the private sector is diminished precisely because the public sector fills the gap? This is a question—different from the crowding out one—that must be addressed in order to prevent decreasing investments by the private sector in areas like R&D, a clear trend in some sectors.

In pharmaceuticals, there is indeed a trend of increasing state investments in areas like research and development, and a decreasing spend by the private sector. As the National Institutes of Health (NIH) have spent more than $300 billion over the last decade ($31 billion in 2012 alone), private pharmaceutical companies have been spending less on research over time, dedicating more of their retained earnings to development, marketing, and to stock buybacks. Some have justified the decreasing spend on research in terms of the crisis in the productivity of R&D. Yet others, like Angell (2004, ex-editor of the *New England Journal of Medicine*), have long insisted that most of the radical new drugs have been coming out of public labs, with private pharmaceutical firms concerned more with 'me too' drugs (i.e. slight variations of existing drugs) and marketing. CEOs of large pharmaceutical companies have admitted that their decision to downsize or in some cases eliminate their R&D labs is due to a belief that in the 'open innovation' model of innovation, most of their research is performed by small biotech and/or public labs (FT, 2011). Their focus has thus turned to searching for new knowledge externally rather than funding R&D internally. At the same time, however, they have been increasing the amount of funds used to repurchase their own shares—a strategy to boost their stock price. For example, Amgen, the largest dedicated biopharma company, has repurchased stock in every year since 1992, and since 2002 the cost of Amgen's stock repurchases has surpassed the company's R&D expenditures in every year except one (Lazonick and Tulum, 2011). The fact that top pharmaceutical companies are spending a decreasing amount of funds on R&D at the same time that the State is spending more—and while increasing the amount they spend on share buybacks—makes this particular innovation ecosystem seem more parasitic than symbiotic. Indeed, in the last decade, Fortune 500 companies have spent $3 trillion in share buybacks. While the largest repurchasers (especially in oil and pharmaceuticals) claim that this is due to the lack of new opportunities, in fact in many cases the most expensive (i.e. capital intensive) investments in new opportunities (with high market and technological risk), in both medicine and renewable energy, are being made by the public sector (GWEC, 2012). This raises the question of whether the so-called 'open innovation' model is in danger of becoming dysfunctional.

Unfortunately, the same problem seems to be appearing now in the emerging clean technology sector. In 2010, the US American Energy Innovation Council (AEIC), an industry association, asked the US government to increase its spending on clean technology by three times to $16 billion annually, with an additional $1 billion given to the Advanced Research Projects Agency for Energy (ARPA-E). However, companies in the council have together spent no less than $237 billion on stock repurchases between 2001 and 2010. The major directors of the AEIC come from companies with collective 2011 net incomes of $37 billion and R&D expenditures of approximately $16 billion. That they believe their own companies' enormous resources are inadequate to foster greater clean technology innovation is indicative of what is going on (Mazzucato, 2013).

10.4. Conclusion

This chapter has offered some provocative thoughts on the relationship between innovation and inequality, thoughts which might guide future research. It has been argued that only through the innovation community becoming directly engaged with this relationship, which was at the heart of 'classical' economics, can we hope to achieve growth that is not only 'smart' but also 'inclusive'. This requires rethinking the role of the State in the innovation ecosystem (i.e. moving beyond fixing failures or creating the right framework conditions), asking whether the public sector receives sufficient return for its high-risk mission-oriented investments, and how value extraction activities by less scrupulous companies can be limited so that innovation 'ecosystems' are more symbiotic and less parasitic.

References

Acemoglu, D. (2002). 'Technical Change, Inequality and the Labor Market', *Journal of Economic Literature*, 40: 7–72.

Aghion, P., Caroli, E., and Garcia-Penalosa, C. (1999). 'Inequality and Economic Growth: The Perspective of the New Growth Theories', *Journal of Economic Literature*, 37: 1615–60.

Angell, M. (2004). *The Truth Behind the Drug Companies*. New York: Random House.

Atkinson, A., Piketty, T., and Saez, E. (2011). 'Top Incomes in the Long Run of History', *Journal of Economic Literature*, 49: 3–71.

Breakthrough Institute (2012). 'Where Do Good Technologies Come From?' (downloaded May 2013 from <http://thebreakthrough.org/archive/presentation_where_good_techno>).

Burlamaqui, L. (2012). 'Knowledge Governance: An Analytical Perspective and its Policy Implications', in L. Burlamaqui, A. C. Castro, and R. Kattel (eds), *Knowledge Governance: Reasserting the Public Interest*. London: Anthem Press, 3–26.

Dosi, G., Malerba, F., Marsili, O., and Orsenigo, L. (1997). 'Industrial Structures and Dynamics: Evidence, Interpretation and Puzzles', *Industrial and Corporate Change*, 6: 3–24.

Duhigg, C. and Kocieniewski, D. (2012). 'How Apple Sidesteps Billions in Taxes', The New York Times iEconomy Series (downloaded on 1 November 2012 from <http://ec.europa.eu/research/innovation-union/pdf/state-of-the-union/2011/state_of_the_innovation_union_2011_brochure_en.pdf#view=fit&pagemode=none>).

European Commission (2011), 'State of the Innovation Union' (downloaded on 1 November 2012 from <http://ec.europa.eu/research/innovation-union/pdf/state-of-the-union/2011/state_of_the_innovation_union_2011_brochure_en.pdf#view=fit&pagemode=none>).

Friedman, B. M. (1979). 'Crowding Out Or Crowding In? The Economic Consequences of Financing Government Deficits', NBER Working Paper, 284.

GWEC (2012), 'Global Wind Report: Annual Market Update 2011', GWEC.org, Global Wind Energy Council, March, Web 19 July (downloaded on 30 November 2012 from <http://www.gwec.net/fileadmin/documents/NewsDocuments/Annual_report_2011_lowres.pdf>).

Laffont, J.-J. (2008), 'Externalities', in S. N. Durlauf, and L. E. Blume (eds), *The New Palgrave Dictionary of Economics*. London: Palgrave.

Lazonick, W. and Mazzucato, M. (2012), 'The Risk-Reward Nexus in Innovation', *Industrial and Corporate Change* (forthcoming) (downloaded May 2013 from <http://www.policy-network.net/publications_detail.aspx?ID=4201>).

Lazonick, W. and Tulum, O. (2011). 'US Biopharmaceutical Finance and the Sustainability of the Biotech Business Model', *Research Policy*, 40: 1170–87.

Lundvall, B.-Å. (ed.) (1992). *National Systems of Innovation: Towards a Theory of Innovation and Interactive Learning*. London: Pinter Publishers.

Mazzucato, M. (2013a). 'Towards a Fairer Capitalism: Let's Burst the 1% Bubble', *The Guardian*, 16 January (downloaded on 18 January 2013 from <http://www.guardian.co.uk/commentisfree/2013/jan/15/fairer-capitalism-bubble-value-creation>).

Mazzucato, M. (2013b). *The Entrepreneurial State: Debunking Private vs. Public Sector Myths*. London: Anthem Press. London: DEMOS.

Mowery, D. C. (2012). 'Defense-Related R&D as a Model for "Grand Challenges" Technology Policies', *Research Policy, 41*: 1703–15.

Nelson, R. R. (2007). 'Building Effective "Innovation Systems" Versus Dealing With "Market Failures" as Ways of Thinking About Technology Policy', 20 October mimeo.

OECD (2012). 'Promoting Inclusive Growth: Challenges and Policies' (downloaded on 18 January 2013 from <http://www.oecd.org/eco/labourmarketshumancapital andinequality/promotinginclusivegrowthchallengesandpolicies.htm>).

Pisano, G. P. (2006). 'Can Science Be a Business? Lessons from Biotech', *Harvard Business Review, 84*: 114–25.

Roush, W. (2010). 'The Story of Siri, from Birth at SRI to Acquisition by Apple— Virtual Personal Assistants Go Mobile', Xconomy.com, 14 June (downloaded on 2 July 2012 from <http://www.xconomy.com/san-francisco/2010/06/14/the-story-of-siri-from-birth-at-sri-to-acquisition-by-apple-virtual-personal-assistants-go-mobile/>).

11

An Agenda for Future Research

Bengt-Åke Lundvall

11.1. Introduction

In the field of innovation studies, progress requires collective research in teams that give room for diversity in terms of disciplines, research style, and methodological competence. Major advances within the field have been made in connection with large research projects. The Yale study, the Sappho project, and the MIKE project all contributed appreciably to our understanding of innovation. The same may be said about the collaborative projects on national innovation systems organized by Nelson and Lundvall.

In the middle of the 1990s, the European Framework programmes made it possible to establish several major projects that brought together scholars from the institutions in Europe most active in innovation studies. The Globelics network with its annual conferences has served as a platform for several major research projects linking innovation to economic development. The BRICS project coordinated by Jose Cassiolato brought together leading scholars from Brazil, Russia, India, China, and South Africa, who studied the role of innovation in these major emerging economies. The Catch-up project, coordinated by Dick Nelson, gave special attention to how catching up takes place in specific sectors. Together with another project involving global participation—the Unidev project that studied the role of universities in innovation systems—these projects have contributed to a new understanding of how innovation relates to economic development (see also Lundvall et al., 2011).

To this should be added that participation in big projects where students combine individual responsibility for their thesis work with contributing to the project offers an ideal form for research training. Apprenticeship learning in relation to supervisors may be combined with opportunities for students to visit other research teams abroad.

Defining projects that address existing and emerging problems is one way to challenge old truths, stimulating the development of theory and new tools when the old ones prove to be inadequate. Engaging junior and senior scholars from different parts of the world in major projects will help to ensure that the field of innovation studies continues to break new ground and remains attractive to creative and curious students.

11.2. Research Projects and Problems

In what follows, I will sketch out 10 areas where major problem-based collective projects could become important stepping stones for consolidating and renewing innovation studies as a field of research. My selection of projects reflects what I see as major global challenges and as neglected problems in innovation research. The selection reflects inspiration from the other chapters in the book. The selection is not exclusive—in parallel with the proposed projects, there will be a lot of demand-driven, applied research on innovation management, regional and sectoral innovation systems, and international competitiveness.

Redefining the Role of National Innovation Systems and Interactive Learning in the Light of Globalization

In the search for a theoretical core for innovation studies, Chapter 2 pointed to 'innovation as an interactive process' as a concept that could be associated with such a core, with the concept of a national innovation system emanating from this perspective. There are at least two reasons to critically revisit these basic concepts.

First, it is becoming increasingly obvious that governance and regulation at the level of nation states are under stress. This reflects the fact that technology and economy are becoming more global while the nation state remains the frame for developing human resources through education, labour market policy, and welfare arrangements. It is far from obvious how this contradiction will be resolved. As mentioned by Steinmueller, one cannot exclude a retreat to more national and protectionist strategies as a possible outcome.

Second, important parts of the innovation process are becoming more dispersed in terms of location. Major multinational firms from the USA and Europe are locating research and development in China. Increasingly multinational companies from BRICS countries are establishing R&D in Silicon Valley and other high technology industrial districts in the USA and Europe.

The project could have a focus upon multinational firms operating worldwide but taking into account national systemic specificities and the role of national government. The ultimate aim would be to test the usefulness of operating with concepts such as interactive learning and national systems of innovation in the new, more globalized context.

The Entrepreneurial and Learning State

Governments do very different things in different national systems and this stands in stark contrast with simplistic stereotypes concerning 'state' versus 'market'. This project would compare the ambitions, activities, and outcomes of state activities that have a direct and indirect impact upon innovation, across national borders. To make it operational, the project might compare the role of the state in sectors such as research, health, and education. The project might make distinctions between reactive and entrepreneurial functions. It could also study to what degree governments make systematic use of research-based knowledge when designing public policy. This question was proposed as a theme for research in the chapter by Carlota Perez.

Family Life in the Information Technology Era

In the modern family the adoption of information technology in the form of media and communication equipment makes a major difference. This includes the boys' toys mentioned by Ben Martin as well as household technology. And it is true both for the middle-class family with a house full of advanced gadgets in the USA and for the villager working in Beijing who can communicate with his family on a mobile phone.

Early studies of the impact of household technology on the time used for different tasks revealed some surprising results. For instance, time saved by new gadgets was often absorbed by maintenance of the gadgets. It is important to understand how technology at different stages of the shift towards the information-intensive household affects the gender dimension, upbringing of children, and the openness of the family. Of course, there is no simple mechanistic causality from technology use to the organization of family life. Context variables that may influence impact have to do with gender equality at work, the education system, and so on. The outcomes of such a project could feed back to regulators, content producers, and developers of software.

Economic Development and the Organization of Work

While the world of business is becoming global, the world of work remains more local. There is great pressure in terms of migration from poor to rich regions, but the high-income nation states are building barriers and this is reflected in national differences in work organization. In a series of papers,

I have joined Lorenz, Valeyre, and others in the analysis of the organization of work in different parts of Europe. The most important results of the international comparison within Europe were, first, that there are quite dramatic differences between different European countries regarding access to learning in the workplace. Second, we find that countries with a large proportion of discretionary learning jobs tend to be the most active when it comes to innovation.

There is great potential in pursuing this kind of analysis on a global scale. In developing countries, it is often difficult to obtain reliable data on work organization and learning via surveys addressed to firms, and a more realistic strategy is often to rely less on statistical analysis and more on case studies. It is an interesting question whether the European Working Conditions Survey design, where employees are interviewed face-to-face at their principal residence, could produce reliable statistical material. Another advantage with this method is that it could help with gaining insights into work, innovation, and learning in the informal sector. In several African countries, more than 50 per cent of households work in this sector and it is important to understand how it interacts with the formal sector when it comes to the diffusion and use of innovation.

The Euro-Crisis and the Catching Up of the South of Europe

There is no shortage of advice on how to solve the Euro-crisis, but most of it is either about abstract ideas of a future fiscal union or about how the European Central Bank can become the central bank for Europe. The current strategy combines fiscal transfer to the peripheral countries with the implementation of severe national austerity and privatization programmes. It is assumed that the structural tensions that lie behind the crisis can be overcome by reducing wages and public expenditure. This research project would look at other reasons for these tensions. What are the characteristics of the peripheral innovation and competence-building systems that undermine their capacity to catch up with the countries in the North of Europe? What elements of social capability and what forms of institutional change are necessary for catching up to take place? The project should involve scholars from different parts of Europe as well as those from outside Europe. One aim would be to develop strategies that make it possible to pursue the European project. Another would be to demonstrate the usefulness of an innovation perspective.

The Financial Industrial Complex, Financial Innovations, and their Contributions to Growth and Stability

This project would require collaboration between critical sociologists, political scientists, innovation scholars, and experts on finance and financial institutions. The ultimate aim would be to analyse how the sector can be made to serve society by channelling saving into innovation and investment, on the one hand, and facilitating national and transnational transactions, on the other.

The project would study 'the financial industrial complex' in specific countries as a community that shares certain basic ideas, and would analyse the mechanisms through which it influences the public and governments. How can this industrial complex be brought under democratic control? Is nationalization of key institutions a necessary step? Other issues would relate to 'financial innovation' and institutions that can assess the utility as well as the risks of diffusing specific innovations, the consequences of automation of speculation through information technology, and the tension between national regulation regimes and banks that operate on a global scale. The project might study how the globalization of finance affects the access to capital for innovation in SMEs that operate locally and in non-metropolitan contexts. It could also look into the possibilities to establish a new global financial architecture, in which the new emerging economies are granted a role that corresponds more directly to their actual significance in the world economy.

The Military Industrial Complex, Warfare, and New Technology

One example of destructive creation not mentioned in the other chapters of the book is the process of developing new arms that make it possible to kill remotely, at a distance. The development of drones and the use of information technology in detecting and destroying enemies have important consequences for barriers to going into war.

A research project that looks into how the collaboration between industry, defence departments, and the military influences the development of new technologies would be helpful in clarifying how new technological trajectories are shaped. This is also important because of the important mutual spillovers between civil technology developments and those developed specifically for military purposes. Such a project might be difficult to design without prestigious public support, since there might the risk of being accused of damaging the national interest. Nonetheless, war is an activity that has a major impact upon citizens in democratic countries and they therefore should have the right to be informed.

Green Innovation and Sustainable Development

One of the most serious threats to the future of human society is the inadequate effort to reduce or eliminate CO_2, resulting in global warming. This challenge is mentioned in several of the other chapters. A major research project would aim at studying and comparing the technical trajectories in specific renewable energy technologies, such as solar, wind, and hydro power. The project would give equal attention to the evolution of the science base, the supply of new technical solutions, and the role of intermediate users and end-users. It would identify lock-in situations, where external intervention might be necessary to make the direction of change more satisfactory. Examples of public policies that help to foster innovation and open up new opportunities could be studied.

The aim of the project would be to clarify what the most important barriers to the development, application, use, and diffusion of renewable energy technologies are. This research could be organized on a global scale, with analysis of applications both in the North and in the South. A major issue would be the need for global coordination and the possibility of establishing positive sum games when it comes to economic benefits and knowledge sharing.

Migration and Innovation

Ultimately, people matter more than anything else. In the future, the patterns of mobility across borders and sometimes across oceans will shape the future of innovation. Historically, the industrial revolution in England was greatly accelerated by the royal state when it stimulated immigration of workers from Continental Europe who were blacksmiths and who helped to build the first iron works and gun factories. Currently demographic development is extremely imbalanced between regions. In Southern Europe the birth rates are low, while in the nearby North African countries there is strong growth in the proportion of young people. The fact that incomes are higher in Europe, while youth unemployment is high on both side of the Mediterranean, increases the tension between the desire of some to emigrate and the willingness of others to welcome newcomers.

The research project should take into account the fact that migration involves brain-circulation as well as brain-drain and brain-gain. Such a perspective may help in developing new forms of international collaboration that offer positive sum games. The fact that rich countries' patents are protected while there is no compensation for poor countries that deliver knowledge in the form of emigration of skilled labour, also needs to be addressed.[1]

---

[1] It is important to note that the euro-crisis, the financial crisis, war technology, sustainable development, and demographic imbalances have in common that technical innovation plays a role in tackling a set of problems crucially important for mankind. But lack of technical innovation is not the most important problem. It is rather the contradiction between the current predominantly nation-state form of governance and the need for global governance with regard to certain issues. It is tempting to regard the nation state as a natural phenomenon and to practice 'methodological nationalism'. But there is also a tendency to regard globalization as a unidirectional

Sources of, and Barriers to, Individual and Collective Creativity

In this field, there is room for an interesting collective project bringing together what can be learnt from neuroscientists trying to understand how the brain responds to stimuli, with those researchers studying the role of culture and religion in supporting or blocking creative thinking. How can different education systems, organizational forms, and incentive systems contribute to collective creativity? Is it only the creative class who are engaged in creative work? To what degree does diversity in terms of experience and in terms of interaction with others within and across organizations contribute to creativity? Another subtheme could focus on what can be learnt from creative industries and from cultural industries. The construction sector could be another interesting case. Here, the creative work of architects has traditionally been separated from the implementation. It is perhaps significant that this sector has long been characterized by low productivity and lack of innovation in the production process.

11.3. A Final Remark on the Future of Innovation Studies

The list of themes that could be addressed by the listed research projects demonstrates that there are many interesting tasks to pursue. They would all require both international and inter-disciplinary consortia of scholars, and they would produce new insights that would feed into what will become the knowledge base of the next generation of innovation scholars. If this were organized carefully with the use of a range of methodological tools and with a good mix of PhD students, senior, and junior scholars, it could make a significant difference in the world while at the same ensuring that innovation studies not only survives but remains an exciting field in which to work.

This is important because doing research should be fun, at least most of the time! One unique positive characteristic of the community working on innovation studies is that the culture at meetings and training events combines critical debate with a friendly and tolerant climate. This culture reflects the

process that always results in progress for mankind. Neither of these two perspectives would seem to offer sustainable paths of global development. The current era is one where the current multi-level governance system requires innovative solutions. Otherwise the various crises are likely to be prolonged and to give rise to nationalist regression and protectionism. In such a context, technical innovation may become more destructive than creative. It tends to be mobilized primarily to fight or compete with 'others', and the knowledge sharing that is crucial to cope with the global challenges will no longer be an option. I have therefore proposed that the Norwegian government set up a new institution: *NOGGI—the Norwegian Observatory for Global Governance Innovation*. The aim of such an institution would be to produce and diffuse research-based ideas on how to reform global governance in such a way that the world becomes sustainable in economic, ecological, and social terms.

fact that the founders—Chris Freeman, Dick Nelson, and others—from the very beginning set high standards, especially when it came to welcoming and mentoring young scholars. When discussing the future of innovation studies in terms of infrastructure and research training, we should be aware of the enormous value of this intangible capital that we have inherited and do all that we can to make sure that it is not lost.

Reference

Lundvall, B.-Å, Joseph, K.J., Chaminade, C., and Vang, J. (2011). *Handbook of Innovation Systems and Developing Countries: Building Domestic Capabilities in a Global Setting.* London: Edward Elgar.

Index

Note: Bold entries refer to figures or tables.